Oxford S

Shakespeare and London

OXFORD SHAKESPEARE TOPICS

Published and Forthcoming Titles Include:

Oxford Shakespeare Topics

GENERAL EDITORS: LENA COWEN ORLIN, PETER HOLLAND,

AND STANLEY WELLS

Shakespeare and London

DUNCAN SALKELD

OXFORD

UNIVERSITY PRESS

OXFORD
UNIVERSITY PRESS

Great Clarendon Street, Oxford, OX2 6DP,
United Kingdom

Oxford University Press is a department of the University of Oxford.
It furthers the University's objective of excellence in research, scholarship,
and education by publishing worldwide. Oxford is a registered trade mark of
Oxford University Press in the UK and in certain other countries

First edition published in 2018
Impression: 2

Published in the United States of America by Oxford University Press
198 Madison Avenue, New York, NY 10016, United States of America

British Library Cataloguing in Publication Data
Data available

Library of Congress Control Number: 2018931541

ISBN 978–0–19–870994–7 (hbk.)
      978–0–19–870995–4 (pbk.)

Printed and bound by
CPI Group (UK) Ltd, Croydon, CR0 4YY

For Tom, Sam, and Ellie

Acknowledgements

I wish to thank the series editors, Stanley Wells, Peter Holland, and Lena Cowen Orlin, for so carefully guiding this book through to completion. I am sincerely grateful for all their detailed comments, criticism, and advice on the manuscript, saving me from numerous potential pitfalls. The errors that remain are, of course, mine alone. My anxieties of influence have become pleasures of indebtedness, and I am especially grateful to my colleague Paul Quinn who read and advised on sections of the book. I've had the huge pleasure of getting to know Roger Cline, the London Topographical Society's indefatigable treasurer. With a keen eye, encyclopaedic knowledge of London, and a dry wit, Roger very generously read the entire manuscript and improved it at innumerable points. I'd like to thank Alan H. Nelson for his great kindness and generosity in discussing aspects of this book. I remain hugely indebted to the work he and William Ingram have done on the Southwark archives. Without their extraordinary labours, I could never have completed the sections on Edmund Shakespeare or John Reasonable. I'd also like to thank Martin Wiggins, Miranda Kaufmann, David Kathman, Heather Knight, Eva Griffith, Andy Kesson, Ann C. Chistensen, Michele Marrapodi, and Dulce Garcia for opportunities to discuss some of this material both formally and informally at academic gatherings. I am grateful, too, for all the help provided by librarians and archivists at the London Metropolitan Archives, the National Archives, the Bodleian Library, the British Library, and colleagues at the University of Chichester. I am much in debt to the staff at OUP, including Jacqueline Norton, Aimee Wright, Eleanor Collins, Clement Raj and copy-editor Dan Harding. I thank my students, past and present, for being such wonderful companions in learning. Paul and Alison Woodfield and Ken, Olivia, and Brian Tottle have helped more than they know. This book is affectionately dedicated to my children.

Contents

List of Illustrations

"Map of London Places Important to Shakespeare's Plays and London Playgoing", from THE NORTON SHAKESPEARE: BASED ON THE OXFORD EDITION, SECOND EDITION, edited by Stephen Greenblatt. Copyright © 2008, 1997 by W. W. Norton & Company, Inc. Used by permission of W. W. Norton & Company, Inc. The exact date of The Curtain is unclear.

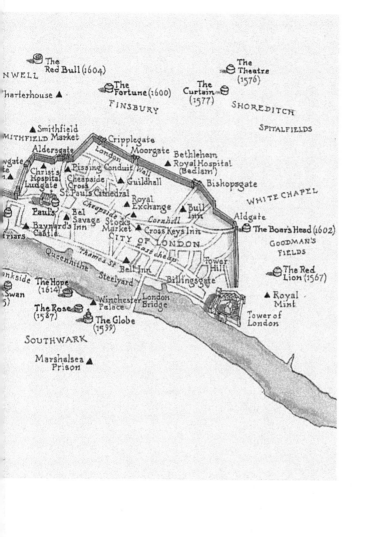

The Red Bull (1604)

NWELL

harterhouse ▲

The Fortune (1600)

The Curtain (1577)

The Theatre (1576)

FINSBURY

SHOREDITCH

SPITALFIELDS

▲ Smithfield Market

MITHFIELD Market

Aldersgate

Cripplegate

London

Moorgate

Bethlehem

▲ Royal Hospital (Bedlam)

wgate
te
n▲

Christ's
Hospital
Ludgate

Pissing Conduit

Wall

Cheapside
Cross

▲ Guildhall

Bishopsgate

WHITE CHAPEL

St.Paul's Cathedral

Cheapside

Royal
Exchange

Bull
Inn

Aldgate

Paul's

Bel
Savage

Stocks
Market

Cornhill

The Boar's Head (1602)

Baynard's Inn
Castle

▲ Cross Keys Inn

GOODMAN'S
FIELDS

friars

CITY OF LONDON

East cheap

The Red
Lion (1567)

Queenhithe

Thames St

Bell Inn

Tower
Hill

Steelyard

Billingsgate

nkside

The Hope
(1614)

Swan
5)

Winchester
Palace

London
Bridge

The Rose
(1587)

The Globe
(1599)

▲ Royal
Mint

Tower of
London

SOUTHWARK

Marshalsea ▲
Prison

Introduction

Ophelia hails a carriage

In her madness, Shakespeare's Ophelia bids everyone goodnight and leaves the stage calling for transport: 'Come, my coach!' (*Hamlet*, 4.5.70). It is a small detail borrowed from Marlowe's character Zabina in *Tamburlaine I*, and one that Ben Jonson picked up on when he co-authored *Eastward Ho* with George Chapman and John Marston in 1605. In *Eastward Ho*, a rather vain young woman calls for her carriage. She is named Gertrude and attended by a hapless servant called Hamlet. A coachman enters in 3.2, his mouth full of half-eaten breakfast, followed by '*Hamlet, a footman, in haste*'. Jonson's Hamlet berates the coachman, anxious that his mistress is ready to leave and this is no time for porridge. Gertrude is keen to see her 'Castle in the east' which she has won by marriage to Sir Petronel Flash. Since her coach is small and doesn't have room for anyone else, Hamlet faces having to run along the street beside her. A tankard-bearer enters and asks, "Sfoot, Hamlet, are you mad?' (3.2.7), a satirical allusion to Shakespeare's play. Fuss is made over Gertrude's appearance and the coach's imminent arrival, but it never comes, and Gertrude merely ends up singing catches that echo those of mad Ophelia.

Jonson excelled at this kind of short, madcap scene. His London-based play *Bartholomew Fair* is full of them. The 'mini-*Hamlet*' of *Eastward Ho* is a comic experiment in refamiliarization. An early-seventeenth-century audience would hardly expect to see Gertrude waving at them from her coach window as she passed through Cheapside with Hamlet jogging along beside her. Jonson brings the forbidding, distant, and strange world of Shakespeare's play home and, for a moment, renders it all ridiculously familiar. This book is partly an attempt to think further about that incongruity, the misfit of Shakespeare's faraway worlds performed in much closer-to-home neighbourhoods in and around the City of London. While Shakespeare owed his success to London, it seems he was always attempting to transport his audience out of it. Characteristically, Jonson played the antagonist and transposed them (along with Gertrude and Hamlet) back into it. In doing so, he told us something. The 1603 printing of *Hamlet* makes no mention of any coach. That detail is only to be found in the 1604 and 1623 imprints.[1] The play Jonson, Chapman, and Marston had seen in performance was that printed in the 1604 second quarto (Q2), or a version of it. The 1603 *Hamlet* (Q1), howsoever derived, may have been assembled solely for the purposes of print.

Fragments

Occasionally, incidental historical details of London life can find an echo in the plays. The parish registers of St Botolph's, Bishopsgate, record the burial of 'Jaques de Boyes' on 23 May 1578, alongside other members of his family.[2] Jaques de Bois is the name of a melancholic character in *As You Like It*. In 1599, Roger and Mary Elsinore kept a victualling house on Bishopsgate Street. 'Elsinore', an Anglicized variant of the Danish town name Helsingor, does not occur in any of the known 'sources' for *Hamlet*. On 8 May 1598, Anne Sweno told that she had been encouraged to sign a complaint against Thomas Wood, minstrel and bailiff of Southwark. 'Sweno' is the name of the Norwegian king in *Macbeth* (1.2.59). The following year, Katherine Cuffe confessed she had dressed as a boy and smuggled herself into the Inner Temple to be with Ambrose Jasper who had given her a ring. Her story is not unlike Viola's in *Twelfth Night*, performed at the next-door Middle Temple in 1602. In the summer of 1606, Mary Berry was raped in her master's slaughterhouse in Pilcock Lane near St Nicholas Shambles. Edgar as Poor Tom in *King Lear* sings, 'Pillicock sat on Pillicock hill' (3.4.75).[3] We cannot be certain that these people and situations were known to Shakespeare. Such details may appear suggestive but, with so much still unknown, they can be little more than that.

There are several questions that arise at the start of a book on this topic. What was it like to live in London? Do we have historical records of Shakespeare's whereabouts, associations, and activities there? Do Shakespeare's works disclose his thoughts or attitudes about urban life? Did Shakespeare settle in London? Did Londoners embrace him as one of their own? To what extent did he refer to, or describe, the City in his works, and did his representation of it change? These are all questions for which we would very much like to have firm and detailed answers. Unfortunately, they can only be answered tangentially or partially, if at all, with many uncertainties acknowledged. We can make inferences on the basis of evidence, but the nature of the evidence varies, and, in weighing it up, plausibility must be sifted from possibility. Much of the time we have to accept that 'we just don't know'. Yet not knowing can also be one of the most exciting aspects of studying Shakespeare. There are always details to follow through, sources to trace, trails to pursue, documents to find, and meanings to weigh up. Often, though, we have to work from fragments.

Encompassing the teeming life of early modern London is a near-impossible task. Paul Griffiths's book *Lost Londons* has perhaps come closest to conveying the complexities of its problems and challenges and the extraordinary multiplicity of human events that filled up the life of its streets. Griffiths explains in close detail the problems of vagrancy, theft, begging, fraud, and disputes of all kinds that weighed on the minds of the City's leaders.[4] In the centre of London, people lived (and died) crammed together in narrow alleyways, housed in crowded tenements whose windows overlooked each other and gave little privacy. A continual influx of itinerant outsiders kept the metropolis shifting into different patterns of connection and service.[5] Many streets were filthy, blocked by fly-tips, or filled with the bustle of wheeled traffic and market-sellers. Cutpurses, nightwalkers, and vagabonds gathered in back lanes or in the fields, away from constables and beadles. Magistrates and officers at the sessions houses, courts, prisons, and 'hospitals' struggled to regulate and manage a confusion of human activity they could not possibly control. Single moments in this struggle can have a telling significance. In the middle of this human 'mass and mess', as Griffiths puts it, two boys, Francis Stavely and William Wheatley, were found huddled up in a hole in 1640, whipped for vagrancy, and returned to their fathers.[6]

Eleanor Hubbard's *City Women: Money, Sex, and the Social Order in Early Modern London* provides a detailed study of 'migrant maids', young women who were drawn into London from the shires in search of work. Hubbard analyses the mix of native and outsider maidens, wives, and widows in different areas of London, their durations of service, age at marriage, and the kinds of skills they brought to the metropolitan economy.[7] Many sought husbands as well as service, since males had the advantage of belonging to a trade that afforded some employment protection. Some found themselves exploited and pregnant outside of wedlock. These women tended to be cut adrift, forced back on the road in the hope of avoiding prosecution. Yet for other women, becoming a household mistress, or 'good wife', was the first step on a life of Christian modesty and respectability. As Hubbard explains, women often forged a kind of solidarity, as best they could. They lived and slept together (without sexual implications) and collaborated in working to establish a rudimentary living for themselves. Most were able to do this legally, but, as Hubbard shows, there were plenty of others who resorted to prostitution simply to get by. Among a host of examples, she tells the story of Em Finch, used virtually as a slave by her master and mistress. Finch was often forced by her mistress to 'go up into a room to be naught[y] with divers men'.[8] The distinctions between abuse, prostitution, and rape in early modern London are not always easy to draw.

Ineluctably, fragments will play a substantial part in this book. What William Ingram has termed 'scraps of information' can suggest much.[9] But the implications of a fragment are delimited by all that remains missing. Any sheet of writing is, of course, a part of the world that produced it. Anecdotes, lines of text, parish register entries, or prosecutions have value as metonyms for a greater whole that can never be fully pieced together. Thankfully, scholarship is adding to our understanding all the time. Influential work has been done, for example, by Lukas Erne on Shakespeare's relationship to London publishers and printers, David Kathman on London actors, Charles Nicholl on Shakespeare's time as a lodger in Silver Street in or around 1604, and James Shapiro on Shakespeare's life and work in 1599 and 1606.[10] But given that there is so much we still have to learn about Shakespeare's London life, this book is inevitably selective. The fragments we do have must serve, in the hope that particular examples can suggest a broader picture.

It is worth pausing over just a few examples of London life that seem to bring us closer to that world. The first concerns a Londoner, an unnamed woman, walking on Thursday 20 December 1576 under the great stone arch of Newgate. As one of the seven fortified gates or 'posterns' of the City of London, it allowed passage into and from 'the City'. But Newgate also had a terrible history as the site of a prison and place of execution. Perhaps the woman paused for a moment, distracted. Standing nearby was Simon Fawkenor. All we know about him is that he snipped her leather purse and tried to make off with it. Inside it were three shillings and a silver thimble. That, at least, is what Fawkenor told the court at his prosecution on Wednesday 2 January. The woman was evidently quite well-off, something he may have guessed from the leather. But he might also have realized that Newgate, being one of London's most feared prisons, was hardly a safe area for a thief. We know no more of this incident. But the fact that, after so long, we can learn what someone kept in their pocket or purse on a given day is (no pun intended) arresting.

Two further fragments carry an element of the farcical. In 1578, Thomas Kyd, a cooper, courted Mistress Eleanor Gilderson (a married woman) by bringing her whistles, combs, and roasted meats as she was drying laundry in the fields. On one occasion when he was with her in an upper chamber, her husband came up the stairs, and Kyd hid under the bed. This Kyd is unlikely to have been the dramatist and author of *The Spanish Tragedy* but may have been a family relation. In a not entirely dissimilar case two years earlier, Thomasine Breame, a brothel madam, was entertaining 'one Mandrell' one evening when constables of the Watch knocked at her door. The gentleman quickly 'lay under the feather bed and Mistress Breame upon him'. By this uncomfortable means, they escaped arrest.[11]

Reports like these may seem merely anecdotal, but they offer detailed verbal snapshots of everyday life at the time. Accounts of people hiding under beds, or carrying trinkets into the fields, convey a sense of being somehow 'close' to the past. The nineteenth-century historian Leopold von Ranke thought such details might enable us to discover history 'as it really happened', but this of course is wishful thinking.

Records can be unreliable, tell only a very distorted or partial account, and leave out much that might change our understanding significantly. We cannot be 'close' to incidents long ago, but we can be to the dark ink on a yellowing page that discloses them. Moreover, from these episodes we have a sense of people being close to one another—Fawkenor beside the unnamed woman, Kyd beneath Gilderson, and Mandrell under Breame, fearing discovery. The proximity of these people to each other, together with that of the magistrates to the offenders, generates for us today an effect of 'nearness by proxy'. The losses and accretions of time separate us from the moment, yet documentary records like these can still translate, and shape how we imagine the past.

Survey of chapters

Chapter 1 begins by asking whether it is useful to speak of 'Shakespeare's London', a very common shorthand phrase readily used by just about all Shakespeareans, including myself. The phrase may obscure the important contributions of other London writers of his day and the fact that Shakespeare seems to have had an uneasy relationship with the metropolis. For these reasons, it is a phrase that generally will not occur in this book. After a brief discussion of Thomas Middleton, Thomas Dekker, Thomas Heywood, and Ben Jonson as London dramatists, the chapter goes on to outline significant links between Stratford-upon-Avon and the capital. Even the Bishop of Winchester, whose palace stood near the Southwark playhouses in the liberty of the Clink, had family relations in Stratford, Warwickshire. Other possible links include members of the Quiney family living in Bucklersbury and a Matthew Shakespeare in Clerkenwell. The chapter argues that, however immersed in London's world he became, Shakespeare was always a 'countryman', one whom the authorities termed 'foreign born'. He began his career in London as an outsider, and despite all the success he enjoyed on stage and in print, a sense of exclusion seems to haunt his work even to the end.

Chapter 2 is devoted to a discussion of Shakespeare-related locations in London. It is designed to give the reader some familiarity with the layout of the capital and its principal sites. But it is not a 'tour guide' through the early modern city. Instead, it argues that aspects of

London's topography have significance at particular moments in his works. The chapter begins by looking at London as a whole, both the City and Westminster, by means of contemporary maps and panoramas, and prose works by Henry Machyn and John Stow. It then traces areas in the capital to the north, south, east, and west of the City's centre. The chapter focuses on Shoreditch, Clerkenwell and Bishopsgate, Southwark and Bankside, the Tower of London, and Tyburn, a dreadful place of execution. These locations all played a part in Shakespeare's life in the metropolis. When a London location is alluded to in the plays, it affords a moment of recognition for the audience, yet often one that is fleeting and set within the play's broader narrative or history.

Chapter 3 discusses people connected with Shakespeare's City life and work. It begins with a discussion of the Burbage family whose support for Shakespeare seems to have been foundational. The discussion then covers two rather less well-known Clerkenwell figures who seem to have had associates in the theatre industry, Gilbert East and Luce Baynam, otherwise known as 'Black Luce'. These two unsavoury characters had links to theatrical activity in the 1590s and are likely to have been known to Shakespeare. The chapter moves on to consider Shakespeare's move from Bishopsgate, an area of some notoriety just south of Shoreditch, to the Bankside in Surrey. Edward Alleyn had made a similar move around 1593 and appears to have taken an interest in Shakespeare's work. He bought a copy of Shakespeare's *Sonnets* for five pence. The chapter turns to discuss Shakespeare's relationship with Sir William Brooke, who for a short period of six months served in the position of Lord Chamberlain. It offers evidence to suggest that in creating Falstaff, Shakespeare caricatured the activities of Brooke's sons. In the polarized politics of the late 1590s, Shakespeare could not avoid taking sides. The chapter closes with consideration of two rather scandalous figures, Christopher Beeston, a co-actor in Shakespeare's company accused of rape, and George Wilkins, a man given to violent misogyny. The chapter argues that, whether he liked it or not, Shakespeare was, through his associations with this range of people, deeply engaged in London's social world.

Chapter 4 explores the ways in which Shakespeare's art confronted power in the form of local London authorities. It begins with a discussion of the role of the livery company system and the constitutional bodies that ran the City of London. The chapter covers the relentless pressure exerted by the Lord Mayor and Court of Aldermen against theatres and highlights just how precarious the situation of both theatre managers and players could be. It shows that Shakespeare responded to some of these pressures in *Measure for Measure*, voicing in figures such as Angelo, Barnardine, and Mistress Overdone an implicit critique of the hypocrisies of the city's ruling bodies. Shakespeare's apparent antipathy to anti-theatrical pressure is aimed largely at the lower levels of authority—beadles, constables, and magistrates. The chapter goes on to argue that Shakespeare's response to coercion from the City authorities and the violence of London life was to produce more 'art'. It considers Shakespeare's intellectual engagement with the arts, especially painting, poetry, and music. With the accession of James I, and Shakespeare's elevation to a member of the 'King's Men', his work enjoyed a greater degree of protection. The chapter closes with a brief discussion of the position of Peter Street, the carpenter who built the Globe in 1599, who also served as a City magistrate.

London's cultural diversity becomes the focus of Chapter 5, which makes clear that although strangers made up a small proportion of early modern London's population, the City harboured groups of very different national and ethnic heritage. Immigrants tended to live near the fringes of the City, in wards close to the old wall. We find a pocket of Africans living in and around Tower Hill and the Italian Bassano family dwelling in Bishopsgate and Shoreditch. The chapter gives an account of Sir Horatio Palavicino's activities in London and suggests that the wealthy merchant Baptista Spinola may have prompted the name of Kate's father in *The Taming of the Shrew*. It goes on to discuss what we know of a black family living on Bankside in the late 1580s and early 1590s. John Reason, sometimes surnamed 'Reasonable', raised a family in the parish of St Olave's, Tooley Street. Unlike many servile Africans in London, 'Reason' had a job as a silkweaver and may have helped in making costumes for performances at the Rose. His name is unusual and may have a bearing on a short dialogue with the clown in *The Merchant of Venice*. The chapter further considers Shakespeare's association with Huguenot families in London and finds, in that part of 'The Book of Sir Thomas More' attributed to Shakespeare, an extraordinary defence of the rights of aliens.

The book finishes with a conclusion that returns to the significance of fragments for reading Shakespeare's London life in the context of its time. Some of these fragments are testimony to lives lost, like Perdita in *The Winter's Tale*. The infant Elizabeth, at the end of *Henry VIII* (*All is True*), by contrast, points to a future of promise. This study's innumerable debts to previous writers on the topic will be evident. Writing on a subject like this, one cannot avoid awareness of the fact that there is so much more to be said. Others, no doubt, will add to the picture. The approach taken in this book is, broadly speaking, historical and empirical. It assumes that language is as real a stuff as any other material and by definition translatable. The plays and poems are not regarded simply as a product of their history. There is plenty of evidence that Shakespeare's works shaped the culture of his time. Appropriately, perhaps, we lack a theory of fragments, and so readers looking for theory will only find it tacit. Others seeking a 'history of London', its demography, topography, or politics, may discover numerous excellent studies elsewhere. Several of them are cited in the notes.[12] Much of the detail in this book rests on the implications of 'scraps of information'. Documents, sources, texts, and objects from the past bear a certain agency, since they qualify and condition what can be made of them today. Sometimes only very little can be said, or guessed at, from a detail that conceals at least as much as it discloses. The weight of all that remains unknown will always be felt.

Stratford to London

Introduction

We commonly encounter the phrase 'Shakespeare's London' in books on the early modern period. It is an easy shortcut that we have all used on some occasion, but it harbours a certain implication: that London somehow belonged to Shakespeare. It suggests a relationship of mastery or dominion, as though Shakespeare at some point took over London's cultural activity and made it his. But just a moment's reflection tells us that this impression is obviously misleading. Shakespeare was just one of many playwrights—among them Christopher Marlowe, Thomas Kyd, Robert Greene, George Peele, Thomas Nashe, and Ben Jonson—who flourished in the era. This book argues that Shakespeare's relationship with the City was a good deal less easy than the phrase would suggest. Shakespeare never eulogized the capital. He never wrote a play set solely in London. He penned no pageant for the Lord Mayor's shows, never brought his wife or children there (so far as we know), and never settled for long in any one London location. In a 1612 dowry dispute at which he made a brief statement, he gave himself as 'William Shakespeare of Stratford upon Avon'.[1] Yet Shakespeare owed everything to the metropolis. Stratford made the man; London created the phenomenon. After 1600, his fellow writers—Thomas Heywood and Ben Jonson among them—started to quote his work in theirs. If Shakespeare has come to dominate our sense of the cultural and literary life of early modern London, he should hardly be blamed for that.

Shakespeare's London?

From our perspective today, it is easy to imagine that Shakespeare was uniquely the most important force in the theatrical world of London in the late sixteenth and early seventeenth centuries. Yet Shakespeare was surrounded by many other Londoners who helped to make his career. Some of these were authors. William Camden, writing in 1605, gave Shakespeare's name as just one among other 'wits of these our times, whom succeeding ages may justly admire'. Edmund Howes, in 1615, made a long list of 'our modern, and present excellent poets which worthily flourish in their own works' and included Shakespeare as just one among so many others.[2] These literary lists serve to underline the fact that Shakespeare belonged to a shared literary culture. In order to get a better idea of 'Shakespeare's London', it is worth considering, however briefly, what we might mean by 'Middleton's London', 'Dekker's London', 'Heywood's London' or 'Jonson's London', should we imagine the capital as assimilable to a single creative perspective.

Middleton, Dekker, Heywood, and Jonson were connected closely to London's civic culture in ways that Shakespeare was not. Middleton was born a Londoner, baptized in the parish of St Lawrence Jewry in 1580 where his parents had married. He attended school in London, went to university in Oxford, and returned to the City where he married in 1603. By the time of James's accession, Middleton had already begun writing drama, specifically for the children's companies of St Paul's and Blackfriars. The following year, he was hired to contribute to *The Magnificent Entertainment*, a celebration of London's new monarch. Subsequently, he wrote quasi-journalistic pamphlets and poems and contributed to City pageants. He sometimes worked collaboratively, with Dekker, Shakespeare, Ford, William Rowley, Webster, and Garret Christmas. In 1613, he teamed up with Anthony Munday to put on his first Lord Mayor's show. Middleton's early prose writing was filled with London's topography. His literary success eventually led to him becoming, in 1621, the official City chronologer, a salaried position devoted to recording life and events in the metropolis. His first play, *The Phoenix* (1603–4), shows him playing an ambiguous game and immersed in an urban culture of legal disputes, smoke-filled taverns, and entanglements with women. The play is notionally set in an Italianate locality, with bawdily suggestive characters named Furtivo, Latronello, Lussurioso, Infesto, and Fucato. But, to remind his audience that what he was really talking about lay not far beyond the playhouse door, he had an officer of the law hail the Counter prisons in the Poultry and Wood Street as the 'two most famous universities' of 'that notable City called London'.

Although he grew up with a latent Calvinism, his literary works show him inclined to urban satire. These were London plays for London audiences. Yet, as Gary Taylor notes, Middleton's favour with the City declined in the 1620s. His annual stipend of £10 was threatened, and projects for the Lord Mayor's pageants of 1625 and 1626 were abandoned.[3] In a discussion of 'Middleton's London', Paul S. Seaver argues that Middleton wrote plays for a 'growing publishing industry' that fed the public's 'insatiable appetite for new plays'. An expanding 'literate laity' combined with 'traditional learned professions' opened up a new market for London dramatists who were no longer entirely dependent upon 'the traditional structure of Crown, Church and nobility'.[4] In short, Middleton—a prolific, celebrated, and officially recognized writer—belonged to London rather than the other way around.

Thomas Dekker also contributed to the 1604 *Magnificent Entertainment* and had a hand in several of the Lord Mayor's pageants. He is known for writing plays for the Admiral's Men based mainly at the Rose on the south bank, and (perhaps with Marston) *Satiromastix* (1601) for the Lord Chamberlain's Men. There is no doubt that Dekker hoped to be considered a Londoner. It has long been supposed that he was born to Dutch immigrant parents, a fact that would mark him always as an outsider. This supposition may be strengthened by a 1599 entry in the parish registers for St Leonard's, Shoreditch: 'Peter Good yͤ son-in-law of Thomas Dycher stranger buried in yͤ same day'. Good is listed as having resided in 'Allen's rents'.[5] If the entry refers, as seems quite possible, to Dekker's father, it would suggest that Thomas the younger grew up in Shoreditch as a neighbour of the Burbages, in the shadow of the Curtain and Theatre playhouses. In his prose writings, Dekker emphasized his claim to citizenship. In *The Seven Deadly Sinnes* (1606), he wrote of himself as a Londoner, declaring to the world that 'from thy womb received I my being, from thy breasts my nourishment'.[6] This was not, of course, a claim Shakespeare could have made.

Among Dekker's works are some thirty lines he contributed to 'The Boke of Sir Thomas More' and a full-length play, listed by Philip Henslowe in 1599 as *The Gentle Craft* which was published the following year as *The Shoemaker's Holiday*. Both of these works were fully London-centred. *The Shoemaker's Holiday* is a dramatization of a tale of 'The Gentle Craft' (1597) written by Thomas Deloney.

In retelling the story of Simon Eyre, a shoemaker who rose to become Lord Mayor, Dekker shows a cartographic imagination, alluding to a host of specific London locations, including military training fields in Westminster, Finsbury, and Mile End, the madhouse at Bedlam, Fleet Street, Tower Street, Whitechapel, Cornhill, the Guildhall, Gracious Street, Cornwall in the Vintry, and St Faith's Church by St Paul's.

Dekker's prose pamphlets depict his most vivid scenes of quotidian London life. In *The Gull's Horn-book* (1609), he gives satirical advice on the virtues of long hair and advice on how a young man should behave in the central public aisle of St Paul's ('Paul's Walk'), how a gallant ought to conduct himself in an 'ordinary' (a tavern), and proper behaviour at playhouses. He also adds hints on how to evade 'the watch', or constables, on the way home. In a 1608 pamphlet, *Lanthorne and Candlelight, or The Bell-mans second Nights walke*, he details the kinds of persons 'the watch' was supposed to catch and outlines a vocabulary of 'canting' terms supposedly used by tricksters in and around the City.[7] The pamphlet draws to a close with an abject focus on London's prisons and abuses perpetrated by those who maintain them. Dekker wrote from painful personal experience. In 1598, Philip Henslowe had lent him money to secure his release from the Counter prison in the Poultry.[8]

We see Dekker in these works alert to the City's many hazards and risks, aiming to get a handle on its ways, ruses, deceits, perils, and, most of all, its forms of language, perhaps so that he might rise above them. He was fascinated by rare and unusual words, especially the picaresque vocabulary he imagines as used by gangs at the lower end of the social scale. He was one of London's most prolific dramatists, working at times in collaboration with Middleton, Jonson, Marston, Webster, and—on *Sir Thomas More*—with Munday, Chettle, Heywood, and Shakespeare. His parentage notwithstanding, Dekker enjoyed sporadic patronage from the City. He wrote a Lord Mayor's pageant called *Troia-Nova Triumphans, London Triumphing* (1612), drawing on the old mythical name for the capital 'Troynovant' ('New Troy'), and penned a variety of other City-based works. These included *The Wonderful Year, Wherein Is Shown the Picture of London Lying Sick of the Plague* (1603), *The Seven Deadly Sins of London* (1616), and *The Bellman of London, Bringing to Light the Most Notorious Villainies* (1608). Overall, it is hard to escape the impression that Dekker's vision of the capital remained broadly pessimistic. The few wistful consolations imagined in his many songs, some of them appended to *Lanthorne and Candlelight*, are quickly snuffed out by allusions to poverty, prison, and the gallows. Between 1613 and 1620, he was incarcerated in the King's Bench, Southwark, for debt. Nevertheless, Dekker always seems to have felt that he belonged in the City. Towards the end of his life, in *A Rod for Run-Awayes* (1625), he called London 'Mother of my life, Nurse of my being'. He and his wife were buried in the parish church of St James in Clerkenwell, in 1626.[9]

What then might be said of Thomas Heywood's literary relationship with the city? Like Dekker, he collaborated with other writers, including Chettle, Munday, and Webster, and (between 1598 and 1600) had an arrangement with Henslowe to write plays for the Admiral's company. Between 1603 and 1604, he took a hand in at least eight plays for Worcester's Men.[10] At the height of his career, he was centrally involved in London's theatrical life. David Kathman explains, 'By the autumn of 1601 Heywood had become a leading member of the Earl of Worcester's company of players, which became Queen Anne's Men in 1603. This company moved among the Boar's Head, Rose, and Curtain theatres before finally finding a permanent home at the Red Bull in 1607.' All this while, he lived in Southwark (1598–1610) and raised children there, before finally settling north of the river, in Clerkenwell (Figure 1.1).[11]

Heywood was responsible, it seems, for a handful of London-based plays whose genres fall somewhere between what we tend to think of as the 'history play' and City comedy. The two-part *King Edward the Fourth* is usually attributed to him, a work set in London that makes a wide range of topographical references. The two parts were licensed and printed together in 1599. A later work attributed to him, *The Fair Maid of the Exchange* (1602), not only has a specific location in its title—London's commercial centre—but adds 'the pleasant humours of the cripple of Fanchurch, very delectable, and full of mirth'. The Royal Exchange was a bourse or merchants' hall designed and built in 1565 by Sir Thomas Gresham and situated just east of the corner between Cornhill and Threadneedle Street (see Chapter 5). Gresham himself lived nearby in a grand Elizabethan house near the wall just west of Bishopsgate Street. In the play, seamstress Phillis Flower and her friend Mall Berry are pursued by fraternal love rivals attempting to

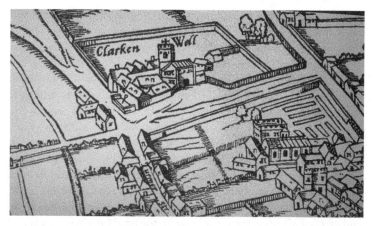

Figure 1.1. Clerkenwell, from the 'Agas' map, (*c.*1561–70). The collection of buildings near the top includes the dissolved priory of St Mary, the church of St James with tower, and adjoining buildings. A water spout over the site of the medieval well is just visible on the left side of the priory, at the corner of the cross-roads (upper left). 'Turner' (Turnbull or Turnmill) Street was London's most infamous street. It was here that brothel-owner Gilbert East resided in the 1570s, near the house of 'Black Luce'. The line of dwellings running north–south (St John's Street, upper right) probably includes the residence of Matthew Shakespeare 'vict-ualer'. The collection of buildings north of Cow Cross comprises the priory of St John (also dissolved). The castellated gatehouse, which still survives, is clearly visible on this map. Reproduced by kind permission of British History Online

outdo each other for the ladies' hearts. The play is set in and around the Cornhill area of north London and makes reference to other locations such as Gracious Street in Bishopsgate and Mile End Green in the east.

Heywood seems to have developed these London interests in his later two-part play, *If You Know Not Me, You Know Nobody* (1603–5). These plays about the accession of Elizabeth I star Gresham as a character. The second part, which focuses centrally on his project of building the Royal Exchange, employs a very specific London topography—St Antholin's church, the Artillery yard, the Rose and Crown in the Poultry, the Dagger Inn at Cheapside, Bridewell prison, St Paul's, Lombard Street, and the Strand—all to lend an air of historicity to the story. It even traces the route Elizabeth I took from Westminster into the City to dine with Gresham and view the bourse.

The play includes an early scene in which Gresham, Sir Thomas and Lady Ramsey, and Dr Alexander Nowell, Dean of St Paul's, shelter from a storm in one of Nowell's chambers and stop to admire the 'pictures' of great London citizens he has on display. Gresham is struck by the charitable foundations that these former aldermen and mayors, and their wives, have established and resolves thereafter to build the Royal Exchange at his own cost. The play zips through time to the defeat of the Spanish Armada and ends with a rousing cheer for Queen Elizabeth. London, for Heywood, was a place of bartering, negotiating, exchange, and winning people over. But it was also a place where the supremacy of the Crown rests upon the endeavours of a rising middle class engaged in international trade. In Heywood's plays, precious commodities like the 'diamond' given to Master Flower at the end of *The Fair Maid of the Exchange*, or the pearl Gresham grinds to a powder and drinks while dancing in his slippers in *2 If You Know Not Me*, have an unsettling, motivating power.

These sketches are necessarily brief, and so much may be said of Jonson's depictions of London that whole books, chapters, and articles have been devoted to the topic.[12] It is worth taking in the view of Ian Donaldson, Jonson's biographer. As Donaldson explains:

Like Dickens, who so admired his plays, Jonson created a vision of the modern city as a busy, mysterious, and labyrinthine place, teeming with eccentric life. He helped to invent the new genre of city comedy that intriguingly reflected the [*sic*] Jacobean London back to itself. He castigated city vice, and thrived on the stimulus of city living.

Jonson's attitude towards the City was a good deal more satirical than Dekker's or Heywood's. In *Bartholomew Fair*, he represents the area of Smithfield (where the annual event was traditionally held, on 24 August) as dotted with stalls and booths and filled with caricature citizens who squabble, brawl, and outdo each other for enterprise or religious zeal. Jonson presents the fair as a Rabelaisian blend of knockabout comedy: it is disorderly, and crammed with cartoon figures. Occasionally, he will refer to real individuals like 'Deaf John' in *The Alchemist* and the lunatic William Whetstone in *Bartholomew Fair*.[13] The relationship between Jonson's civic satire and Shakespeare's work has been illuminatingly explored by David Riggs, but however much each responded to the other's work, even at the most superficial level it is easy to see a strong contrast.[14] Shakespeare presented his audiences with depictions of remote lands populated by largely alien characters. It is almost as if Shakespeare regarded drama and poetry as a means of removing the mind away from the immediate hardships of urban life, perhaps a making of imaginative 'amends' (to use Puck's word at the end of *A Midsummer Night's Dream*) for its many privations. But he was not unrealistic. He did not adopt Sir Philip Sidney's argument in *The Defence of Poesie* that poetry should present not what is (or is not) but what ought to be. Instead, for him, poetry and drama opened up worlds of possibility, sometimes strange, at other times wild, and sometimes powerfully discomfiting.

If Shakespeare aimed to keep London largely (though not entirely) out of his plays, his name had, by the early seventeenth century, become central to the capital's literary culture. The accession of James in 1603 confirmed his position as a leading member of the King's Men. He enjoyed royal patronage, performed at court, and had the admiration, and perhaps envy, of his peers. Heywood, for example, recycled Shakespearean lines through echoes and fragments that an audience would probably have recognized. Early on in *A Woman Killed With Kindness*, the servants' jokes about dancing echo Sir Andrew Aguecheek and remind, following Dogberry, that 'comparisons are odious' (*Woman Killed*, 1.2.15–18). Captain Goodlack, in the first part of *The Fair Maid of the West*, dwells on the notion of 'Opportunity', saying, 'She's the best bawd' (1.3.40–1), recalling the distractions of Lucrece in Shakespeare's 1594 poem. In the same scene, a tavern drawer echoes Shakespeare's serving-boy Francis, 'Anon, anon' (1.3.67), and the same prank is later played by Clem at The Windmill Tavern in Foy (3.2.3). Heywood's parodic drama *The Rape of Lucrece* quips on the phrase 'sick at heart' from the opening of *Hamlet*, and the phrase 'much ado' recurs a number of times throughout all of these works. Similar linguistic traits continue in *The Fair Maid of the Exchange* where echoes of *Venus and Adonis*, *The Merchant of Venice*, *Much Ado About Nothing*, and *Twelfth Night* all surface. Other writers, like Robert Tofte and John Weever, were citing Shakespeare by 1600, and his name was beginning to appear on the title pages of his plays in quarto.[15] As the parody of *Hamlet* in *Eastward Ho* indicates, Shakespeare was rapidly becoming publicly quotable, a sign of his growing regard in London's literary world.

Stratford and London links

Nothing about Shakespeare's dramatic success was inevitable. Possibly the most remarkable feature of his life is that he survived at all, especially to the mature age of fifty-two. Whatever the truth of stories that Shakespeare fled Stratford for London after having risked a flogging for poaching one of Sir Thomas Lucy's deer, or that he joined up with a company of players visiting Stratford called the Queen's Men, it remains the case that Stratford was a risky place to live. Infant mortality rates were high. The town's burial register records a total of fifty-six deaths in 1562, forty-seven of them children (84 per cent). The picture improved slightly the following year, with fifty-one burials in total, including thirty-four children (66.5 per cent). A total of eighty-two baptisms were registered in 1562, but just about half that number of children died the same year. In 1563, eighty-one baptisms were recorded, but well over a third of that number had died by the end of the year, including 'Margareta filia Johannis Shakspere' on 30 April.

The situation was about to get worse. Next to the burial entry for apprentice Oliver Gunne on 11 July 1564, the 'minister' Richard Bifield (or one of his clerks) added, 'Hic incepit pestis', which translates as 'here began the plague'. That year, there were 253 burials in Stratford, 134 of them children. Shakespeare's was one of only thirty-nine baptisms in the entire year. Multiple burials on the same day start to appear in the parish register. Throughout August, September, and October 1564, the daily routine of the church officers seems to have involved little else but the grim work of collecting bodies ready for burial, a task that would only diminish once the air grew cooler in the winter months.[16] Deaths outstripped births and looked set to rid the town of young people altogether. Having lost his daughters Joan and Margaret in 1559 and 1563 respectively, Stratford alderman John Shakespeare might have removed his son to the relative safety of Snitterfield where his own father kept a farm with oxen. Against the odds, Shakespeare, unlike his two elder sisters, somehow survived.[17]

When Shakespeare writes in his earlier plays of departing and arriving, he strikes a genuinely optimistic note: 'Cease to persuade, my loving Proteus. | Home-keeping youth have ever homely wits.' The words are Valentine's, at the opening of *The Two Gentlemen of Verona*, just as he is about to set off for the court of Milan. Proteus wishes his well-willing adventurer safe progress and 'good hap' in setting forth, anticipating that Valentine might see some 'rare noteworthy object' in his travel (1.1.1–15). The prospect of encountering something new, rare, or marvellous on a long journey is not something that a Midlands youth leaving his home town for the first time was likely to forget.

There is a mood of excitement and promise at the beginning of *The Two Gentlemen of Verona*, in anticipation of what the future may hold. Even Lance's wailful account of his own home-leaving (2.3) is turned into sparkling comedy. Petruccio, in *The Taming of the Shrew*, is another newcomer, a third gentleman of Verona who strides into Padua in hope of a wife. The amorous Lucentio arrives in Padua with this father's 'good will' and the 'good company' of Tranio his servant (1.1.6). Setting eyes on Bianca, he is immediately love-struck, and thereafter a madcap series of disguises and ruses ensues until at last every Jack has his Jill. Shakespeare's newcomers, like Antipholus and Dromio of Syracuse in *The Comedy of Errors*, are quickly caught up in a delightful, chaotic hilarity.

We might wonder what it was that generated for Shakespeare this optimistic sense of the city as a place of opportunity and adventure. It possibly stemmed from the example of Stratford's most famous son. Everyone in 1560s Stratford would have known the story of Hugh Clopton, a young man who went to London, became extraordinarily successful and wealthy, and returned to build and live in one of the largest houses in the town, called New Place. A local mercer (or fine-cloth merchant) by trade, Clopton rose to become a prominent London alderman and was elected Lord Mayor of London in 1491. John Stow, in his 1598 *Survey of London*, listed Clopton as one of the City's honourable citizens, a man noted for his charitable works and civic generosity. For the younger Shakespeare, growing up in agrarian Stratford, it was Clopton more than any other figure who had pioneered the journey and come to symbolize all that the capital city could offer. When Shakespeare eventually bought New Place in 1596, just across the road from the Guild chapel (also built by Clopton), he must have seen himself as the great man's heir. Other Stratfordians now regarded him as a man of means. On 25 October 1598, Richard Quiney wrote to Shakespeare from the Bell Inn in Carter Lane, just south of St Paul's Cathedral, asking for a loan of £30. Whether or not Shakespeare responded to this request remains unknown.

Clopton and Shakespeare were not the only Stratfordians with London links. Another Stratford mercer, Humphrey Brace, requested in his will of 1591 that he should be buried in the parish of Stratford and left money for church repairs. A trader in fabrics and textiles, Brace owed a substantial total of over £250 to individuals in both London and Stratford, including alderman Sir John Allott, Master Bartholomew Soames, and Master Allen ('haberdasher'), the first and last being well-placed members of London's ruling Common Council. Brace died owing money also to local Stratford associates, and his will orders that £5 be paid to a 'Mr Queenye' (probably Adrian Quiney). He left a further £5 to the town poor. Another Stratford person linked with the capital was Alice Smith, widow of Stratford and sister of the late Bishop of Winchester, John Watson. He had bequeathed her a gilt bowl and lid which she now passed on to her son-in-law. The Bishop of Winchester's palace stood near the Clink prison on London's Bankside, not just a familiar landmark to all who lived nearby or visited the south bank playhouses but a centre of local authority.

It would be a mistake to suppose that Stratford was totally isolated from the economic and cultural heartland of London. We know that John Shakespeare, the poet's father, represented the Stratford borough in London in the early 1570s. John Hall tells us that his daughter Elizabeth 'went to London' in early April (year unspecified) but had returned by 22 April, ill with a 'distemper' on the side of her face.[18] Other Stratfordians had significant London connections. John Bell, warden of Stratford-upon-Avon and Bishop of Worcester, had been a canon at Westminster and royal chaplain under Henry VIII. Edward Aglionby was member of Parliament for Warwick and recorder of Stratford-upon-Avon in 1571. Peter Smart, clergyman, was born in Stratford and educated at Westminster School. Richard Field, Shakespeare's countryman, also made the journey, becoming apprentice to the printer Thomas Vautrollier who kept a shop in Blackfriars. Field printed *Venus and Adonis* (1593) and *The Rape of Lucrece* (1594). Shakespeare even wrote his fellow Stratfordian into his drama. Shakespeare alludes to Richard Field as 'Richard du Champ' in *Cymbeline* (4.2.379). Under pressure to change character names in *Henry V*, he went back to his roots and chose surnames from among his father's Stratford neighbours—Bardolph, Fluellen, and Court—names probably meaningless in the metropolis but listed in a 1592 citation of hometown recusants alongside John Shakespeare.[19]

There was more than one route from Stratford to London. The most direct journey passed through Banbury, Aylesbury, Uxbridge, and Tyburn (now Marble Arch) in London's western suburbs. A slightly different route was taken by Stratford petitioners John Jeffreyes and Thomas Barber 'of the Bear' who stopped overnight at Oxford in 1590 before making their way to Uxbridge the following day. Once in London, they hooked up with Thomas Greene, a lawyer. Their business done, they returned via Banbury rather than Oxford. Richard Quiney, Adrian's son and one of Shakespeare's close Stratford neighbours, was another traveller between Stratford and London. We know from his letter to Shakespeare that he sojourned at an inn near St Paul's. At the Bell in Carter Lane, he received a letter from Abraham Sturley in anticipation of Shakespeare's procuring £30 or £40 on their behalf. A further letter, from Adrian Quiney to his son Richard, sent to 'the Bell in Carter Lane', urged him to bring some of the money home.[20] But there were Quineys already in London, with apparent Warwickshire connections, and they too had something of a wayward reputation.

In the mid-1570s, Bartholomew Quiney, a clothworker like Adrian the Stratford mercer, was investigated at London's Bridewell Hospital for keeping ill rule in his house. A servant, Thomas Clark, testified on 21 December 1575 regarding the improper conduct of Joan, Bartholomew's wife, with a 'Master Farmer'. Farmer and Joan denied everything but were 'detained prisoner' since neither seemed to be telling the truth. The same court later heard of a Roger Quiney, son to an apothecary living in Bucklersbury, who sought to introduce an associate to 'two handsome wenches in Shoreditch at the pump under the wall, which were light housewives'.[21] Bucklersbury was a short lane popularly known for its perfumeries, tobacco stalls, and grocers (see chapter 5). Coincidentally, it was where Richard Quiney's son, also called Richard, later set up shop as a grocer.[22]

Shakespeare writes of Bucklersbury as being fragrant. In *The Merry Wives of Windsor* Falstaff quips of lovers who lisp like women in men's apparel and 'smell like Bucklersbury in simple time' (3.3.67). John Stow, describing Bucklersbury in 1598, states, 'The whole street called Buckles bury on both sides throughout is possessed of Grocers and Apothecaries'. Of the vials and distillations in this lane, Thomas Becon wrote in 1563, 'If one devil be in so little portion of incense, what a number of devils be there in all the apothecaries' shops that are in Bucklersbury'. Walsingham wrote to Burghley in 1581, hoping 'that his absence will do him more good than all the drugs in Bucklersbury'.[23] In Sonnet 5, a delicately lyrical poem, Shakespeare writes of youth as a distillation of summer's essence, like a fragrance, 'A liquid prisoner pent in walls of glass' whose 'substance still lives sweet'. In the next sonnet, he exhorts the young man to 'make sweet some vial' (No. 6, l. 3). Poetry preserves beauty like a flower in an apothecary's bottle, or like the healing 'Honey of Roses' and 'sugar dissolved in Rosewater' we find in John Hall's casebook (published 1657).[24]

That young Richard Quiney of Stratford should have relocated to Bucklersbury hints at the possibility that he may have gone to reside with relatives there. It is not implausible that Shakespeare might have had London cousins too. We know that Thomas Greene, who lodged with Shakespeare at New Place, called himself Shakespeare's 'cousin', but this may not necessarily imply a kindred relationship. Intriguingly, a Matthew Shakespeare appears in the parish registers of Clerkenwell, a north-western London suburb, throughout the 1570s. He had eight children, all of whom except for the last, Thomas, died in infancy. Matthew Shakespeare appears in the Middlesex County Sessions records, where he is cited as a 'victualler' living in St John's Street (Figure 1.1). Trouble seems to have followed him around. Two servants of Sir John Perrot took against him for an unspecified reason, and later he found a dead body outside his front door, the loser in a duel that had taken place in nearby Wood's Close. The body seems just to have been dumped there. These details add local colour, but what makes Matthew Shakespeare of greater interest is his marriage in 1569 to Isabel Peele at Christchurch Greyfriars, Newgate. Christchurch stood directly next door to Christ's Hospital where James Peele was school bursar and where his son, the dramatist George Peele, was educated before going on to Oxford. Marriage to a Peele in this church almost certainly means that Isabel Peele was George's sister. When Shakespeare sat down to write *Titus Andronicus* in the early 1590s, Peele's sister was, or had been, Mistress Isabel Shakespeare married to Matthew Shakespeare of St John's Street, Clerkenwell.[25]

In 1592, Shakespeare seems to have been a relatively new arrival to London. A pamphlet titled *Greene's Groatsworth of Wit* (1592), ostensibly by the dramatist and prose writer Robert Greene (but possibly by

Henry Chettle, its printer), criticized Shakespeare as an 'upstart crow' beautifying himself with the feathers of other writers, while remaining a 'Johannes fac totum' or mere dogsbody. Punning on a line from Shakespeare's *3 Henry VI*, the author sees this upstart as arrogant, having a 'tiger's heart wrapped in a player's hide', one who thinks himself 'the only Shake-scene in a country'. The misquotation and pejorative 'Shake-scene' is a clear hint as to who this *parvenu* is. The word 'country' here refers to a home area or town from the shires and emphasizes that this new writer is an outsider. Greene (or Chettle) calls men like this 'buckram Gentlemen', 'peasants', and 'new-comers' (sig. F1ʳ).[26] The *Groatsworth* author might have written 'the only Shake-scene in a city' but seems to deliberately specify the countryside instead. Buckram, as Falstaff declares in his lines about the Gads Hill robbery in *1 Henry IV*, was a coarse cloth or canvas starched for durability with a gum or paste, the apparel of 'rogues' (2.4.185). The *Groatsworth of Wit* author is out to warn his fellows that this 'Shake-scene' is an overambitious country boy new to the game.

Coming from the 'country', Shakespeare could never really be a Londoner. As we shall see in Chapter 5, the terms 'alien' or 'stranger' usually designated visitors from overseas. The word 'foreigner' applied to English people from outside the City.[27] London's authorities regarded the growing number of vagrants in the city streets as particularly worrying. Unwanted outsiders from the shires were sometimes labelled 'foreign born' before being sent home. As anxieties about vagrancy grew, Elizabeth's Parliament passed the first of its 'poor laws', the famous '43rd' of 1601. This act ordered the expulsion of masterless and idle persons from the City, and pressure was applied to put it into effect. From 22 May 1602 to 17 March 1603, vagrants 'born in foreign counties' were herded through the courts, whipped, and packed off to the provinces from whence they came. On 16 April 1603, Richard Burton and Thomas Bartlet were both whipped as vagrants and returned via a network of constables to Warwick, with tuppence each to see them on their way. Arriving from Stratford prior to 1592, Shakespeare too was 'foreign born'. When Orlando, in *As You Like It*, tells Duke Senior that 'this boy is forest-born' (5.4.30), he does so to attest to Ganymede's innocence as an outsider to the court, and so, too, as a person without reproach.

Stratford had important historical, economic, and religious links with the capital city. With Shakespeare, it had unique cultural and artistic links too. Shakespeare kept his home in Stratford, and when in London he seems to have resided in areas populated with strangers of various kinds. He may have travelled with his acting company, as well as moving between Stratford and London. Even in London, he seems to have been itinerant, moving addresses on at least four occasions. He could never really embrace London or call it his own. Intellectually, his interests lay in stories about people and places far distant either in time or geography. In *The Two Gentlemen of Verona*, *The Taming of the Shrew*, and *The Comedy of Errors*, he captured the excitement he himself might have felt as a new arrival in an unfamiliar city. But this eagerness begins to fade. The plays become absorbed by different kinds of exclusion—lovers caught in a mazy woodland, exiles holding court in a French forest, a black general hated by his friend, a daughter 'strangered' by her father, a military hero banished from Rome, a misanthrope hiding in a cave outside the city, and a savage who ends as sole possessor of a remote island somewhere in the Mediterranean or 'Bermoothes'. These are all stories that tell of personal estrangement. Even in his most city-based play of the 1590s, *The Merchant of Venice*, Shakespeare presents an already alienated protagonist, Shylock, only to humiliate and exclude him further at the end. The dominant perspective in all these plays is that of an outsider whose place in society is uncertain. We might almost think Shakespeare to have been a reluctant Londoner.

Places

Even in Shakespeare's most continental plays, London locations occasionally surface. *The Taming of the Shrew* seems decidedly Italian: with Kate of the Minola family and Lucentio of the Bentivolii (1.1.13), we seem to be in the heart of Italy. But when Petruccio arranges to ride with Kate to her father's house, they dismount at the end of 'Long Lane' (4.3.183), a London street that led from Barbican to Smithfield market.[1] Just before the dance in *Much Ado about Nothing*, Beatrice tells a masked Benedick what she thinks of him: 'I am sure he [Benedick] is in the fleet' (2.1.134). Both the 1600 and 1623 editions of the play capitalize the word 'fleet', as though it were a proper noun. The River Fleet, which ran from underground springs near Clerkenwell southwards to the Thames, past the Fleet prison, was notorious for its filth and stench. Beatrice seems to imply that Benedick is up to his neck in it. Isolated as these allusions are, they connect the play to its audience in moments of recognition. In order to clarify these moments, and to lay out the topographical context for this book, this chapter sets out key areas of the capital, its principal landmarks and locations, and highlights their connections with Shakespeare's work. It is inevitably selective. It begins by considering the metropolis as a whole, via contemporary maps and panoramas and prose accounts of the capital, by John Stow and Henry Machyn. It then focuses on specific areas to the north, south, east, and west, to highlight some of the ways in which these locations had a bearing on Shakespeare's life and work.

The story of England's capital is in fact a tale of two cities, London and Westminster, and these were very much divided in terms of jurisdiction, power, wealth, and population (see Figures 4.3 and 5.1). Not surprisingly, Westminster stood to the west of the walled City of

London. It followed the curve of the river leading east towards the City of London and comprised mainly the royal court at Whitehall, the historic abbey, St James's Park, and the grand houses along the Strand with spacious gardens opening onto the Thames that belonged to the aristocracy. By contrast, the City of London was a place of narrow thoroughfares, lanes, and alleyways and filled with the 'middling', labouring, or 'common' sorts of people. It was a diverse, bustling place, bounded by the landmarks of Temple Bar at its western edge and the Tower of London on its eastern side (Figure 2.1). The City covered an area of just over a square mile. It was divided into twenty-six 'wards' or districts, each responsible for electing an alderman to represent it at the Common Council, the City's largest administrative body. The old City wall, built by the Romans and fortified over the centuries, marked a physical limit but was not technically the official boundary. The 'wards' of Farringdon Without, Cripplegate, Bishopsgate, and Portsoken, for example, all extended outside ('without') the wall. On the south side of the Thames lay Southwark, a borough placed under the jurisdiction of the City as the twenty-sixth ward, known as Bridge Ward Without.[2] Since 1215, London had been able to elect its own mayor, and over time it had evolved an efficient system of government with the mayor presiding over sheriffs, the Court of Aldermen, and Court of Common Council.

One might be inclined to think that the early modern 'sights' of London would be fairly few and easy to list: the Thames, Westminster Abbey, St Paul's Cathedral, the Bridge, the Tower of London, the Middle and Inner Temples, the Royal Exchange, and the grim place of execution at Tyburn. But there were and are, of course, many other important sites, some of them less immediately visible. One of these is a misshapen lump of limestone that for many years lay hidden behind an unremarkable grille in the wall of 111 Cannon (formerly 'Candlewick') Street.[3] The rock probably dates from Roman times and a plaque over the grille explains its significance: 'This is a fragment of the original piece of limestone once securely fixed in the ground now fronting Cannon Street Station. Removed in 1742 to the north side of the street, in 1798 it was built into the south wall of the Church of St Swithun London Stone which stood here until demolished in 1962. Its origin and purpose are unknown but in 1188 there was a reference to Henry, son of Eylwin de Lundenstane, subsequently Lord Mayor of London' (Figure 2.2).

© The Hebrew University of Jerusalem & The Jewish National & University Library

Figure 2.1. The Braun and Hogenberg bird's-eye map of London (c.1572), showing the stretch of the Thames from Westminster (west) to the Tower of London (east). The old Roman wall reached from the Tower to Blackfriars. London Bridge led to Southwark. On this map, the Bull and Bear baiting rings are visible on Bankside. Public domain

Figure 2.2. The plaque and grille marking the location of London Stone at 111 Cannon Street. Photo by the author

This stone features as a theatrical prop in *2 Henry VI* after Jack Cade, the wild Kentish rebel, has fought his way northwards across London Bridge to Candlewick Street (now Cannon Street). A stage direction at the start of 4.6 reads, 'Enter Jack Cade and the rest, and strikes his sword upon London stone'. Shakespeare took this action from Edward Hall's 1548 chronicle, the play's main source. John Stow similarly noted it in 1598: 'In the year 1450, Jack Cade, and other rebels of Kent, by this bridge entered the City, he struck his sword on London Stone, and said himself then to be Lord of the City'.[4] In the play, Cade presumptuously sits on the stone (probably a painted wooden prop), and declares, 'Now is Mortimer lord of this city' (4.6.1). His progress into north London signals the contested nature of the City: a messenger tells that 'the rascal people', London's ne'er-do-wells, have joined his cause. In the politically volatile years of the early 1590s, announcing oneself lord of the City was daring even when spoken on a playhouse stage.

Theatre made it possible to memorialize those who had once lived among London's spaces. Stow tells us that Margaret, Countess of Shrewsbury, 'late wife of the true and victorious knight and redoubtable warrior, John Talbot', was buried in the Jesus Chapel in St Paul's.[5] Thomas Nashe's prose pamphlet *Pierce Penniless, his Supplication to the*

Devil (entered in the Stationers' Register on 8 August 1592) breaks off its tale to reflect,

How it would have joyed brave *Talbot* (the terror of the French) to think that after he had lain two hundred years in his tomb, he should triumph again on the stage, and have his bones new embalmed with the tears of ten thousand spectators at least (at several times), who, in the tragedian that represents his person, imagine they behold him fresh bleeding.[6]

Nashe's tone here is almost celebratory. In *1 Henry VI*, Sir John Talbot is England's great war-hero, a man whose very name causes the enemy to flee. Nashe regarded the play as a theatrical triumph—after all, he seems to have written its first act.[7] Yet Nashe also knew London's darker side. In *Pierce Penniless, his Supplication to the Devil* (1592), he asks, 'is there any place so lewd, as this Lady London?' Ambivalent regarding most things—politics, religion, gender, and even skin colour—Shakespeare seems more decided than Nashe about London. This chapter explores not just the urban places Shakespeare might have known but also his attitude to them, so far as we may be able to gauge it. For while there were plenty of writers willing to eulogize the City by various means—in panegyrics, encomia, and even in topographical maps and surveys—Shakespeare, it seems, was not one of them.[8]

Maps and panoramas

London Stone, preserved in the heart of the City, is just visible on one of the finest early modern maps, the so-called 'Agas' map. This map, named after a supposed but unlikely association with the Elizabethan surveyor Ralph Agas, is one of several extraordinarily detailed and beautiful images of mid- to late-sixteenth-century London. Produced between 1561 and 1570, it shows not just the streets and lanes of a thriving city but many of the more rural surrounding areas as well. The Thames stretches placidly across its wood-cut panels, left to right, from Westminster to the Tower of London. Open fields surround a compact hub of houses, churches, streets, and alleyways crammed into the walled City. Spacious fields dotted with hamlets and thoroughfares bordered the great wall on all sides. The 'Agas' map shows London as a place of ordered activity: men herd sheep into pens at Smithfield; archers practise in Moorfields and Finsbury; women dry laundry in nearby St Giles; watermen ferry passengers across the Thames as the royal barge passes upstream; a couple walk their dog along the river in Paris Garden; and men prepare for a bull-baiting as dogs in nearby kennels strain upon their leashes. At the Steelyard or Dowgate, cattle are watered on the Thames' shore. The impression is of an organized, well-governed, and settled city, a place in which one might like to live.

Another map, printed at Cologne in *Civitates Orbis Terrarum* (1572) by topographers Georg Braun and Frans Hogenberg, clearly relies on the earlier 'Agas' design for much of its detail (Figure 2.1). But it largely omits the human populace, save for an occasional waterman on the river and two men and women greeting each other in the foreground. Both this and the 'Agas' map almost certainly derive from an earlier 'Copperplate Map' from the 1550s, so called because it was printed from engraved copper sheets, of which only three sections are known to be extant. The Copperplate Map gives a lively, if more quirky, sense of human activity in the capital: archers shoot in the northern limits, pigs are herded along paths, young women play with dogs, men enjoy musket practice, and a woman defecates out of the way near St Mary Spital. The Copperplate Map clearly shows the well in St Helen's Bishopsgate at which Shakespeare must have drawn water, or met friends, when he was staying there in the mid-1590s. Again, apart from the occasional set of gallows at Charing Cross, Newgate, or Tower Hill, and the traitors' heads over the City gates, one might think the City a place of calm and pleasant aspect.

These pictorial representations of London were probably made as guides for foreign visitors and merchants. We gain more detailed impressions—especially regarding the architectural outlines of particular buildings—from the panoramas of London that have survived from the sixteenth and seventeenth centuries. The earliest of these panoramas are the sketches of Flemish artist Anthonis van den Wyngaerde between 1554 and 1557 (Figure 2.3). Wyngaerde's drawings represent London in breathtaking detail. We get a clear sense from his meticulous craftsmanship of how compressed the City was as a centre of life, work, and worship. One of Wyngaerde's sections shows London Bridge resting on its nineteen supporting piers, heavily built up with fortified buildings lined with traitors' heads on pikes. Traffic across the river was clearly a great deal easier by boat. Anyone wishing (as the Burbages did) to transport the timbers of an old theatre to Bankside

Figure 2.3. A detail of London Bridge, from a later redrawing of Wyngaerde's panoramic sketches of London (*c.*1554–57), showing (right to left) St Olave's, Tooley Street, London Bridge, the church of St Mary Overy (St Saviour's). Public domain

and reconstruct it there is likely to have chosen a 'lighter' or barge as the preferred means of transport. Guarded by the Tower to its east, the Bridge acted as a barrier to foreign invasion.

Remarkable as Wyngaerde's drawings are, other 'views' of London by Claes Janszoon Visscher (Figure 2.4) and Wenceslaus Hollar in *c.*1625 and *c.*1647 respectively are of especial interest to theatre historians. These 'rooftop' panoramas show a crowded, neatly packed urban centre, the sky spiked with church steeples. Both Visscher and Hollar depict St Paul's Cathedral without its spire: it caught fire after a storm in 1561 and was not replaced before Wren's rebuilding after the Great Fire of 1666. Hollar's long westward view along the Thames shows the houses of the nobility along the Strand on the northern bank, and, on the south side, the second Globe and Bear-baiting arenas with their labels mistakenly reversed. Visscher presents a view of London from a vantage point south-west of the Bridge and shows St Paul's dominating the skyline. He adds audience members making their way to the Bear Garden and the Globe. While Hollar represents the Globe as circular, and Visscher gives it as octagonal, archaeological discoveries have demonstrated that the Globe was probably a sixteen-sided (possibly

Figure 2.4. A section from Claes Janszoon Visscher's panorama, titled *Londinium Florentissima Britanniae Urbs* (1625, from an original made in 1616), showing the Globe on Bankside. The property with chimney smoke towards the right appears to have been, or included, 'The Vyne'. Reproduced from a tinted Victorian lithograph by kind permission of Peter Harrington Rare Books

eighteen-sided) polygonal structure. Excavations have shown that its replacement structure in 1614 had a tiring-house door and an additional stair tower, shown in Hollar's engraving.[9] So although these illustrations give fascinating detail, their accuracy is variable to say the least. And, as much as we value them, they cannot show the life that went on inside the buildings they depict. For the human life of the City, we have to turn to other sources.

John Stow

When John Stow dedicated his *Survey of London* (1598) to the Lord Mayor, Robert Lee, and the citizens of London, he explained he had wanted to show 'what London hath been of ancient time'.[10] His work has sometimes been regarded as antiquarian, restricted to worthies and benefactors who over the centuries had sustained the City's 'temporal government'. But laced into his narrative are some personal opinions. He disapproved of the 'enclosure' of common land for private gain, building on fields and open spaces, the number of towers and tall structures, and the increase in carts, coaches, and 'whirlicotes' that blocked up narrow lanes. But he also lived in the real world. As a young man, he'd witnessed an execution that took place outside his house in Cornhill. He quarrelled with his family, especially his brother Thomas, and with Richard Grafton, a rival London historian. We see him in the *Survey* denouncing Grafton's claims as 'incredible, & altogether unpossible' and mocking him for taking a stone to be the very tooth of 'Gerrard the Giant'.[11]

Stow begins his *Survey* with an account of those aspects most fundamental to London—the various springs and water sources that sustained it. Noting the legend of London's origins as the city of 'Troynovant' (founded by Brutus and built up by King Lud before the arrival of Julius Caesar), Stow turns to the various wells, bourns, brooks, and rivers that for centuries had served the people living there. He notes the 'marvellous quiet course' of the Thames, from Oxfordshire to London, but also the 'diverse fair wells and fresh springs' with 'sweet and fresh waters' that allowed the City to flourish. Walbrook, running southwards from Finsbury to the Thames, was one of the earliest-known central tributaries for fresh water. Other important water courses included the Tyburn and Fleet rivers, the 'River of the Wells', Turnmill and Langbourne brooks, Holy Well (Holywell, Shoreditch), Clerks' Well (Clerkenwell), Skinners' Well, Clement's Well, and St Bride's Well (Bridewell). Stow notes that plays had for a long time been staged close to the Clerks' and Skinners' wells. Cisterns, 'bosses', and water conduits had been established through the medieval period at Cheapside, Cornhill, Billingsgate, Cripplegate, and the gaols of Ludgate and Newgate. Clean water was essential and made available through an increasing number of channels. It was even directed through lead pipes to houses of the wealthy. But, as Stow observes, many of these brooks and streams had over time filled up with filth and were now 'sore decayed'. He notes historic attempts to 'scour', 'cleanse', or dredge them. Without drains, London had a serious problem with pollution.

Stow's thoughts then turn to security, and he devotes the next sections of his *Survey* to the ditch or moat around the City wall, various bridges, the City's fortified gates and water inlets, and its towers, castles, and citadels, including the Tower of London, Mint and Royal Exchange, Barnard's Castle, Barbican, and fortifications on London Bridge itself. Stow makes clear that these fortifications are institutions not only for control but also for protection of England's

'Treasury of the ornaments and Jewels of the Crown'. The safety of the state depended upon them. Stow follows these observations with accounts of the London law colleges, the Inns of Court and Chancery, customs and practices in the City, sports and pastimes, neighbourhood watch arrangements, and commoners, including several women, who rose to become citizens with important legacies in funding or founding London charitable schemes. Poor relief, repair of roads, bridges, and buildings, education, and water supply are all listed as areas of key investment made by wealthier Londoners to develop a robust infrastructure by the late sixteenth century.

The rest of his *Survey* is devoted to a ward-by-ward walk-through of streets and civic spaces, starting from the east by the Tower of London and moving gradually westwards, beyond the boundary at Temple Bar and into the City of Westminster. Stow begins with Portsoken (just north and east of the Tower) and follows with the wards of Aldgate, Lime Street, Bishopsgate, Broadstreet, Cornhill, Langbourne, Billingsgate, Bridgeward within, Candlewick Street, Walbrook, Dowgate, the Vintry, Cordwainer Street, Cheapside, Coleman Street, Bassinghall, Cripplegate, Aldersgate, Farringdon within and Farringdon without (within or outside the City wall respectively), Bread Street, Queenhithe, Castle Baynard, and Bridge ward (Southwark). The historical significance of landmarks in these areas is noted, as Stow tracks his way through suburbs and liberties such as the Tower, Norton Folgate (north of Bishopsgate), St Martin's, the Glasshouse (near Charterhouse), Saffron Hill, the Temple, St Paul's, Blackfriars, Bridewell, and Whitefriars—areas that lay technically outside the jurisdiction of the City itself and paid a subsidy for this freedom. Stow depicts the City as united through a network of shared responsibilities. The Bridge House, he notes, was used for housing materials necessary for the repair of the Bridge. But it also had garners and granaries for storing corn, and ten ovens (six of them 'very large') to bake bread 'for relief of the poor citizens, when need should require'. Aside from his own personal irritations, Stow represents the City as a place of grand accomplishment. Quoting the Roman poet Livy, he writes that the purpose of his *Survey* is 'to make the first foundation of [the City] more honourable, more sacred, and as it were of greater majesty'.[12] To some extent, Stow's London is a fossil, its life entombed in stone in monuments to the good and great. It is only in his personal and family recollections that the abrasive quality of everyday life emerges. His sister-in-law declared that, having looked after Stow's mother, 'I forsake God, if I have not washed 10 bucks of shitten clouts that she hath shitten'.[13]

Henry Machyn

Stow's lists of illustrious London citizens—former Lord Mayors, aldermen, benefactors, and figures of esteem—serve as a kind of textual funerary monument, the work of the stonemason carried over into the medium of print. A rather different London commentator, one who probably never imagined his jottings would ever be published, was himself an arranger of funerals. Henry Machyn was parish clerk for Holy Trinity-the-Less and frequently involved in elaborate funerals for people whose estates, or relatives, could afford them. Machyn made banners, rolls, and heraldic escutcheons (sometimes called 'impresas') for these occasions. Decorative banners or palls might be made of expensive materials such as velvet or silk, while heraldic shields were often formed from papier mâché, similar in construction perhaps to those used as props in stage plays such as *Pericles* or Middleton's *Your Five Gallants*. After his death, Machyn left behind a detailed diary covering significant London historical and political events, especially for the years 1550–63.

Machyn's diary is a fascinating record of life in the City. He notes occasions for merriment. May celebrations in Fenchurch Street involved a 'goodly May-pole', morris dancing, a giant, moors, and a model castle. Wrestling matches were held at Clerkenwell and Bartholomew Fair in Smithfield, and shooting matches in Finsbury. A great 'scaffold' was set up for a play at the Queen's hall in Westminster, performed by the gentlemen of the Middle Temple. Crowds gathered in 1552 at a stage or scaffold built near the cross at Cheapside to await the procession of the 'king's lord of misrule', with a similar festive event the following year. At a feast hosted by the Company of Skinners, the diners enjoyed spiced breads, cherries, strawberries, apples, marmalade, sugar, comfits, oranges, Hippocras, Rhenish and Claret wines, 'and beer and ale great plenty'.

But Machyn's interest is also caught by more grisly events. He notes the hanging of John Mosbie and his sister in Smithfield, on 14 March 1550, and executions of their associates, for the murder of Master

Arden of Faversham, Kent. This conspiracy became the substance of the play now known as *Arden of Faversham* (printed in 1592) in which Shakespeare may have had a hand.[14] Machyn records the arrest and execution of Sir Thomas Wyatt the Younger whose uprising against Mary Tudor failed in 1554, adding the gruesome fact that Wyatt's head was placed in a basket to be carried 'to Newgate to be parboiled'. In the event, it was stolen as a martyr's relic. Other pitiful scenes he records include brandings for heresy, fatalities, suicides, and horrifying accidents—a man fatally wounded after a blind bear bit out a piece of his leg, or a startled horse kicking out the brains of its rider. The *Diary* tells of rebels drawn on hurdles to execution at Tyburn, petty offenders carted or set in the pillory, public whippings, and mothers who killed their offspring—including 'a man's daughter', in the riverside Worcester House, who 'was delivered with a child, and after cast it out of a window into [the] Thames' (Worcester House was used as a brothel in the 1570s, and perhaps earlier).

Alongside such detail, Machyn records major historical events: the arrest of Lady Jane Grey and her followers, the coronation procession of Mary Tudor in 1553, Wyatt's rebellion of 1554, a 'blazing star' or comet in 1556, the lightning strike that brought down the steeples of St Martin's Ludgate and St Paul's, the death and funeral of Mary Tudor, and the coronation of Elizabeth I.[15] The funerals in which Machyn took such interest were rich in theatrical implication. The wealthier sort often left instruction in their wills for bells to be rung, prayers to be said, and bread to be given out to the poor. Obsequies for an important citizen could involve chief mourners, the priest or minister, heralds, friends and business associates of the deceased, the executors, women, and children. Banners, standards, rolls, drapes, palls, hearse-cloth, and shields all added to the sense of a ceremonial occasion. The contrast between criminals carted out of town to be strung up before a gaping crowd at Tyburn, and the stately honours on show at funerals of worthy citizens, could hardly be more stark, and this huge social differentiation is evident in the strangely moving but sometimes shocking document Machyn left behind. London may have been a place of great opportunity for Shakespeare, but, as Machyn shows, it was also a place of horrors. As we trace across the City, from north to south, and east to west, we tend to find this gloomier aspect predominant in the plays.

North

Shakespeare had several connections with the northern fringes of London. We know from documents in the National Archives, and from a detailed study by Charles Nicholl, that Shakespeare lodged in the year 1604 at a house in north London on the corner of Mugwell Street and Silver Street. The house, visible on the 'Agas' map, should not be assumed to be merely generic. It seems that while here, in the home of Christopher Mountjoy, a Huguenot 'tire-maker', Shakespeare may have drafted *King Lear*, and come into contact with George Wilkins, his co-writer on *Pericles*. But Silver Street was not Shakespeare's only north London residence. According to John Aubrey, Shakespeare had once 'lived in Shoreditch', a possibility Nicholl accepts as likely.[16] Yet although a joke about coarse language spoken in nearby Finsbury occurs in *1 Henry IV* (3.1.248), Shakespeare nowhere mentions Shoreditch, Holywell, Clerkenwell, or Islington despite the fact that—prior to 1599—his plays were routinely performed there at the Curtain or Theatre playhouses. These two buildings emphatically link Shakespeare to London's northern suburbs in the 1590s. John Stow visited Shoreditch but had little to say about its theatre industry, noting only a marginal reference to the 'Theatre and Curtain for Comedies and other shows'. He gives the north end of Bishopsgate Street the name Be[a]rwards Lane, presumably because men led bears in and out of London by this route.[17]

It is worth pursuing what we know about the Curtain a little further, since archaeological evidence has found it to have had a distinctive, rectangular shape. Consequently, a good deal of reappraisal about this playhouse has taken place.[18] It is sometimes said that the Curtain began life as a playhouse in 1577. In fact, we do not know when the Curtain was built. In 1577, the puritan-minded John Northbrooke mentioned it as one of London's many schools for 'wickedness and vice to be learned in'.[19] This allusion to the playhouse as a place of learning is worth noting. The following year, a foreign visitor to London, L. Grenade, recorded his impressions of Shoreditch:

At one end of this meadow are two very fine theatres, one of which is magnificent in comparison with the other and has an imposing appearance on the outside. This theatre can hold from 4 to 5,000 people and it is said that a great Lord had it erected. Now, both of these were erected and dedicated for the performance of some plays and other spectacles, most of which comprise actions made up for pleasure rather than ones that have actually taken place.[20]

Grenade probably exaggerated his audience figures here. Some critics have argued that early playhouses could accommodate up to around 3,000 audience members, although this may be an optimistic estimate. All the same, these structures were very popular social spaces and for that reason they had to be built, as Grenade points out, 'outside the city'. Grenade explains further that these venues were used for 'plays and other spectacles', and we know that fencing matches, or 'prizes', took place at the Curtain between 1575 and 1590. He adds that 'a great Lord' erected the more ornate and attractive of the two playhouses. Since James Burbage had been the leading player in the Earl of Leicester's company, it seems possible that Leicester was the implied 'lord'. But Leicester did not build, or fund, the Theatre. The lease of property in Holywell taken out for the Theatre in 1576 states repeatedly that Burbage had undertaken to construct, repair, or even dismantle property on the site 'at his own proper costs and charges'. Moreover, his business partner's widow, Margaret Brayne, complained in 1592 that 'it was her husband's wealth that built the Theatre, as everyone knoweth'.[21]

But Grenade's account helps us to reinterpret a puzzle that has long attached to the Curtain. In 1592, the then-owner of the playhouse, Henry Lanman, agreed that James Burbage and his brother-in-law John Brayne could share in its profits, since they were 'taking the Curtain as an Esore to their playhouse'.[22] This word 'Esore' has often been rendered as 'easer' and interpreted as referring to a financial 'easement', here established by way of a neighbourly agreement. In truth, we do not know what this word means. But we might hazard a guess that it meant something a good deal less unusual or complicated than a financial arrangement. The two playhouses have traditionally been understood as relatively contemporaneous with one another. Speaking of them together, Grenade says that one of the two theatres was more magnificent than the other. The inevitable question is: which one? In 1613, Antimo Galli reported on the visit of the Venetian ambassador Foscarini to the Curtain. Galli speaks of the playhouse as, 'an infamous place in which no good citizen or gentleman would show his face'.[23] John Aubrey, writing somewhat unreliably of Ben Jonson in the 1680s, alleged that he 'acted and wrote, but both ill, at the Green Curtain, a kind of nursery or obscure playhouse'.[24] The *OED* cites the theatrical meaning of the word 'nursery' as '†2c. A theatre established in London for the training of actors. Obs[olete].' Both Northbrooke and Aubrey seem to imply the Curtain was a location where actors learned their art and rehearsed, in addition to putting on performances. From the evidence, it would seem that it was the meaner or more rudimentary of the two playhouses. The word 'Esore' may imply that it was also the earlier.

The biblical character Esau was a rougher, more despised elder brother, the first of twins. The first-born son of patriarch Isaac, and robbed of an inheritance by his younger brother Jacob, Esau had been coarse in appearance from birth. Jacob tells his mother Rebekah in Genesis 27:11, 'Esau my brother is a hairy man, and I am a smooth man'. St Paul, in Romans 9:13, quotes the prophet Malachi, 'Jacob have I loved, but Esau have I hated'. In 1584, John Jewel, Bishop of Salisbury, wrote in his exposition of Thessalonians, 'In this world, as there is a Jacob, so is there an Esau' (sig. P4ʳ), and similarly, John Bate observed in his dialogue *The Portraiture of Hypocrisy* (1589), 'where there is a Jacob, there is an Esau' (sig. K1ʳ). Phonetic spellings are common in the era. We find them in wills, and repeatedly in Henslowe's 'Diary': for example, 'the gresyan comody' and 'sege of london'.[25] The document in which the word occurs is hastily written in an ordinary English cursive hand (Figure 2.5).[26] The Curtain, then, may have been an Esau to the Theatre's Jacob, rough and plain since its inception, a slightly elder brother to the younger, more attractive sibling. This explanation at least fits with the syntax and cultural context of the line, and it is the kind of metaphor an actor like Burbage

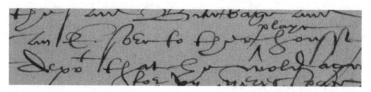

Figure 2.5. Document recording James Burbage and John Brayne's understanding of the Curtain as an 'Esore' to the Theatre, TNA C14/226/11/(Pt 1): 'the said Burbage and Braynes taking the Curtain as an Esore to ther playe housse' Reproduced by permission from the National Archives

might have enjoyed. The Curtain and the Theatre were perhaps London's twin playhouses, the Curtain earlier but not by much. Burbage and Brayne may have felt this priority gave them a *de facto* right to its profits. Much remains uncertain, but the explanation seems also to accord with archaeological discoveries at the excavation of the playhouse on Curtain Road.

Shoreditch was an area of some cultural diversity. In the parish registers of St Leonard, Shoreditch, we find a thriving, populous community, its life set down in baptisms, marriages, and burials. The registers make specific references to addresses in Shoreditch: Halliwell (Holywell) Street, New Rents, Rose Alley, Hoxton, Curtain Rents, Cock Alley, Church End, Talbot Alley, Allen's Rents, Crown Rents, and Cross Key Alley. Some of these locations, such as Church End near St Leonard, Cross Key Alley by St Mary's Spital, Rose Alley, and Talbot Alley just south of Hog Lane are clearly marked on the 1738–47 London map by John Rocque. Thanks to archaeological work on the nearby playhouses, we can hazard a reasonable guess at where 'Curtain Rents' may have stood. But the precise situations of the other addresses are harder to identify. We learn from the burial register that the parish was home to a number of strangers, including Katherine Winckell ('a Frenchwoman'), Sapio Berhone, Edward Bassano and his son Valentine, Patricio and Anne Ubaldino with their daughter and son Lowrye and Roberto, Boone Provoio, Charles de la Moy, and, as we saw in Chapter 1, Thomas Dycher (Dekker?), whose son-in-law was buried in 1599. Other, more familiar names, feature in the registers too. Cuthbert Burbage of 'Halliwell' buried his son James on 15 July 1597, and the actor John Duke of 'Three Cups Alley' interred his children Susan and William on 11 July 1600 and 3 February 1606. Intriguingly, a burial entry occurs for 'Elizabeth Pope ye wife of Thomas Pope' on 25 October 1584. If this is a reference to the future Lord Strange's and Lord Chamberlain's actor, it is the earliest such reference we have. It also shows this Thomas Pope living in at the 'Three Cups' alley, a neighbour to John Duke, and of course to the Burbages in Holywell Street.

Living outside the City wall perimeter, even near the greener spaces of Shoreditch, offered little protection against disease. The printer of Shakespeare's First Folio, William Jaggard, also living in 'Hollowell street', lost his daughters Jane and Elizabeth, son William, and servant Thomas Greene to the plague of 1603. The same infection took Richard Burbage's daughter Francis and Christopher Beeston's son Augustine, apparently named after Lord Chamberlain's actor Augustine Phillips who was probably the child's godfather.[27] If Shakespeare lived nearby, perhaps in not-so-far-away Bishopsgate, these were not just his colleagues or associates but neighbours and fellow worshippers. The lively and controversial Welsh clergyman Meredith Hanmer was vicar at St Leonard's, Shoreditch, until 1592 and is likely to have given entertaining sermons. But the life of the plays seemed to matter just as much. Richard Burbage (who very probably played the part of Romeo) named his daughter Juliet and buried her at St Leonard's in 1608. She was just six years old. Shakespeare's fellow actors William Sly and Richard Cowley also appear in the register, interred in 1608 and 1616 respectively.

For more cheerful occasions, Shoreditch hosted nine alehouses, according to a survey made in the reign of Edward VI, and these included (from the Bridewell Hospital archives) the Bell, the Greyhound, the Galley, the Horseshoe, and the Old Swan. Good cheer could quickly turn sour. On 2 November 1605, Margaret Warren, residing at the Horseshoe, was arrested for being drunk at the 'Sign of the Pie without Aldgate'. John Price faced punishment on 19 September 1607 for having lain with Margaret Havis on 'a bottle [bundle] of hay' in a stable belonging to 'the sign of the old Swan'. We can get a sense of the kind of goods people had in their homes from prosecutions in the County Sessions records. In 1553, John Hill was charged with having stolen 'two yards of woollen cloth of a violet colour worth sixteen shillings, a frieze tunic worth five shillings, a pair of white stockings worth three shillings and fourpence'. In 1590, Morgan Dolling was sentenced to hang for stealing from a Shoreditch house a foot-cloth of velvet worth three pounds, six yards of velvet worth three pounds and ten shillings, four ells of silk called 'green taffeta' worth thirty shillings, a pair of pillowbers (pillowcases) worth ten shillings, a pair of sheets worth sixteen shillings, another pair of pillowbers worth eight shillings, and various items of linen and lawn. In 1596, Christopher Manson and Edward West were branded for stealing sugar, cheese, almonds, and embroidery or lace ('points') from a Shoreditch home.

We know something of the Burbages' possessions as a result of a crime. In 1615, Henry Elliott, his wife Emma, and Thomas Pierson broke 'burglariously' into the Burbages' houses at midnight. We learn from the resulting prosecution that Cuthbert owned two French russet-coloured cloaks worth forty shillings each, another cloak of 'couleur de roy' (light tawny brown) worth twenty shillings, and a green 'saye' (a light, twilled woollen material usually coloured green) apron. Richard, his more famous brother, possessed a dornix carpet worth six shillings, a hunting gun worth twenty-four shillings, forty pieces of pewter, three Holland aprons, a smock, bands, cuffs, other laced bands and cuffs, a handkerchief worth twelve shillings, other handkerchiefs, headbands, five ladies' cross-cloths, children's aprons, women's bands and handkerchiefs, and other fabric items. The three had taken a huge haul, together worth around £20. Arrested and charged, Pierson pleaded 'benefit of clergy' (which meant those who could read escaped execution) and was branded and released. Elliott's wife stood 'Not Guilty' and was acquitted. Elliott himself said nothing. He remained mute, thereby avoiding forfeiture of his goods and estate.

This choice came at a particularly unpleasant cost. His family might inherit, but he faced an excruciating punishment termed 'peine fort et dure', better known as 'pressing to death'. Carried out in 'the pressing yard of Newgate', this sentence ordered the gradual crushing of the accused by heavy weights. It must have made a quick death by hanging seem almost desirable by comparison. Five years earlier, in 1611, a Henry Elliott had been caught burgling another house and on that occasion successfully pleaded 'Not Guilty'. In 1615, Elliott was not so lucky. Cuthbert's French-style russet-coloured cloaks were highly valuable at sixty shillings apiece, and he clearly had a taste for fine, expensive clothes. We may assume that both Richard and Shakespeare owned similar items. We know rather little of the personal items Shakespeare owned. In his will Shakespeare left his 'wearing apparel' to his sister Joan, his sword to Thomas Combe, all his 'plate' to his granddaughter Elizabeth Hall except for his 'broad silver and gilt bowl', which went to his daughter Judith, and famously his 'second-best bed' to his wife Anne. But wills do not always tell the whole story. If we were to judge Richard Burbage's possessions merely from the contents of his will, we might think he barely owned anything at all.[28]

About a mile and a half west of Shoreditch lay the small suburb of Clerkenwell, situated outside the City wall (Figure 1.1). Clerkenwell was situated a mile north of the Thames. To find it from the north bank, all one had to do was to follow the course of the (filthy) River Fleet. By 1540, its nunnery of St Mary and priory of St John had both been dissolved. In rooms above the entrance to the old priory, St John's Gate (which still survives), the Master of the Revels, Edmund Tilney, kept his office. Tilney's role was to assess, allow, or censor books registered with the Stationers' Company sent to him prior to, and occasionally after, publication. In 1597, his post was granted 'in reversion' to Sir George Buc which simply meant that should the office become vacant, Buc would succeed to it. On the title page of a 1599 imprint of Robert Greene's posthumously published play *George-a-Greene, The Pinner of Wakefield*, Buc left a handwritten query as to who the play's author might have been. Just beneath the title, Buc wrote, 'Written by............a minister who ac[ted] the pinders p[ar]t in it himself. Teste W. Shakespea[re]'. The Latin word 'Teste' was a legal term that cited a named person as a witness or authority. Buc had evidently consulted Shakespeare's opinion on the authorship of the play and gained some intriguing information about who played in it. He added a further note, just beneath: 'Ed. Juby saith that this play was made by Ro. Gree[ne]'. This was not the only edition of a play on which Buc made inscriptions. His handwriting appears on playbooks by George Peele and Shakespeare too.[29]

That Shakespeare knew the reputation of Clerkenwell is indicated by a reference in *2 Henry IV* to 'Turnbull Street', the most notorious red-light area in London. Turnbull (or sometimes 'Turnmill') Street was (and is) a short lane that linked Clerkenwell Green with the open area of Smithfield which Stow describes as 'enclosed with inns, brew-houses and large tenements'. Witches were occasionally burned at Smithfield, but the area was more familiarly known for its sheep pens and market days. Turnbull Street was notorious for its bawdy houses. Falstaff soliloquizes in *2 Henry IV* about Justice Shallow's exaggerations, the 'wildness of his youth', 'the feats he hath done about Turnbull Street: and every third word a lie' (3.2.301-2) Of course it is Falstaff, especially in *Part One*, who is so given to lying, but Shakespeare gives just enough of a history to Shallow, a former student at the lawyers' college Clement's Inn, to make him a plausible target for Falstaff's detractions. Shakespeare's connection of the lawyers' inns with Turnbull Street rested on an open secret that the bawdy houses of Clerkenwell were frequented by the students at the inns, especially from Gray's which lay just a fifteen-minute walk away to the south-west. Nor was it unknown for a woman to be discovered in a Gray's Inn gentleman's chamber.

We learn from tax returns that, in the mid-1590s, Shakespeare lived in Bishopsgate, in the parish of St Helen's. On 15 November 1597, he was listed as having failed to pay a subsidy of five shillings on goods estimated at the value of five pounds (a small sum by the standards of the day). On 1 October 1598, he was rated as owing a further thirteen shillings and fourpence on goods again valued at five pounds. These amounts were arrears from taxes initially levied as long ago as 1593. Once more, he failed to pay. Shakespeare had twice missed the due date for payment, and was noted as being among those who lacked possessions or estate in the area. In the margin against Shakespeare's name in the subsequent report, the Exchequer clerk wrote 'Surrey' and 'Residuum Sussex', implying a new location for this particular taxpayer. At this time, Surrey and Sussex shared the same sheriff so the note need not indicate that Shakespeare had travelled far. But from this scrap of evidence that pinpoints merely his absence, we learn that Shakespeare had already moved to what Antonio in *Twelfth Night* calls 'the south suburbs' (3.3.39), in all probability to Southwark's Bankside.

South

We will come back to this question of tax arrears shortly since the Court of Exchequer was unwilling to let the matter go. But it may be useful first to gain a sense of the area to which Shakespeare moved. Southwark is often described as having been a rather dissolute place, of baiting arenas, rowdy playhouses, and, most notoriously of all, brothel houses or 'stews' lined up along the Thames.[30] But this is something of a myth since the Bankside bawdy houses had long been turned into ordinary houses, tenements, and dwelling chambers. It is true that Southwark held a fair in the main street called 'Long Southwark' each September, but it seems to have passed off peacefully each time, and relatively few people from the area were prosecuted for sexual offences.[31] But like any area associated with the playhouses, including Shoreditch or Gracious Street, a reputation for scandal and licentiousness lingered, and disproportionately outweighed the usually calmer reality.

London's south 'wark', bulwark or fortification, was originally Roman and is likely to have developed with the first bridge. In the late sixteenth century, Southwark was a borough in the county of Surrey and included 'Bridge Ward Without', the twenty-sixth and last of London's wards by Stow's count.[32] Significant buildings in early modern Southwark included St Mary Overy (now Southwark Cathedral), St Thomas's Hospital, the Bridge House, Winchester Palace, the Mint, and five prisons—the Clink, Counter, Marshalsea, White Lion, and King's Bench. A 1542 sketch map of streets, lanes, and buildings just south of the Bridge gives a fascinating glimpse of the layout of the streets, lanes, houses, taverns, and prisons in the area. The map is reproduced at the beginning of William Rendle's book *Old Southwark and its People* (1878). The King's Bench and Marshalsea are clearly marked on the east side of St Margaret's Hill, as are St Saviour's Church, Winchester Palace, St Thomas's Hospital, and a number of taverns or victualling houses. The 'Agas' and 'Braun and Hogenberg' maps give valuable representations of the Bankside area with its bull- and bear-baiting arenas. William Smith's 'Panorama of London' of 1588 provides another fine illustration of the broad area of Bankside, showing St Saviour's, the Bishop of Winchester's residence, and the animal-baiting amphitheatres but omitting the Rose playhouse which Henslowe had built in 1587. The Rose appears as 'The Playe howse' in the 1593 map by John Norden, engraved by Pieter van den Keere, and the Swan can be seen in a detail from a 1627 plan of Paris Garden.[33]

From the north, Southwark was accessible by the Bridge or by water. A passport was required to go in and out of Southwark via the Bridge. In 1596, the printer John Wolfe was commissioned to print 1,000 passports to be issued to those wishing to enter Southwark. On foot, one would have to negotiate the gates with their heavy portcullises, a drawbridge, and several buildings, including a chapel, built on the Bridge. Paying a waterman the penny fare to cross the river was clearly the least troublesome means of crossing, and most illustrations of the era show the Thames filled with the traffic of small boats. The Henslowe-Alleyn papers preserve a 1593 petition to Charles Howard,

Lord Admiral, by the London watermen to allow Philip Henslowe to reopen the Rose after its closure during a time of plague. Play-going had become an essential part of the Southwark economy and was regarded by watermen as crucial to their livelihood.[34]

A view of Southwark from the northern side of the Thames, designed to commemorate the coronation procession of Edward VI in 1547, gives some idea of what the Bankside area might have looked like. The image is an eighteenth-century version of a mural at Cowdray Park, Sussex, lost to a fire in 1793 (see Figure 2.6). But

(a)

(b)

Figure 2.6. (a) A view from the north looking south across the Thames of the eve-of-coronation procession of Edward VI (1547), showing the former stews arranged along Bankside on the south side of the river, by Samuel Hieronymus Grimm and James Basire, England, eighteenth century; (b) a detail of the eve-of-coronation procession of Edward VI showing Bankside. © Victoria and Albert Museum, London

even in a reproduction by a later copyist, the picture is remarkable. It shows a long procession emerging from the Tower of London and making its way past St Lawrence Poultney, 'Eleanor's Cross' in Cheapside, through a triumphal arch near St Paul's, beyond Temple Bar, and away into the distance towards Westminster. The coronation design shows the gentrified ranks of prominent London citizens neatly lining the Cheapside thoroughfare, granting legitimacy to the transfer of power that is taking place. While liverymen of the worshipful companies respectfully watch the gorgeous train of knights and heralds trooping by, everyday life continues on the other side of the river as folk climb out of boats, meet up, or take a stroll by the Thames. The whole image is unique for the way it compresses so many London landmarks into a story of orderly governance and kingly succession, all visually narrated along thoroughfares of the City where wealth and power are concentrated, north of the Thames. But it gives us a rare view of the south side of the river and suggests an economic contrast. Bankside seems subdued, mundane, and sparsely populated by comparison.

This is of course 1547, well before the building of the Rose, Swan, and Globe playhouses, but the economic differentiation between north and south must have been stark and made the entrepreneurial endeavour of theatre owners such as Henslowe, Francis Langley, and the Burbages all the more distinctive. Elizabeth I would have seen her brother's coronation image during her stay at Cowdray in 1591. Perhaps her eye would have rested on the show of courtly decorum in the foreground, rather than on the infamous Bankside 'stews' across the river. But they too had their own order, colour, and spectacle. Before they were closed by Henry VIII in 1546, they were subject to official regulations and known, as Stow explains, by painted signs on their walls depicting 'a Boar's head, the Cross Keyes, the Gun, the Castle, the Crane, the Cardinal's Hat, the Bell, the Swan etc'.[35]

Stow proves a valuable guide to the area of Southwark. On the riverbank, he notes a 'continual building of tenements about half a mile in length to the bridge', houses visible in the Cowdray mural. He mentions Blackman Street, St Olave's, and Bermondsey Street, the church of St Saviour's, formerly called St Mary Overy, and 'St Thomas in the Hospital', a priory devoted to tending the sick suppressed in 1539 but given over to the City in 1553. Among the area's 'most notable' houses, he includes the Bishop of Winchester's palace, which stood almost adjacent to the Clink prison on Bankside, the Tabard Inn (of Chaucerian fame), the Bridge House, the Stews, and the Bear Gardens. Stow explains that the Clink was often used to incarcerate those who were disorderly or caused affray and disturbed the peace, especially men who had been frequenting 'the Brothel houses'. East of the Clink stood the palace of the Bishop of Winchester, the remains of which can still be seen. Built in 1107, in the reign of Henry I, Stow describes it as 'a very fair house well repaired, and hath a large wharf and landing place called the Bishop of Winchester's stairs'.

Moving eastwards along the south bank, the next building of note was the grand church of St Mary Overy (or St Mary Over the River). After the dissolution of the monasteries in the late 1530s, the church was rededicated to St Saviour. Stow explains that the church stood on the site of an early 'house of sisters' founded by a woman named Mary who also established a ferry service across the river. Later, under Henry I, it expanded to include the dissolved church of St Margaret's on the Hill within its jurisdiction. It also housed a new chapel dedicated to St Mary Magdalen, an appropriate biblical figure for what Stow calls 'the brothel houses'. The Mint was established, he records, in 'a large and most sumptuous house' built in the reign of Henry VIII by the Duke of Suffolk, Charles Brandon, Marshal of the King's Bench and Marshalsea prisons, but confiscated by the king and renamed Southwark Place.[36]

Stow gives some discussion to Southwark's prisons. He notes that the White Lion had initially been an inn for travellers but was used, after 1560, as a lock-up in conjunction with the prison at Newington further south. Nineteenth-century historian William Rendle suggests that Stow here seems to conflate the White Lion tavern which stood near the Bridge, in the parish of St Mary Magdalen and by the north end of St Thomas's Hospital, with the prison of the same name which was situated further south on Borough High Street near St George's Church. Stow tells a vivid story of the Marshalsea. A squire who murdered a mariner was seized by fellow ship-men while still in shackles and stabbed repeatedly 'as if he had been a hog'. He was then tied by his leg irons to a rope, dragged to the gallows, and there hanged to an accompanying fanfare of trumpets, 'as though they had done a great act'.

The locations of the Marshalsea and King's Bench prisons are visible on the 1542 map but some further impression of their relative size and layout can be gauged from the 1738–47 map of London made by John Rocque. Both prisons stood on the east side of the High Street leading south to St George's Church and were mainly used to incarcerate debtors, but also—throughout the 1580s—recusants and papists. Machyn tells us that in 1561, the 'gatherer' or rent-collector of the King's Bench was set in the pillory for giving away nose-gays to people in the street and boasting he 'should be married'. Nine of Essex's followers in February 1601 were tried at the King's Bench, or 'Queen's bench' as it was sometimes called in the reign of Elizabeth. The building seems to have incorporated some dwelling chambers: on 2 November 1605, one Joane Legate, single and with child, gave her abode as the King's Bench, Southwark. The case of Michael Bankes is especially shocking. He had been held in the King's Bench for an unstated offence but, in 1610, was 'executed & did revive again & was in the old Vestry at the last, and then he was carried back & was executed again'.[37]

The Marshalsea stood adjacent to St George's churchyard and was a more substantial collection of buildings than the King's Bench. As Stow points out, in 1381 Wat Tyler's men attacked both it and the King's Bench and ruined the Marshal's house. In 1592, the Marshalsea was again broken open after a riot by textile workers, cloth-weavers, and felt-makers. This unrest is unlikely to have inspired the representation of the Cade rebellion in *2 Henry VI* because the play was written probably a good deal earlier (*1 Henry VI*, a 'prequel' written last in the trilogy, was already in performance by the summer of 1592). Nevertheless, in depicting Cade's hard-fought progress across London Bridge and as far as London Stone, the play focuses the contest for the crown sharply on a fierce battle for the City.

Cade's route to London begins south of the river. A Messenger enters to tell the King, 'The rebels are in Southwark; fly my lord! Jack Cade proclaims himself Lord Mortimer... | And vows to crown himself in Westminster' (4.4.26–30). Cade has set forth from the White Hart Inn in Southwark, a place he is loath to see again (4.7.177). This threat to the security of London grows incrementally. A second Messenger brings news that 'Jack Cade hath almost gotten London Bridge'. The good citizens are in flight, and the 'rascal people' of the town, looking for revenge, 'Join with the traitor; and they jointly swear | To spoil the city and your royal court' (4.4.48–52). Both the City and Westminster are now imminently at risk. Once Cade has crossed the river, he has just a few yards to go up New Fish Street and then turn either east at St Magnus' Church for the Tower or west towards Westminster. An out-of-control political clown, Cade speaks in a kind of rollicking, reckless nursery rhyme: 'Up Fish Street! Down Saint Magnus' Corner! Kill and knock down! Throw them into Thames!' (4.7.155–6). While Cade is reported to have set the Bridge on fire and to be heading for the Tower, the King's forces gather half a mile away at Smithfield (4.5.9–10). Cade goes to meet them shouting, 'pull down the Savoy' and 'th' Inns of Court—down with them all!' (4.7.1–2). The potency of Cade's words, even as his own followers laugh at him, is striking. He warns Lord Saye, 'I am the besom that must sweep the court clean of such filth as thou art' (4.7.27–9)— daring words even in the mouth of a clown.

Hall's chronicle explains that, while in Southwark, Cade broke open the Marshalsea and King's Bench prisons. Another feared lock-up he might also have attacked (though Hall doesn't record it) is the Southwark 'Compter' or Counter. The Counter stood in a triangular section on the west side of Borough High Street, just where the road forked at St Margaret's Hill and opposite the George and Tabard Inns. The 1542 map shows it as a collection of buildings with an entrance or gateway in the middle, facing a marketplace. As Rendle explains, the parish of St Margaret's was merged in 1540 with that of St Mary Magdalen and renamed as the parish of St Saviour. Formerly the site of the church of St Margaret's, the building had diverse uses, as a courthouse, a prison, a town hall, and private rents. In Southwark, St Saviour's would have been Shakespeare's parish church, and in one of its recesses it held the tomb of John Gower, the Choric figure who introduces and explains the action of Shakespeare and Wilkins's play *Pericles*.

Is it possible to know where Shakespeare lived south of the river? Unfortunately, we have no precise location for him after he left Bishopsgate. But documents relating to his tax arrears once more bear on the question. In 1796, the great Shakespeare scholar Edmond Malone wrote, 'From a paper now before me, which formerly belonged to Edward Alleyn, the player, our poet appears to have lived in Southwark near the Bear-Garden, in 1596'.[38] The paper Malone had before him seems now to be lost and cannot be corroborated, but records from the Court of Exchequer help to narrow the location a little. A list of those owing subsidies, dated 6 October 1600 and copied into the Surrey and Sussex Pipe Roll for 1599-1600, cites Shakespeare as owing thirteen shillings and fourpence. In the margin are abbreviated notes in Latin made by the court clerk: 'London R̶: o nⁱ Episcopo Wintonensi T'. These marginalia provide some clues.

As E. K. Chambers explains, 'London R̶' refers to the place in which the default occurred. The 'R̶' is a note that a response was needed and has been struck through at a later point after the query had been satisfied. The 'o nⁱⁱ' is an abbreviation of the phrase 'oneratur nisi', meaning that the tax collector, in this case the sheriff of Surrey, would be liable for the money unless he could show otherwise. The words 'Episcopo Wintonensi' are a reference to the Bishop of Winchester whose palace, and jurisdiction, lay in the liberty of the Clink on Bankside (Figure 2.6b). Effectively, the Exchequer was expecting the Bishop's men to collect the sum. The capital letter 'T' is thought to have been a later addition because, as a contraction for 'Tot[us]', meaning 'whole', it indicated that the money had indeed now been collected. What these rather obscure Latin contractions confirm is that Shakespeare was indeed living in the liberty of the Clink at this time. This is a conclusion the usually cautious Chambers was himself willing to accept.[39] The Bishop's liberty stretched from Winchester Palace, adjacent to St Saviour's, to the Pike Gardens, some 500 metres, or a third of a mile, to the west. It was small enough to warrant the fact that just about anywhere in this locality could reasonably be said to be 'near the Bear-Garden' as Malone had claimed.

It may be that Shakespeare had a personal reason for moving to the liberty of the Clink. On 31 December 1607, his brother Edmund was buried in the church of St Saviour. A fee book records the expense of the funeral at twenty shillings: 'Edmund Shakespeare, a player, buried in the church, with a forenoone knell of the great bell, xxˢ'. Bronze circles sounding from the church tower would carry the solemnity of the occasion to all around. Edmund had been a parishioner nearby for at least a year and maybe longer. It was common practice for parish wardens to note down in sacramental 'token books' the names of those attending holy communion at Easter. In a list of names for 1607, the year Edmund died, his name appears but is crossed through. He is set down in the token book as 'Edmund Shakespeare', one of several residents living at a house called 'the Vine', a building almost adjacent to the Clink (Figures 2.4, 2.7, and 2.8). Also living there was Shakespeare's co-actor Lawrence Fletcher.

The same token book lists Philip Henslowe and Edward Alleyn as living by 'The Bell' at the east end of Bankside. The Vine and The Bell had, prior to 1547, served as Southwark 'stews' but were now, as far as we know, ordinary dwelling-houses. The sites of some of these houses are shown on a plan of Bankside based upon the 1875 Ordnance Survey, published in the Bankside volume of the Survey of London. Along a 300-foot stretch of the riverside, from the corner of the Clink to the Bear Garden, stood a series of properties—the Castle, Vine, Bull's Head & Swan, the Crane, the Elephant, and the George. Close to the Rose playhouse lay 'The Bell'. The Castle was also known as

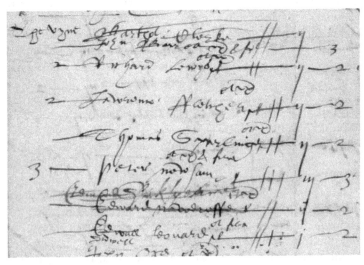

Figure 2.7. A page from the Southwark Token Book for 1607 showing 'Edmund Shakespeare' and 'Lawrence Fletcher' as dwelling at 'The Vyne'. The name 'Edmund Shakespeare', written above that of 'Edward Woodruff, is crossed through (Southwark Token Book, 1607, LMA P92/SAV/256, p. 6, l. 28). The name of the King's Men actor 'Lawrence Fletcher' is given above it at l. 23. London Metropolitan Archives P92/SAV/256, p. 6, l. 28; courtesy of the London Metropolitan Archives

The Beare bayting

Figure 2.8. The 'Agas' map (*c*.1561–70), showing the former 'stews' of Bankside, with 'the Castle' on the corner (upper right) and, adjacent left, 'the Vine' where Shakespeare's brother Edmund lived in 1607 with Lawrence Fletcher. The 'Elephant' stood to the west. Near the bear-baiting pit, kennelled dogs strain on their leashes. Reproduced by kind permission of British History Online

the 'Castle upon the Hope or Hoope', and it is now the site of The Anchor public house, near the present-day Globe. It seems that next door to the Castle, on its western side, was the Vine, a building that on the 'Agas' map appears rather attractive, with two back doors, a spacious back garden, two chimneys, and two gabled upper windows (Figure 2.8). In 1605, a dispute arose as to whether the garden attached to the Vine belonged in fact to a Master Jeffrey Butler of 'The Elephant', three doors along to the west.[40] Shakespeare never mentions the Vine, but he does seem to have recommended (perhaps ironically) The Elephant. In *Twelfth Night*, Antonio throws Sebastian his purse and tells him,

> In the south suburbs, at the Elephant,
> Is best to lodge: I will bespeak our diet
> Whiles you beguile the time and feed your knowledge
> With viewing of the town: there shall you have me.

> (3.3.38-42)

Later, after Antonio has been arrested, Sebastian declares he could not find him at The Elephant. Perhaps when the assessors called on Edmund Shakespeare, he was in no fit state to attend church. His name appears in the 1607 token book but has been scratched out.

This fleeting record of him gives us a glimpse of his brother's connection with Southwark just where we would expect him to be. It would make sense for playhouse owners or bear-pit managers like Henslowe and Alleyn to live in close proximity to their investments where they could keep an eye on them. If Shakespeare ever stayed at the Elephant or the Vine after 1599, he was just a stone's throw away from the Globe.

East

Early modern London's 'east end' was a good deal more rural than the nineteenth-century ghetto we might imagine from Dickens's era. St Katherine's, Wapping, and Mile End Green all housed residents towards the eastern edge of the City, especially near inlets and docks on the Thames such as Billingsgate or Rotherhithe on the southern side. The eastern limit of the City was guarded by the Tower of London, the City's most imposing and historic fortification. The Tower was a place that had a long, macabre history. A grim monstrosity, it casts its shadow over *Richard III* like a piece of medieval 'brutalism'. The Tower is mentioned here and there in the play's sources, from Sir Thomas More's history to Holinshed's *Chronicles* of 1587, but Shakespeare makes it central. A precursor play belonging to the Queen's Men company, *The True Tragedy of Richard III*, mentions it on eight occasions: it is referred to in Shakespeare's play some twenty-seven times. Setting the play so deliberately in its dark corridors, Shakespeare writes his own blood-soaked 'true tragedy' under the shadow of this infamous London fortification.

The 1594 imprint of *The True Tragedy of Richard III* advertises on its title page that it shows 'the smothering of the two young Princes in the Tower'. That moment in the play is handled with brutal efficiency: 'Jack: Come press them down, it boots not to cry again, Jack upon them so lustily. But Master Forest now they are dead what shall we do with them?'[41] The deed is over in seconds. Although the quarto title page of Shakespeare's *Richard III* advertised it as showing 'the pitiful murder of his innocent nephews', in fact the Lord Chamberlain's play omits the horrific scene, relegating it to a report of prior offstage action by the assassin Tyrrell (4.3). Excision of the princes' murder is just one of several significant differences between the two plays that suggest their broad independence from each other.

The primal scene for Shakespeare's *Richard III* is an event dramatized earlier in *3 Henry VI*, the murder of King Henry by Richard in the Tower (5.6.57–60). Close and unseen, such killings seem a quick and easy matter. Henry's coffin, brought in by pall-bearers in the second scene of *Richard III*, is a sign of Gloucester's preferred manner of assassination—done in obscurity and easily explained away or clouded by lies and protestations. But one of the play's most shocking lines has a plain, open lucidity. With all the detachment of a death-camp clerk, Richard's ruthless agent Ratcliffe coldly seals the fates of Rivers, Grey, and Vaughan: 'Make haste. The hour of death is expiate' (3.3.23). A hint of Pauline theology in the word 'expiate' makes it ironically callous, but in their stark meaning Ratcliffe's words generate for the victims a sudden consciousness of their own imminent end.

Other murders in this play are committed with quick brutality. Locked in his cell (1.4), Clarence has guilty dreams about deeds he has done in his brother's name, but, faced with murderers, he pleads his innocence. The second murderer seems to soften, just for a moment, with a teasing hint of pity before Clarence is stabbed from behind and famously dumped in a butt of malmsey (Madeira) wine. The ironies are palpable: Hastings, having been released from the Tower just as Clarence was committed to it, thinks himself safe. Catesby, Buckingham, Ratcliffe, and even his ally Stanley all know differently. Hastings pays no heed to his horse's stumbles as it nears the Tower, the animal 'loath to bear me to the slaughter-house' (3.4.86). As with Clarence, Richard turns against Hastings without warning. According to both Sir Thomas More's history and the *Chronicles*, Richard banged his fist on the table as he did so. Richard's sudden, violent, yet calculated irascibility, matched with Ratcliffe's lethal, cold detachment, illustrate the risks of power in the hands of a few self-interested zealots who lack any capacity for empathy.

The Tower is the play's *éminence grise*, a place befitting any blood-stained tyrant. The young Prince, with his brother, is afraid to go there: 'I do not like the Tower of any place' (3.1.68). The Prince asks Buckingham whether Julius Caesar originally built the Tower. It is a schoolboy's question, but one that seeks to distinguish truth from report, a division Richard likes to obscure. The Tower's history is not reassuring, and when the young Duke of York declares, 'I shall not sleep in quiet at the Tower' (3.1.142), we sense that he too fears what is coming. Shakespeare uses the Tower's intimidating reputation to build the approaching doom. When Edward IV's wife Elizabeth is prevented from visiting her sons there, she justly fears for their safety: 'Stay, yet look back with me unto the Tower.– | Pity, you ancient stones, those tender babes | Whom envy hath immured within your walls. | Rough cradle for such little pretty ones, | Rude ragged nurse, old sullen playfellow | For tender princes' (Folio, 4.1.97–102). The lines may be rhetorical, but their juxtapositions are stark and memorable: the words 'nurse' and 'playfellow' are unlikely metaphors for the Tower. Historically, the princes were twelve and nine years old when they entered the Tower. In 1592, when the play was probably written, Shakespeare's own son, Hamnet, was only seven. The Tower was no place for a child.

But the Tower was an instrument of state policy. In a cultural atmosphere that was often paranoid and febrile, it was frequently used throughout the 1580s and 1590s to detain, torture, and interrogate the more notable renegade Catholics, including Shakespeare's own distant relatives Edward Arden and John Somerville. A list of prisoners in 1594 mentions Philip Howard (Earl of Arundel), Roger Lopez (the Queen's physician), his associates Estevan de Gama and Manuel Tinoco, Edmund Neville, Peter Wentworth, Robert Southwell, and others. An accompanying note adds, 'There are also diverse priests and other dangerous persons in the Marshalsea, Gatehouse and other prisons'. Government anxieties regarding dangerous recusants were close to obsessive. In October 1586, Sir Francis Walsingham, Elizabeth's spymaster, received a papist confession and 'treasonable letter' together with a note advising, 'The common gaols are overcharged with Recusants'.

Walsingham's agent in the Tower was Richard Topcliffe, by reputation a sadist who oversaw the breaking and execution of many Catholics, including Robert Southwell and priests John Gerard and Henry Garnet. Topcliffe's remedy for the papist threat was straightforward: imprisonment, torture, and death. He wrote in 1590 that 'Jesuits and seminary priests' were 'men chosen out from among the traitorous and most bloody-minded wits among the fugitives'.[42] If merely banished, they would simply serve as guides to the invaders from Spain. Topcliffe knew the theatres and they knew him. In the 1580s, he employed Anthony Munday, and later, in 1597, he would be instrumental in the suppression of Jonson and Nashe's *The Isle of Dogs* on grounds of sedition. From what we know of him, he seems to have enjoyed his reputation for cruelty. His manner seems not to have been so very different to that of Shakespeare's cold-hearted desk clerk. It would hardly be surprising if, on hearing the name 'Richard Ratcliffe' (3.3.1), some in the playhouse brought to mind Richard Topcliffe.

West

London's 'West End', as we think of it today, barely existed in the early modern era. Covent Garden was simply a convent garden, Drury Lane lazed its way beside grazing cows, and Haymarket was a lane in which one bought fodder. Nevertheless, the heart of power in England lay west of the City of London, in Westminster. It was here that the royal palace was situated, beside Westminster Abbey and Westminster Hall. Westminster was where the nation's monarchs were crowned, held court, and (some of them) buried. The town of Westminster was granted 'City' status in 1540, and thereafter it sent its own MPs to Parliament. But it was not a city like the City of London. It had none of the governmental structures—the Common Council, Lord Mayor, gilds, or worshipful companies—that served London east of the boundary at Temple Bar. The Abbey, which owned land in the local parishes of St Margaret's, St Martin's in the Fields, and St Clement Danes, held sway over much of the locality through its Court of Burgesses, a body set up to deal with local disorder, disputes, and petty criminality.[43] St Margaret's, Westminster's principal parish, gradually adapted to the new restrictions following the Reformation, slowly relinquishing its ties to the old fraternities and the Abbey, and evolving with the growth of the court. In 1532, Henry VIII built St James's Palace on the site of an old hospital and refurbished York Place, Wolsey's former residence (held by virtue of Wolsey's title as Archbishop of York), as the new palace of Whitehall, with an indoor tennis court, bowling alley, and cock pit. At the same time, the parish of St Margaret's expanded to accommodate the growing service industry on which the court increasingly came to rely.

We can imagine Shakespeare walking around Westminster Abbey and taking in its extraordinary historical treasures, especially the ornately carved tomb of Richard II in the chapel of Edward the Confessor, with its gilt bronze effigies, behind the ancient Coronation

Chair, or the stately tomb of Henry V situated aloft. Standing in the choir, he might have viewed a fourteenth-century portrait of Richard II seated in the Coronation Chair. We have no evidence that he did, but it is not an unreasonable supposition. He refers directly to the Coronation Chair in the early play *2 Henry VI*. Eleanor Cobham, wife of Humphrey, Duke of Gloucester and Lord Protector for the young King Henry VI, has her own dreams of rising to become Queen of England:

> Methought I sat in seat of majesty
> In the cathedral church of Westminster,
> And in that chair where kings and queens are crowned,
> Where Henry and Dame Margaret kneeled to me,
> And on my head did set the diadem.
>
> (1.2.36–40)

It is a dramatic and vivid image, and one so treasonable that the shocked Gloucester chides her for it. Eleanor is indignant at her husband's reproof and declares, 'Next time I'll keep my dreams unto myself, | And not be checked' (1.2.53–4). Their tense but private conversation has some tenderness. Gloucester shows affection, saying, 'Nay, be not angry, I am pleased again' and calling her 'Nell' (ll. 55, 59), but Eleanor's appetite for power is not blunted. As Hall explains in his chronicle, the historical Eleanor went on to seek out sorcerers in the hope of making her dream a reality. Hall's account of her associations with Roger Bolingbroke, 'a cunning necromancer', and 'Margery Jourdayne, surnamed the witch of Eye', lends Shakespeare's play its stunning Faustian pyrotechnics in 1.4. But Eleanor's dream of sitting in the chair of state with her rivals kneeling before her is entirely Shakespeare's invention, a precursor to the aspirations of Lady Macbeth.

Shakespeare refers elsewhere to the 'chair of state', 'The supreme seat, the throne majestical' (*Richard III*, 3.7.118), and 'the regal throne' (*Richard II*, 4.1.104), but by these terms he seems to have had in mind the throne in Parliament rather than the Coronation Chair in Westminster Abbey. The playing company certainly had a chair among their properties, one that probably doubled occasionally as a throne. A stage direction in *3 Henry VI* has Edward IV sitting in a 'chair' in 4.4.0, and at 3.5.0 of *Henry VI Part 1*, the Duke of Bedford is 'brought in sick, in a chair' (in this case clearly not a throne). Sometimes by 'seat' is meant merely place or status in the social hierarchy, for example when Richard II says, 'Now, by my seat's right royal majesty' (2.1.121). The chair authorizes his position as monarch, physically representing his instalment and legitimacy. The image of the Coronation Chair occurs in *Richard III*, when Buckingham calls Catesby over and bids him sound Hastings out about the prospect of Richard becoming king: 'What think'st thou? Is it not an easy matter | To make William Lord Hastings of our mind, | For the instalment of this noble duke | In the seat royal of this famous isle?' (3.1.160-4). The crown is not enough for Richard: he also wants acclaim and looks forward eagerly to his coronation. Throughout the history plays, power is represented via topography, and sometimes with a single chair. The bloody question of who should be monarch is a matter of who wins Westminster. Whoever governs in Westminster rules England, Scotland, Wales, Ireland, and France.

Shakespeare's adaptation of historical fact gravitates around Westminster in *Richard II*. Under Richard, Westminster Hall had been reroofed and decorated with his own emblem—a white hart (a mature white stag)—and statues of preceding English monarchs. These ornaments all served to accentuate the sanctity of his role as monarch. Creating drama of huge paradox, Shakespeare switched the play's nervy scene of resignation from the Tower (as Raphael Holinshed has it) to the Hall (4.1.153–318). This is the famous 'deposition scene' (4.1.146–308), cut from the 1597 quarto apparently for its potential radicalism, in which Richard agonizes over handing the crown to Bolingbroke. Richard repeatedly demurs as the reality of formal abdication weighs upon him. Slowly, he relents. By the end of the scene, he has yielded his right to rule, and Bolingbroke orders him to the Tower, a detail Shakespeare took from Hall and one that marks a literal reversal: Richard must tread the reverse path of his coronation progress, from west to east, a journey that sees him humiliatingly 'unkinged' (4.1.210).

In the event, Richard is moved instead to Pontefract Castle in Yorkshire where he feels himself utterly reduced, as if to 'nothing' (5.5.38). There he is killed in brutal circumstances by Sir Piers Exton and his men. Richard manages to kill four of his attackers before, as Hall explains, Exton leaps into his chair and slays him 'with a stroke of a pollax...upon the head'.[44] Even in his dying words, Richard is thinking hierarchically. He tells Exton, 'Thy seat is up on high, | Whilst my gross flesh sinks downward here to die' (5.5.111–12), words that hint at stage action—a chair, perhaps with Exton on it, and Richard slumping to the floor. Bolingbroke himself died fourteen years later (in 1413), in the Jerusalem chamber at Westminster Abbey, a detail in Holinshed that Shakespeare expands near the end of *2 Henry IV* to bring the two plays full circle, as 'far as to the sepulchre of Christ' (*1 Henry IV*, 1.1.19). Appropriately, one of his successor's first acts as King Henry V was to return Richard's body to Westminster Abbey.

The western limits were the site of another, more grimly famous structure—the fearful triangular gallows at Tyburn. The location and appearance of this apparatus is clearly visible on the London map produced by John Rocque (1738–47), situated at the north-eastern corner of Hyde Park near (what is now) Marble Arch. Condemned prisoners would be tied to the end of a cart and whipped from London's sessions houses and gaols through the City streets, along what is now Oxford Street, westwards to Tyburn. 'Carting' was a punishment designed partly to humiliate and partly to hurt. Those repeatedly found guilty of incontinent behaviour or fraud might be made to ride backwards on a horse with a paper hat on their head, or 'whipped at a cart's arse' through the streets with 'rough music' or a clanging of domestic basins to accompany them. Whipping at either end of the process would probably deter further offences.

Those condemned at the sessions to be hanged had just a one-way route out of the city, either southward to St Thomas-a-Watering or, more often, westward to Tyburn. The Middlesex County Sessions records are filled with instances of prisoners routinely—almost casually at times—sentenced 'to be hung', briefly returned to Newgate, the Fleet, or some other London gaol, before being carted off to Tyburn. Shakespeare mentions the site only once by name, and light-heartedly. The three friends, Ferdinand, Biron, and Longaville, form a trium-virate, as Biron ironically suggests to Longaville, invoking its distinctive triangular shape: 'Thou makest the triumviry, the corner-cap of soci-ety, | The shape of Love's Tyburn that hangs up simplicity' (*Love's Labour's Lost*, 4.3.51). The line's conflation of the three-horned 'corner-cap' worn by divines and ministers, with the shape of the infamous gibbet and shared bonds of friendship, is quick but complex. The gallows' frame could apparently hold seven 'simplicities' per beam, as many as twenty-one at a time, if required. It was efficient and predictably served as a place of macabre entertainment.

Countless innocents must have died at Tyburn. Something of the arbitrariness of judicial hanging at the time is captured in *Titus Andronicus* when Saturninus, Emperor of Rome, suddenly condemns a clown to the gallows: 'Go, take him away and hang him presently' (4.4.45). The clown has earlier comically mistaken the name 'Jupiter' for 'gibbet-maker' (4.3.80–1) and now committed no other crime than bringing a letter from Titus and a gift of two pigeons. Saturninus has just before protested, 'As who would say, in Rome no justice were' (4.4.20). When a fool encounters a despot, dark, sardonic humour ensues and the banality of execution is heightened. A deeply moral play, *Titus Andronicus* repeatedly questions the irrationality of violence and injustice. After Titus kills his son Mutius, Lucius tells his father, 'My lord, you are unjust; and more than so...' (1.1.288). Later, Marcus asks why the self-mutilated Titus should mock his own agonies: 'Why dost thou laugh?' (3.1.264). Once Aaron has killed the nurse who has brought Tamora's black baby, Demetrius exclaims, 'What mean'st thou, Aaron? Wherefore didst thou this?' (4.2.146). After Titus has killed his daughter Lavinia, even the murderous Saturninus is astonished: 'What hast thou done, unnatural and unkind?' (5.3.47). At crucial moments when violence seems inexplicable, the play puts the questions to which an audience will want answers, and, finding none, makes an implicit point.

Shakespeare's ability to compress unsettling ideas into just a line or two is nowhere more striking than in a veiled allusion to Tyburn in *Romeo and Juliet*. Juliet begins 3.2 alone and speaks a declamation to night, asking that it pass with speed: 'Gallop apace, you fiery-footed steeds, | Towards Phoebus's lodging' (3.2.1–2). The line reverses Faustus's climactic appeal, 'O lente, lente, currite equi noctis' ('O slowly, slowly run, you horses of the night'), in Marlowe's powerful tragedy. Juliet continues with an image of Phaeton, the classical divinity who drove Phoebus's chariot too near earth and, struck down by Jupiter's lightning, hurtled from the sky. But her words connect this literary downfall with a more familiar, dreadfully real rough cart:

> ... Such a wagoner
> As Phaeton would whip you to the west
> And bring in cloudy night immediately.
>
> (3.2.2–4)

Only one sort of person might be whipped to the west and pitched out of a wagon when these lines were written. Prisoners from the gaols at

Ludgate and Newgate would be flogged westwards to Tyburn, hanged, and so cloudy night brought upon them in an instant. Titus Oates was famously 'Whipt from Aldgate to Newgate by the common Hang-man; on Friday from Newgate to Tyburn'.[45] Juliet's lines in the 1597 quarto are followed by the Nurse holding 'cords' (the ladder Romeo used) and talking ominously. They may well have reminded the play's audience of their own London topography, turning epic classical legend to stark, grim realism. As every mature Londoner was probably aware, where the day ended, life ended too.

In such instances, Shakespeare set into his plays moments of audience self-recognition, as if to seal an implicit contract between the play and those who watched it. But, as his allusions to the Tower and Tyburn show, such moments could have sobering effects. If he ever felt a sense of wonder in the capital, it probably quickly faded. London held a great many threats to Shakespeare's art—the risks of playhouses pulled down, plague, incarceration, and possible execution—all serious forces that weighed against it. As we shall see in Chapter 4, Shakespeare's answer seems to have been to produce more art. Textual allusions to the spectators' London world tend to be latent or oblique in Shakespeare, part of a deeper background, as though at a distance from the plays' central concerns. Other early modern writers liked either to blame or praise London. As Lawrence Manley has shown, Tudor verse complaints repeatedly criticized the capital as a centre of crime, corruption, and undesirable immigration. Puritans denounced London's sinfulness as akin to that of Babylon, Tyre, Sodom, or Gomorrah.[46] Alternatively, writers from John Lydgate to Edmund Spenser and Sir William Davenant praised the capital as 'of true meaning, and faithful observance', 'the famous Troynovant', and as 'royal' London.[47] Shakespeare seems to have avoided either of these approaches, although we might infer that he took a rather pessimistic view of urban life overall. But, as we shall see in chapter 3, this does not mean he could avoid taking sides.

People

When we come to consider the people Shakespeare might have known in London, we perhaps most readily think of his fellow writers, Christopher Marlowe, Thomas Kyd, or Ben Jonson. We might even suppose that he had some acquaintance with Elizabeth I since his company acted before her on at least twenty-five occasions. But it readily becomes apparent that Shakespeare must have come across very many people when in London, most of them largely unknown to us: carpenters, joiners, thatchers, doorkeepers, gatherers, prompters, scribes, musicians, tailors, and play-house painters. Shakespeare lived among parishioners, tradesmen, shop-keepers, lawyers, merchants, and citizens of all kinds. As the tribune Sicinius observes in *Coriolanus*, 'What is the city but the people?' (3.1.197). This chapter aims to see Shakespeare's writing in London in conjunction with these others among whom he lived and worked. It focuses on his co-actors, and those who lived near them, including Edward Alleyn who shared the stage with them in the early 1590s. It adds details of some of the men and women involved in the seamier aspects of life in the suburbs, including Sir William Brooke, co-actor Christopher Beeston, and co-author George Wilkins. The information we have about many of these lives remains sketchy, but what emerges is that particular individuals and events seem to have had either an impact or a shaping influence on Shakespeare's writing.

Shakespeare's company: The Lord Chamberlain's Men and the Burbages

Shakespeare's art flourished in London because others enabled it to do so. We may imagine a solitary poet at work alone in his garret, studiously turning out sheets of blank verse, but the reality was that Shakespeare depended on those around him. In this respect, the Burbage family's contribution to Shakespeare's development as a writer can hardly be overstated. James Burbage was initially by trade a joiner, a maker of furniture and fittings, and he would later become a carpenter, someone able to oversee the construction of an entire building. He was also an actor and had risen to become the leading figure in the Earl of Leicester's troupe of players. By the early 1570s, this group was looking for a more permanent home in London. Burbage petitioned the Privy Council in May 1574 to license them to play within the City of London and its liberties (areas of devolved administration independent of the mayor's jurisdiction), under conditions set by the Master of the Revels.[1] The benefits of having a base in London were obvious: days otherwise spent on the road could be used for rehearsal or performances, and players could enjoy both some financial stability by working (when not touring) closer to home and family life.

In April 1576, James Burbage took out a lease from Giles Allen on a property in Holywell, Shoreditch, that had been part of the old, now dissolved, Augustinian priory. The lease was designed to enable him to both build and dismantle (should he so desire) a theatre there. Shoreditch was where Burbage made his home, near the church of St Leonard where he worshipped each Sunday and saw his children baptized. He formed a contract with his wealthy brother-in-law, John Brayne, and, probably with his brother Robert (also a carpenter), set about establishing the Curtain and Theatre playhouses. These ventures were both huge financial risks and led to trouble between the Burbages and Braynes from the start. Those quarrels did not end when Brayne died a bankrupt in 1586. In 1592, when Brayne's wife Margaret tried to claim the rights to half of the Theatre, Burbage was reported as saying, 'Hang her, whore ... she getteth nothing here'.[2] Eventually, Giles Allen's refusal to renew the Holywell lease provoked Burbage's son Cuthbert into having the Theatre taken down and its timbers reused to build the Globe on Bankside. James had died and been buried at St Leonard's in early 1597. His widow, Helen (Brayne's sister), was interred alongside him in 1613. The parish registers show the family as residing in Halliwell or Holywell Street, just south of the Theatre and north of the Curtain. Cuthbert and Richard,

James's sons, lived there—as the Henry Elliott case showed—in separate 'dwelling-houses'.

Mary Edmond has described James Burbage as 'a rumbustious character'.[3] After a quarrel at the Theatre in 1584 involving some 500 persons, the Lord Mayor dispatched two aldermen to the Court at Westminster to request the 'suppressing and pulling down of the Theatre and Curtain'. The Queen's Men advised Fleetwood to summon James Burbage, 'who was a stubborn fellow', and have him bound over to keep the peace. Burbage refused to present himself and said that he was Lord Hunsdon's man and that he would appear before his lord the following morning. Fleetwood instructed a sheriff to bring Burbage before him. But, as he explained in a letter to William Cecil, 'he stouted [braved] me out very hasty'. When Fleetwood threatened him with imprisonment, Burbage insisted the issue go before a sessions court, claiming that since he was 'a councillor's man' he must avoid any such constraint. Fleetwood relented but added that 'he shall be sure to be bound or else is like to do worse'. He evidently regarded Burbage as a man heading for the pillory or whip.[4]

Many of the intricacies of how these early playing companies were formed, and their associations with each other, remain obscure. If the quarto title page of *Titus Andronicus* is to be trusted, Shakespeare may have had close connections with Strange's, Pembroke's, and Sussex's companies in the early 1590s. But it was his integration into the Lord Chamberlain's Men in 1594 that proved formative for his career. The abstract of a play called *The Second Part of the Seven Deadly Sins* provides an insight into how the company organized its staging and props (including seats, weapons, jewels, robes, and a severed head in a dish) and made use of a dumb show. An important and rare document, it takes us close to Shakespeare's company live on stage at either the Curtain or the Theatre.[5] It shows that leading parts are given to Richard Burbage, and 'Mr Brian', 'Mr Pope' and 'Mr Phillips'. These last three names refer to George Brian, Thomas Pope, and Augustine Phillips. Lesser roles are taken by William Sly, John Holland, John Duke, Richard Cowley, Robert Pallant, Thomas Goodale, John Sincler, and others simply named Kitt, Harry, and Vincent. The names 'Kitt' and 'Harry' possibly designate Christopher Beeston and Henry Condell, the 1623 Folio's co-editor. Parts given to female roles in this play are taken by younger actors named as Nick, Robert, Saunder (Alexander Cooke?), Ned, Will, and T[homas] Belt. A direction indicating 'Th. Goodale to him will foole running' may signal an entrance for the company clown, Will Kemp. The document, which David Kathman has redated to the second half of the 1590s, is the best guide we have as to the kinds of roles actors took in the Chamberlain's Men, although two significant names—John Heminges and William Shakespeare—are missing.[6] There are unascribed roles, such as that of Lydgate or 'a Captaine', that either might have played. This group formed Shakespeare's closest associates in London. The First Folio of 1623 lists the names of the actors who, through the evolution from Chamberlain's Men to King's Men, performed the plays: William Shakespeare, Richard Burbage, John Heminges, Augustine Phillips, William Kemp, Thomas Pope, George Bryan, Henry Condell, William Sly, Richard Cowley, John Lowin, Samuel Crosse, Alexander Cooke, Samuel Gilburne, Robert Armin, William Ostler, Nathan Field, John Underwood, Nicholas Tooley, William Ecclestone, Joseph Taylor, Robert Benfield, Robert Gough, Richard Robinson, John Shank, and John Rice. They comprised quite a tightly knit company: John Underwood named one of his sons 'Burbage', Heminges and Lowin were 'overseers' for Underwood's will, John Holland lived in a tenement that adjoined Thomas Pope's house in a London 'liberty', probably the liberty of the Clink on Bankside, Christopher Beeston named a son 'Augustyne', Phillips's sister married Robert Gough, and Nicholas Tooley lived late in life with Cuthbert Burbage in Shoreditch.[7]

It is possible also to pin down fairly precisely where some of these actors lived, at least in the early stages of their careers. It would make sense for those with a financial stake in the playhouses to live near their investments, since no one had a stronger interest in keeping them safe from accident or damage. In Southwark, house visitations were made each Easter to sell tokens that permitted householders to take the sacrament. Consequently, the token books provide us with a kind of census of parish inhabitants. In the books for St Saviour's, we find the following names all in the liberty of the Clink and Paris Garden: Augustine Phillips in 'Horseshoe Court' (1593–7), Will Kemp living in 'Samson's Rents' (1593–1600), Thomas Pope now in 'Blamer's Rents' (1593–6), George Bryan in 'Oare's Rents' (1596), Alexander Cooke in 'Hill's Rents' (1604–10), Robert Gough in 'Hill's Rents' (1605) and later 'Samson's Rents' (1609–10), William Sly in 'Horseshoe

Court' (1593) and 'Rose Alley' (1594–8), and Robert Benfield at 'Henslowe's Rents' in 1621. A John Shank is listed in 1621 as at 'the Vine', the place in which Edmund Shakespeare ended his days in 1607. The tenement 'Hill's Rents' was usually surveyed just prior to 'the Vine' in the token books and so probably stood either next door or in very close proximity to it.

Naturally, we have to treat these references with some caution. There were undoubtedly others living in Southwark named Sly, Gough, or Kemp, and we cannot always be secure in identifying a name with an actor. But it is fairly certain that Augustine Phillips was the actor living in 'Horseshoe Court' in 1593, since he baptized his children at St Saviour's, although by 1605, when he died, he owned a house in Mortlake near Richmond. We are also safe to assume that the 'William Sly' living there in the same year is his player-colleague. 'Horseshoe Alley' ran north–south between the Thames and Maiden Lane, just to the east of the Bear Garden.[8] We may never determine the exact locations of all these tenements, but we can work out from the arrangement of the token books that several of them were situated along the stretch of riverbank on Bankside in what had formerly been the old 'stews'.

Gilbert East and 'Black Luce'

The Southwark token books record a 'Gilbard East' as dwelling in a house called 'The Purpendyne' ('Porpentine') in 1593. The name 'Porpentine' occurs also in *The Comedy of Errors* as the sign of a victualling house and refuge for Antipholus of Ephesus, who dines there with a courtesan. Angelo the goldsmith is instructed to bring a gold chain, Antipholus's gift for his wife, to this bawdy ordinary (3.1.118–22). From the token books, it seems that the Southwark 'Porpentine' adjoined Boar's Head Alley, for some of its residents listed with East, including John Street (son of the carpenter who built the Globe Theatre in 1599) are recorded by Henslowe in his 'Diary' as 'tenants' at 'The Bores heade'.[9] This tenement is not to be confused with two other locations north of the river: the 'Boar's Head' in Eastcheap, the setting for tavern scenes in *1* and *2 Henry IV*; or the Boar's Head inn, near Aldgate, that hosted performances within its yard.

The illicit urban economy was predictably sustained by men with money to spend, including members of the Inns of Court. We know that Shakespeare had affiliations with the lawyers' colleges in London—Gray's Inn, the Middle and Inner Temples, and perhaps other Inns of Court and chancery. Thomas Greene, who described himself as a 'cousin' of Shakespeare's and stayed at New Place, Stratford, in 1609, trained as a lawyer at Staple Inn and the Middle Temple. His brother John, who acted for Shakespeare's daughter Susanna over the Blackfriars gatehouse, was a member of Clement's Inn. Justice Shallow in *2 Henry IV* recalls his days as a young man at Clement's Inn, when a much younger Falstaff fought with one 'Samson Stockfish' in Gray's Inn gardens (3.1.31). The scene makes repeated veiled allusions to the women Shallow and his lawyer friends enjoyed. Shakespeare had several connections with Gray's Inn—not least the fact that Sir Henry Carey, the Lord Chamberlain, Henry Wriothesley, third Earl of Southampton, and Edmund Tilney, the Master of the Revels, were all members of this inn. It was there, on 28 December 1594, that *The Comedy of Errors* was performed.

The *Gesta Grayorum*, printed in 1688, explains that on 20 December 1594, St Thomas's Eve, members of Gray's Inn gathered in the Great Hall for the start of their Christmas revels. They had invited a number of guests, including friends from the Inner Temple, Staple and Barnard's Inns. The festivities that night inaugurated a mock 'Prince of Purpoole' (Portpool was a name for the Gray's Inn locale), and the list of invited guests contains several extremely bawdy puns. Third in the list is 'Lucy Negro, Abbess de Clerkenwell', leader of a so-called nunnery, whose 'choir of nuns' with 'burning lamps' will perform 'Night-Service in *Cauda*' and 'chaunt *Placebo* to the gentlemen of the Prince's Privy-Chamber, on the day of his Excellencie's Coronation'. 'Cauda' is Latin for 'penis' or 'tail', and the phrase 'to sing Placebo' means to make oneself servile. The nunnery at Clerkenwell had been dissolved by Henry VIII and the 'nuns' who now resided there were prostitutes with the pox ('burning lamps'). In a series of prosecutions at Bridewell, Lucy Negro is named as 'Black Luce', and her real name given as Luce Baynam (Figure 4.2). As far as we know, she herself was never charged.

The court hearings show that Luce had been a prostitute since at least 1573 and ran a brothel in association with her Turnmill Street neighbour, Gilbert East, and a pimp named Henry Boyer. Together, Luce and East hosted a number of itinerant women at their houses in

Clerkenwell, including Anne Levens, who earned substantial sums from prostitution until her arrest in 1576 (Figure 1.1). 'Black Luce' appears to have had connections with the world of the theatres. She is referenced by name in Thomas Heywood's *1 Edward IV* (1600) and Barnabe Barnes's *The Devil's Charter* (1606). The *Gesta Grayorum* indicates that she was present at Gray's Inn on the night of 20 December 1594. We know too that unnamed 'Gentlewomen' attended the performance of *The Comedy of Errors* at Gray's Inn on the night of 28 December. In that play, Shakespeare alters the kitchen wench's name from 'Nell' to 'Luce', describes her as dark or 'swart' (3.2.100), and puns on the sound of her name (3.1.53–4). When Dromio of Syracuse spies the courtesan, he sees her wearing 'the habit of a light wench': 'It is written, they appear to men like angels of light; light is an effect of fire, and fire will burn; ergo, light wenches will burn; come not near her' (4.3.51–7). Shakespeare's Gray's Inn audience are likely to have understood how the Italian word 'luce' both translated and sounded in English (i.e. 'light' and 'loose'). Dromio's words strikingly echo the description of Lucy Negro in the *Gesta Grayorum*.

In the sonnets, Shakespeare writes about his mistress as though she is dark-skinned, promiscuous, and liable to pass on a venereal infection. The last line of Sonnet 144 makes reference to an angel likely to 'fire' (or sexually infect) another man. Elsewhere, in *Timon of Athens*, Timon exclaims to the courtesans Phrynia and Timandra, 'Be strong in whore, allure him, burn him up. | Let your close fire predominate his smoke' (4.3.142–3). These opaque references tap into the dramatic power of London's illicit economy. After life as a brothel owner, East, it seems, had become Philip Henslowe's 'bailiff', probably a rent-collector and enforcer. What happened to Black Luce, we do not know. She appears still to have been alive in 1601, and it may be that the 1604 inscription 'Lewce East' in Henslowe's 'Diary' has some connection with her, but the facts remain obscure. Even so, anyone reading the sonnets in 1609 might plausibly have brought her to mind, something Shakespeare was likely to have anticipated.[10] But we are left only with surmises.

Black Luce's brothel housed a number of young women, most prominently Mary Dornelly, who wore a silk gown and was kept to serve 'great guests', and Meg Goldsmith, who also went by the name of 'Mistress Tarleton'. Many other itinerant women either drifted or were persuaded into the sex trade, largely as a result of poverty. In 1598, a Stratford-upon-Avon woman named Elizabeth Evans was arraigned at Bridewell under suspicion of incontinent living. She was daughter to a Stratford cutler who had been executed for 'coining', a word that refers to counterfeiting or defacing the queen's coin. She moved between a number of London addresses, escaping arrest by fleeing from 'Tutle' (Tothill) Street in Westminster, then into Southwark, and then again north of the river to Abchurch Lane, just north-east of London Stone. Here she hooked up with an unnamed gentleman from Gray's Inn.

According to testimony at her trial, Evans had boasted that she was worth three hundred pounds per year, a sensational sum of money for the time. Witness statements show that Evans had received some schooling at Stratford, and this provision may lie behind Helena's reference to her 'schooldays' in *A Midsummer Night's Dream* (3.2.203). Beneath her confession, Evans left a remarkably elegant signature. She had been hunted down by the City Recorder, John Croke, and for just about any other woman this moment would have been terrifying. But she must have known she was safe, for present in court that day was Sir William Howard, brother to the Lord High Admiral Charles Howard, who 'did sue for her enlargement', claiming that she was 'a kin' to him. Reluctantly, the Bridewell bench felt compelled to release her despite the fact that Howard was almost certainly lying.[11] We may guess that Evans was a little less than kin and more than kind to him. Either way, she was notably resourceful and took extraordinary risks. Her case is very unusual and full of drama, for few such women escaped Bridewell's whipping post. Whether Shakespeare knew of her from Stratford, or possibly via the Admiral's Men, we cannot say. But, as we shall see, he tended to represent women such as Evans in a sympathetic rather than judgemental light.

Edward Alleyn and Shakespeare

Living close to the Porpentine, the Vine, and Horseshoe Alley on Bankside were actor Edward Alleyn and his father-in-law, Philip Henslowe. Together, they shared extensive business interests in Southwark, at the Rose and Newington Butts playhouses and, after

1604, the Bear Gardens. Henslowe owned the Rose, and his famous 'Diary' of memoranda gives invaluable information about the routine business of running shows there in repertory. Although evidence for Shakespeare's links with Alleyn is relatively scarce, they would have been familiar with one another's work. There is a certain parallel in the paths of Alleyn and Shakespeare across London. John Aubrey, writing in the late seventeenth century, reported (on evidence supplied by Sir William Davenant) that Shakespeare settled near Shoreditch when he first arrived in London.[12] In 1596, official returns from the parish of St Helen's Bishopsgate show that Shakespeare had lived there but moved south of the river. Malone referred to a (now lost) paper that seemed to confirm Shakespeare's move to Bankside.[13] The evidence appears to show Shakespeare and Alleyn tracing a similar London movement, with Shakespeare following Alleyn's course from Bishopsgate to the Bankside.

That course followed an arc, from Bishopsgate, just south of the Shoreditch playhouses, down Gracechurch Street, and across the river to Southwark. Alleyn had been raised at an inn called 'the Sign of the Pie' in Bishopsgate, just outside the city wall. After his father's death, his elder brother John (also an actor) took over the inn, and it would remain in the family for the next 200 years. The Alleyns' portfolio of properties steadily grew to include tenements in St Saviour's, Southwark, among them 'the Unicorn and other messuages'. The Unicorn stood in the liberty of the Clink between the Pike Gardens and the bull-baiting ring that became in 1614 the Hope Playhouse, about 800 feet west along the riverbank from the Vine. The 'Sign of the Pie' was just one of several taverns situated in and around Shoreditch and Bishopsgate. Others included the Woolsack run by ale-wife Widow Browne, the Flower de Luce, the Dolphin, the King's Head, the Swan, the Bell and Bull inns where the Queen's Men had been licensed to play in 1583, and the Bell Inn just north of St Leonard's Church. The north-eastern suburb of Shoreditch, close to the Curtain and Theatre playhouses and with Bethlem Hospital (Bedlam) to the south, just outside Bishopsgate, had gained a certain notoriety (Figure 4.3).

Just a handful of examples will serve to indicate the dubious reputation of this area. John and Lawrence Dutton, both actors with the Queen's Men, were alleged to have pimped out their wives from the

Bell in Shoreditch. In 1576, brothel owner John Shaw was prosecuted for keeping bawdy houses, including one in Bishopsgate. The following year, Anne Smith, residing at the King's Head, was detained for sleeping with a man and accepting a ring by way of payment. Elizabeth Everys, an ill-treated married woman living at 'Arthur's Halls in Bishopsgate street', confessed in 1578 that 'she went to a play at the Bell at Bishopsgate' (on Gracious Street) where she met with a Master Benjamin Gunston and thereafter received gifts and favours from him. Gunston promised her that 'her husband should do her no wrong'.

These were not isolated incidents. In May 1598, Margaret Browne, wife of a stationer living in St Botolph's Bishopsgate, told the court at Bridewell that, spying through a chink in her wall, she saw her next-door neighbour Clement Underhill making merry and being intimate with one Michael Fludd. Clement's husband was away from home.[14] The following year, Agnes Ward, Anne Colimore, Anne Gybbes, Anne Webster, and Margaret Askew were all prosecuted as 'bawdy and lewd women'. They resided at a house rented by Roger Holden at the gate of St Mary Spital on Bishopsgate Street just over the road from Holywell. Holden's house was noisy 'at inconvenient hours', gentlemen of various kinds turned up late at night, including three Spanish merchants, and a back door had been broken to let the women out into the Spital gardens when they feared the house was about to be searched by the watch. The Bridewell magistrates subsequently ordered that 'all the bawds and lewd women sent into this house by the deputy of the ward of Bishopsgate shall be arraigned at the Guild Hall'.[15] This reputation for dissolute behaviour among the playhouse hinterlands would prove impossible to dispel.

By 1593, and probably earlier, Alleyn had moved south to Bankside, leasing out his properties in Bishopsgate. Some years later, he made a list of them in a book of memoranda, along with details of property bonds and leases in and around the Bear Garden. In 1603, the Sign of the Pie was mentioned in the prosecution of Widow Hill and her daughter Judith, a couple with an especially scandalous reputation:

Judith Hill a notorious harlot examined saith that one Master Tilney a gentleman of Gray's Inn had the use of her body at Clarkenwell and he gave her v^s at an alehouse called the Sign of the Pie a quarter of a year since he is an old bachelor brother to Master Tilney a councillor of Gray's Inn. Ordered to be punished and kept.[16]

Edmund Tilney was the official censor of all published plays. He and his brother Robert lived in Clerkenwell, less than a mile north-east of Gray's Inn. The fact that the brother of the Master of the Revels was one of the men frequenting bawdy houses in north London would have done nothing to allay concerns about the immorality of plays. Now at Bankside, Southwark, Alleyn resided in the liberty of the Clink, a locality that housed, according to a survey *c*.1608, 250 watermen, 100 or so tradesmen, and about 150 poor people, widows, and others 'all being ready to take, and not one of them fit to give'.

In summer 1593, plague hit London and Alleyn, now a member of Lord Strange's Men, had gone with the company to the provinces. Members of the company included Shakespeare's future colleagues, Will Kemp, Thomas Pope, John Heminges, Augustine Phillips, and George Bryan.[17] Alleyn wrote touching letters home to his wife Joan, Henslowe's step-daughter, one addressed 'To E. Alline on the banck side' and another (seemingly dated 24 July 1593) to 'Mr Hinslo, one of the grooms of his Majesty's chamber, dwelling on the Bankside right over against the Clink'. Unfortunately, we lack any such precise address for Shakespeare south of the river. It seems plausible that he might have lived close to his brother near the Vine or the Elephant. At the same time, he was making adventurous plans in both Stratford and London. He bought New Place in his home town, a spacious residence with twelve hearths and an impressive array of windows and chimneys. But he and the Burbages were also looking for a new performance space and had their eye on a collection of rooms in the old priory at Blackfriars. Alleyn too would later have property interests in Blackfriars.[18]

Alleyn was also a bibliophile, buying books for himself and his children. Some he gave away, like the one he had decorated in silver and illustrated by the renowned painter Rowland Buckett for Katherine Howard, Countess of Suffolk. The total value of this gift was £15.[19] One of the cheaper books he purchased was by Shakespeare.

On the back of an early modern letter is an inscription apparently in Alleyn's hand that refers to a purchase he had recently made. The letter bears a date of 19 June 1609. At the bottom of a list of purchases, rents, earnings, and apparel is a last note: 'Howshowld Stuff a book Shaksper sonetts 5^{d}' (Figure 3.1). It has been argued that this entry is a

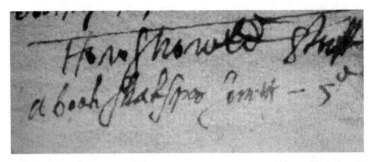

Figure 3.1. A letter from Thomas Bowker to Edward Alleyn showing the latter's purchase of a volume of Shakespeare's Sonnets for '5d'. MSS 2, 12.1ᵛ. 'Howshowld Stuff a book Shaksper Sonetts—5ᵈ' written in Alleyn's hand. Reproduced with kind permission of the Governors of Dulwich College

nineteenth-century forgery by John Payne Collier. It occurs at the end of a list, and Alleyn nowhere else uses the phrase 'Household Stuff', although he does use the words 'Howshowld' and 'Howshowld Charges'.[20] Neither G. F. Warner, a scrupulous Alleyn scholar sensitive to the possibilities of forgery by Collier and others, nor R. A. Foakes, another highly respected Henslowe-Alleyn scholar, raised any query as to the authenticity of this record. Arthur and Janet Ing Freeman, authors of a monumental and rigorous study of Collier's life and work, in which all his Shakespeare fabrications are carefully reassessed, see no reason to think it a deception: 'It seems perfectly genuine to us'. In their book on the sonnets for this series, Paul Edmondson and Stanley Wells note, 'The authenticity of the entry has been questioned...unnecessarily in our view'. Alan H. Nelson has added his authority to the question: 'the entry is unquestionably authentic, far beyond the imitative skills of any known forger, including Collier'.[21]

Close comparison between the words of the entry and similar words and letter formations elsewhere in Alleyn's documents point to Alleyn's hand. In particular, Alleyn regularly used a spurred 'p', as we see in the word 'Shaksper'; he routinely preferred a 'tt' spelling as evident in 'sonett'; the tail of the final 'd' curls through the centre of the letter to the right; and the formation of the 's' and 'h', and the word 'Stuff', are all characteristically Alleyn's. Furthermore, when Shakespeare's name is forged in other documents, it is given in full, which is not the case here. We know that the sonnets were listed in the Stationers' Register on 20 May 1609. Alleyn's scribbled note seems to suggest that the book was available in print within a month of that date and at a penny less than a regular play in quarto. They were poems in which Alleyn had an interest.

Shakespeare and Alleyn resided near each other in Bishopsgate and Bankside. Both were hugely successful in their dramatic careers and professionally connected with the same group of actors. As Roslyn Knutson has valuably pointed out, 'commerce among the playing companies was built on patterns of fraternity'.[22] Parallel experiences are perhaps what we might expect of players in this period, and we can point to other examples. As noted in Chapter 2, the burial of Shakespeare's brother Edmund at St Saviour's Church, Southwark, in 1607, was recorded with the following note: 'Edmond Shakespeare, a player, buried in the church, with a forenoon knell of the great bell, 20s'. On 12 September 1608, the actor Lawrence Fletcher was interred in a similar manner: 'Lawrence Fletcher, a player, the King's servant, buried in the church, with an afternoon's knell of the great bell, 20s'.[23] The duplicate wording might imply payment for this honour by the company rather than an individual.

The Southwark token books show that Fletcher was one of the people living at the Vine with Edmund Shakespeare in 1607 (Figure 2.7). Like Thomas Pope living alongside John Duke in 'Three Cups Alley' in Shoreditch, or Cuthbert and Richard Burbage in Holywell, a life in tandem is suggested. But of these relationships, nothing further is known. We are reminded that the residual traces of Shakespeare's personal connections often survive through scraps and fragments.

Falstaff and the Lord Chamberlain

In 1594, Shakespeare became a member of the Lord Chamberlain's players. But when Sir Henry Carey, the Lord Chamberlain, died at the age of seventy-two in 1596, his position, and that of his company, must have seemed momentarily in doubt. In the event, the position of Lord Chamberlain passed to Sir William Brooke, tenth Lord Cobham, and, under new management, the company's cohesion seemed newly assured. But this arrangement would test Shakespeare's allegiances. Early modern Londoners could not avoid having loyalties, debts of gratitude, or duties and obligations. Shakespeare's dedications to the Earl of Southampton in *Venus and Adonis* (1593) and *The Rape of Lucrece* (1594) are some evidence of his. Southampton was allied to Robert Devereux, the second Earl of Essex. In the last Chorus of *Henry V*, Shakespeare famously acclaims the expected return of Essex from Ireland, bring 'rebellion broachèd on his sword' (5.0.33). It would quickly become clear that the Cobham and Essex households hated each other.

Cobham was only one year younger than Carey. He had been made Lord Warden of the coastal Cinque Ports of Hastings, New Romney, Hythe, Dover, and Sandwich, and constable of Dover Castle, in 1558. He was also Vice-Admiral and a Justice of the Peace for the county of Kent. These were highly responsible positions and a sign of royal favour. A remarkable Cobham family portrait survives, showing Brooke with his second wife, Frances née Newton, her sister Johanna, and his six children, Maximilian, twins Elizabeth and Frances, Margaret, Henry, and William. The setting is likely to have been the dining hall in Cobham Hall, Kent, about twenty-five miles south-east of London Bridge. On the table is a dish of fruit—including cherries, grapes, pears, apples, and plums—a table bell, a knife, and a parrot. Four of the children are holding or tending pets, a lapdog, a rabbit, a chaffinch, and a marmoset. The portrait shows a privileged family enjoying all the benefits of life enriched by domestic and imported luxuries.

Proudly descended (by marriage) from the Lollard martyr Sir John Oldcastle, Brooke became Lord Chamberlain on 8 August 1596. He has been regarded (without much evidence) as no great friend of either plays or players. Around this time, Shakespeare was writing his second set of history plays, including *Henry IV Part 1* and *Part 2*, and in particular creating one of his most celebrated characters, Sir John Falstaff, the famous 'fat knight'. Falstaff stuffs his belly with capon and beer, haunts taverns and bawdy houses, and likes to 'keep' women (mostly by neglect), including the Hostess of the Tavern, Mistress Quickly, and the prostitute Doll Tearsheet. He is a thief, a coward, a witty inventor of excuses, an occasionally callous melancholic, but also a *bon viveur*. He's a character an audience loves but can never admire, an anatomy of parts, or 'trunk of humours' as Hal puts it in *Henry IV Part 1* (2.5.454). Hal's list of grotesque comparisons anatomizes Falstaff as a composite figure.

Controversy has long attached to Falstaff's name. We know from two seventeenth-century sources that Shakespeare's original name for this character was 'Sir John Oldcastle'. A letter by Richard James to Sir Harry Bourchier, dating to around 1625, states that, 'in Shakespeare's first shew of Harrie the fift [*1 Henry IV*] the person with which he undertook to play a buffoon was not Falstaff, but Sir John Oldcastle'. The letter adds that 'offence being worthily taken by Personages descended from his title ... the poet was put to make an ignorant shift of abusing Sir John Falstaff'. As if to confirm the story, Thomas Fuller, writing in 1662, added that 'the *Stage* hath been overbold with his memory, making him a *Thrasonical Puff*, & emblem of *Mock-valour*. True it is, *Sir John Oldcastle* did first bear the brunt of the one, being made the *make-sport* in all plays for a *coward* ... Now as I am glad that *Sir John Oldcastle* is *put out*, so I am sorry that *Sir John Falstaff* is *put in*'. Evidently, Falstaff's original name of 'Oldcastle' caused trouble, but it was not erased entirely. The earliest editions of the plays, printed in 1598 (Q *1 Henry IV*) and 1600 (Q *2 Henry IV*) bear faint residual traces: Hal's 'my old lad of the castle' and an uncorrected speech-prefix—'Old.' (*2 Henry IV*, 1.2.114). The phrase 'old lad of the castle' may be an allusion to the 'Castle on the Hoop' tavern, just west of the Clink prison, next door to the Vine. Other names were changed too. The quarto's 'Sir John Russell' and 'Harvey' became the Folio's Bardolph and Peto.

It has seemed odd that Shakespeare should have risked offending the new Lord Chamberlain, Sir William Brooke, by using the name 'Oldcastle' (even though Oldcastle was only an ancestor by virtue of his marriage to Lady Joan Cobham). The Cobham family, Sir William or his heirs, apparently objected to their distant ancestor being publicly traduced as a drunken, cowardly whore-master. As David Scott Kastan states: 'It seems certain that Shakespeare in *1 Henry IV* origin-ally called his fat knight "Oldcastle" and under pressure changed it ... Cobham ... was a dangerous man to offend ... No one has put forth any credible motive for the pragmatic Shakespeare to engage in such uncharacteristically imprudent behaviour'.[24] Not only this, Shakespeare went on to give jealous Master Ford in *The Merry Wives of Windsor* the alias 'Brooke'. *The Merry Wives of Windsor* was probably written not long after *1 Henry IV* in the years 1598–1600. The word 'brook' is close in meaning to 'ford', but Shakespeare did not have to select that name, and on the surface at least it looks like a second deliberate provocation of the Cobham family.

In the Henry IV plays, Shakespeare takes his audience inside London's victualling houses. We get a vivid impression of inn parlours and by-rooms, the 'fat room' (*1 Henry IV*, 2.5.1), 'the Half Moon' (l. 27), and the 'Pomegranate' (l. 36). Mistress Quickly recalls the exact time and place when Falstaff promised her marriage, 'sitting in my Dolphin chamber' (*2 Henry IV*, 2.1.90). These scenes work in a different linguistic register to those in the main plot of 'civil butchery' (*1 Henry IV*, 1.1.13). They have a comic verbal dexterity that contrasts with matters of national importance, but they also carry a sense of localism. In 1576, Alice Wickham reported illicit merry-making with 'a noise of minstrels' in a lower parlour called 'The Pomegranate' of the Bear tavern in Wood Street. Katherine Dorrett, suspected bawdy house owner, resided at 'the backside of the Half Moon' in Aldersgate Street. One of the Earl of Oxford's men unsuccessfully tried to entice a woman to a banquet at 'the Dolphin' at 'the backside of Old Fish Street' in 1576.[25] Shakespeare drops in echoes of his audience's world, giving them recognizable situations.

A handful of verbal fragments in *2 Henry IV* may have derived from a very specific set of events that concerned the Cobham family. At the start of Act 2 in *2 Henry IV*, Mistress Quickly attempts to have Falstaff arrested, ostensibly for a historical debt of a hundred marks, but more for her latest loan of 'thirty shillings' (2.1.32, 104). Fang, the constable, is concerned that Falstaff may resist and stab someone, and oblivious to innuendo, Mistress Quickly confirms the risk: 'he stabbed me in mine own house, most beastly, in good faith . . . if his weapon be out, he will foin like any devil' (2.1.15, 17). When Fang attempts the arrest, a melee ensues. Falstaff roars, 'Away varlets! Draw Bardolph, cut me off the villain's head, throw the quean in the channel' (2.1.46–7). In the first quarto edition (1600), Mistress Quickly cries, 'Throw me in the channel? I'll throw thee in the channel . . . Murder, murder!' (sig. C2ʳ, 2.1.48). When all the fuss over the 'thirty shillings' has died down, she relents and just wants him home: 'Well, you shall have it, though I pawn my gown. I hope you'll come to supper. You'll pay me altogether? (2.1.160–2). These details of the quarrel—the thirty shillings, stabbing, knocking the hostess into the river, a cry of murder, and the pawned gown—seem insignificant, but they lend an incidental

Figure 3.2. A detail from the 'Agas' map showing Broken Wharf, an inlet on the northern edge of the Thames, just west of Queenhithe dock. Reproduced by kind permission of British History Online

realism to the moment. They are very particular authorial choices and it seems Shakespeare did not entirely invent them, for they may also be found in the prosecution of a procuress in 1598.

Sir William Brooke's tenure as Lord Chamberlain lasted only six months. He died on 6 March 1597. In what follows, his sons William and George play an important part. Almost a year after Brooke senior's death, on 4 March 1598, charges were levelled against Agnes Wilkinson, wife of Michael Wilkinson, dwelling at Broken Wharf, for harbouring prostitutes and taking them to the private chambers of young William and George at the court in Westminster. Broken Wharf comprised a cluster of houses on the north bank of the Thames beside Paul's Wharf, almost directly opposite the bull-baiting ring on the south side (Figure 3.2). A Master Allen had knocked at Agnes Wilkinson's door and offered to take her serving girl, Alice Partridge (alias Woodstock), into the service of 'one Master Brooke'. Alice had owned a 'gentlewoman's gown' but had left it 'in pawn with her'. Allen led Alice westwards 'to the said Master Brooke to the court'. When she returned, Alice was now the owner of a new gown.

We get a few more biographical details from Partridge's testimony. She had been born and raised in Holborn and found service for six months with 'the Lady Hobbie'. Margaret Hoby was powerfully connected through her three marriages: first, to the Earl of Essex, then to the Sidneys, and finally to the Hoby family. Alice, it seems, was a poor worker and soon got the sack. Subsequently, she found shelter with the Wilkinsons at Broken Wharf. It was there that she had lately been arrested by Master Reade, the Marshal. She confessed that Wilkinson had escorted her to 'Master Brooke at the court, being the Lord Cobham's brother, to his chamber'; in other words, to young George Brooke. On the way back from this assignation, Wilkinson fell out with Master Allen when he gave her less money than he'd promised. The row became heated: Allen drew his dagger and threatened to stab her if she did not keep quiet. Wilkinson complained all the more vehemently, and thereupon Allen 'thrust the said Wilkinson's wife into the Thames near White Hall and there [she] had been drowned if the husband of the said Agnes Wilkinson had not been there'.

Master Reade arrested a second girl at Broken Wharf. Barbara Allen confessed that she too had been 'carried' by Wilkinson to 'Master Brooke' who'd paid her thirty shillings in return for 'the use of her body'. Wilkinson, she said, took half of the money. Two men had been at the house when she was apprehended but they 'escaped away', one racing back for a cap he had left by mistake. 'Diverse others', she confessed, resorted to the house and there had 'the use of her body'.[26]

On Monday 6 March, Wilkinson was detained for a week at Bridewell for 'being a common bawd' while the case was referred to the Guildhall. Alice and Barbara were held for nine days. Wilkinson made a fuller confession, saying that she had kept Barbara especially for Sir William Brooke (the younger) who would send for her as and when he pleased. She had taken Barbara to his chamber just 'two days or three before the said Sir William was slain'. She told the court how Brooke would give Barbara thirty shillings for her services. She added that she kept Alice Woodstock especially for George Brooke and had taken her to him just two weeks ago. Wilkinson confessed that others frequented the girls at her house, one paying a French crown and another giving just a shilling each. She added that her gown was now 'in pawn'. She had made, she acknowledged, 'a secret place in her house to keep wenches and lewd women in, in which place the marshal found the women aforesaid when he apprehended them'. Alice was flogged on 8 March 'for that she confessed that Master Brooke had the use and carnal knowledge of her body'. Agnes Wilkinson was whipped at Bridewell on Wednesday 15 March, banned from her house, and exiled altogether from the City of London. Thereafter, Wilkinson and the other girls disappear.

Young William Brooke (1565–97) had started his career in the service of the Earl of Essex. He was preferred to Parliament by his father but failed to win support as an MP for Kent in the autumn of 1597, partly it seems by reason of debt. He made his will on 17 June 1597 before setting out with the Earl of Essex's Islands voyage against the Spanish fleet. Back in London, on the morning of 24 December that year, he added a rushed codicil leaving everything to his brother George, writing, 'Your geast [guest?] and my haste would not suffer me to acquaint you with what I am gone about this morning—what hath called me out so early'. Brooke was heading out to the artillery ranges at Mile End Green to take part in a duel at dawn with the young Sir Thomas Lucas. The cause of this dispute is unknown but, in the event, Brooke was mortally wounded and died later that day. The Privy Council ordered the arrest of Lucas who reportedly had fled to France. Agnes Wilkinson's testimony refers to the fact that Brooke was 'slain' and makes it possible that George's 'geast' was Alice Partridge (alias Woodstock).[27]

Barbara Allen testified that she had been with Wilkinson for half a year which, given that the prosecution was heard in March 1598, would seem to place the events of the case between September and December 1597. Shakespeare's apparent knowledge of some of the details involved would seem to indicate a date of November–December 1597 for the composition of *2 Henry IV*. This is fairly well in line with current thinking regarding the play's date. Although Justice Shallow mentions Mile End Green, possibly even as a place for duelling (3.2.268), there is no hint that Shakespeare knew at the time of writing of the events that led to Cobham's killing, suggesting composition prior to 24 December 1597. The play's epilogue (or epilogues) are a different matter. It has often been thought that the last three paragraphs of the play might have been added at a later stage to suit different kinds of performance. The first paragraph ends with a prayer for the Queen and so may have fitted a production either at court or at one of the Inns of Court. The second (and perhaps third) paragraph requires a dancer or clown to end the play with a jig. The third and closing paragraph openly addresses the controversy attaching to Falstaff's name. The 'humble author' promises to continue the story 'with Sir John in it', a reference to the future play *Henry V*, possibly under way. It seems that Shakespeare planned Falstaff's death in *Henry V*, but the epilogue in *2 Henry IV* leaves open just how that might happen: 'for anything I know, Falstaff shall die of a sweat, unless already a be killed with your hard opinions. For Oldcastle died a martyr, and this is not the man' (Epilogue, 25–9). The word 'killed' may hint at Brooke's demise.[28]

Cobham's sons were behaving just like Shakespeare's whore-mongering rogue during the time their father was Lord Chamberlain. Cobham and his family would have had every reason to want to distance themselves from a comic, lecherous glutton who bore the name of their ancestor on the public stage. Shakespeare could always claim he had simply taken the name from *The Famous Victories of Henry V*. It is faintly possible that he simply had not known Cobham's pedigree, especially via its ancient marriages. Unlikely as that may seem, he gave to the name a character that echoed all too familiarly young William and George's reputation. Thereafter, the relationship between the Earl of Essex and the Cobhams worsened dramatically. In this enmity lay a possible reason for Shakespeare's provocations.

Henry Brooke, old Cobham's eldest son and heir, was loathed by Essex's faction.[29] Essex might have laughed as he wrote to Robert Cecil in February 1598 that in marrying Brooke, Margaret Ratcliffe 'is married to Sir John Falstaff'. The following year, the Countess of Southampton sent gossip to her husband, who was in Ireland with Essex, regarding Henry Brooke's illegitimate newborn son: 'All the news I can send you that I think will make you merry is that I read in a letter from London that Sir John Falstaff is by his Mistress Dame Pintpot made father of a goodly miller's thumb, a boy that's all head and very little body, but this is a secret'. It may be that Shakespeare is quoted here. The phrase 'Dame Pint Pot' echoes Falstaff's admonition to Mistress Quickly in *1 Henry IV*: 'Peace, good pint-pot; peace, good tickle-brain' (2.4.387). By 1600, the Cobhams were clearly identified with Falstaff by their enemies. It is not surprising then that, on the day Essex launched his doomed campaign in London in 1601, Henry Brooke, old Cobham's heir, should have placed 'an ambuscado of musketeers' in a boat on the Thames, to cut the Earl and his followers to pieces as they marched down the Strand.[30]

As Falstaff strolled the stage, Southampton and Essex would have relished knowing that unseemly aspects of the Cobhams' private lives were being publicly aired to London audiences. Shakespeare might have been willing to provoke the Cobham family in *Henry IV* and *Merry Wives*, at the instigation of Southampton, Essex's close friend and associate. Falstaff getting thrown into the Thames in a buck basket in *The Merry Wives of Windsor* might look like recompense for Agnes Wilkinson. A ridiculous attempt at a duel (between Dr Caius and Sir Hugh Evans) is staged at the centre of *Merry Wives* (3.1). There remains of course much that we don't know about these details. But what emerges from them is not an apolitical Shakespeare lacking any affiliations but a writer ineluctably caught up in the factional politics of his time, willing to invoke Essex as a conquering hero in *Henry V*, stage *Richard II* in his support, hint at him as Achilles in *Troilus and Cressida*, and risk conflict with a dangerous, rival dynasty.[31] Since the Cobham affair undoubtedly involved circumstances now lost, there is no full or simple story to tell. The intriguing question that remains is not why Shakespeare made Falstaff such a figure of mockery but why he made him so likeable and forgivable.

The case of Christopher Beeston

We get a glimpse of the friendly rivalry between Shakespeare and Richard Burbage from John Manningham, a law student at the Middle Temple, whose 'Diary' records a memorable tale of the two actors. Manningham liked to note details of sermons, stories, and amusing anecdotes about people and events, picked up from gossip and conversations at the Inns of Court. In one entry, he remarked on a performance of *Twelfth Night* at the Middle Temple on Candlemas night (2 February 1602). In another, dated 13 March that year, he noted a piece of gossip relating to Richard Burbage and Shakespeare:

Upon a time when Burbidge played Rich. 3. there was a citizen grew so far in liking with him, that before she went from the play she appointed him to come that night unto her by the name of Ri: the 3. Shakespeare overhearing their conclusion, went before, was entertained, and at his game ere Burbidge came. Then message being brought that Rich, the 3d. was at the door, Shakespeare caused return to be made that William the Conqueror was before Rich, the 3.

This often retold tale is probably not an invention, for it chimes with all we know of the bawdy incidents so favoured by young lawyers at the Inns of Court. Burbage had played Richard III prior to October 1597 when the play was registered: the first quarto that year announced on its title page that it had been 'lately acted' by 'the Lord Chamber-laine his servants'. As the concluding part of the first tetralogy, *Richard III* is usually regarded as quite an early play, probably written around 1593-4, so we cannot put a date on exactly when this assignation might have taken place. It is a jocular tale. Another story, involving the actor Christopher Beeston, is a good deal more serious.

The Beeston case is an unsavoury episode. On Wednesday 27 October 1602, Margaret or Margary White was charged at Bridewell with bearing a child out of wedlock. In her testimony, she named one Henry Noone as the father but also alleged that she had been raped by Christopher Beeston. At the time of the alleged offence, Beeston was one of the main players in Shakespeare's company and he was due to be married. The record of the case is as follows:

Margary White sent into this house by Mr Recorder's warrant for having a child begotten in whoredom and otherwise living in incontinency examined saith that one Henrye Noone dwelling in Fenchurch Street at the Star and Cock is the father of her child and that he hath put it out and gave ix^{li} [nine pounds] with it. And further she saith that one Christopher Beeston a player at one Winter's house in Star Alley without Bishopsgate had the use of her body but as she saith he did it forcibly, for said he I have lain with a hundred wenches in my time. Ordered to be kept till the cause be further tried.

Nine days later, Beeston appeared before the Bridewell magistrates to deny the allegation as a malicious lie. This was a risky strategy. Defendants who lied in court could expect much harsher punishment. He was bailed to return 'within four days'. The Bridewell governors included London aldermen. After so many complaints to the Privy Council about the licentiousness of plays, they now had a key target in their sights and wanted to proceed against him. When Beeston returned on Saturday 13 April, the bench first took a statement from a Master Knevett, clerk to Sir Henry Billingsley, who denied that he had been instructed to put it about that Beeston had bragged 'he had lain with an hundred women in his time'. This was a curious inter-vention and might suggest that Beeston was alleging a conspiracy against himself, one he traced back to Billingsley, a former Lord Mayor and prominent alderman. What then transpired was extraordinary:

And forasmuch as the said Christopher Beeston is by one Margaret White a prisoner of this house accused to have committed with her the abominable sin of adultery in most filthy and brutish manner in one Winter's house in an alley without Bishopsgate on midsummer eve last. For which he was convented before certain of the governors of this house, and he being examined utterly denieth the fact (notwithstanding she justifieth it to his face). At which time also the said Beeston and others his confederates players did very unreverently demean them-selves to certain governors and much abused the place, and yet upon some reports made known to this court greatly suspected to have committed the fact. And because at this court also some in the said Beeston's behalf hath contrary to all good order taken exceptions against some of the governors of this house it is ordered by a general consent that such a course shall be in law proceeded against him as is and shall be thought fit for so great a crime.

Perhaps the most important phrase in this summation of events is the line roughly half-way through: 'she justifieth it to his face'. For any woman to detail a rape offence face to face with her attacker would require huge resilience and conviction. Beeston was 'greatly suspected' of having committed the 'fact' or deed but his response was breath-takingly arrogant. He brought in actor-friends who 'unreverently' took exception to the magistrates and 'much abused the place'. The above entry expresses the governors' displeasure by insisting on the 'abom-inable' nature of 'so great a crime'. Beeston's act was 'brutish', animal-like—the kind of act Iago lewdly imagines: making 'the beast with two backs' (*Othello*, 1.1.115).[32] We can be sure that Shakespeare knew of this event, and it is possible that he bore it in mind when writing *Measure for Measure*, a play written not so long after 1602. In that play, it is the magistrate Angelo who attempts a rape, a prisoner refuses to be punished, and a clownish character behaves 'unreverently' to the Duke.

The key question about this episode is: who were those 'others his confederates players'? Was Shakespeare among them? Beeston had left the Lord Chamberlain's Men in the summer of that year, perhaps kicked out. By August he had followed Will Kemp, who left earlier in 1599, and joined the Earl of Worcester's troupe. So perhaps the group included some of Worcester's Men. In any event, Augustine Phillips was likely to be among them. He and Beeston appear to have been long-standing friends. On 16 November 1604, Beeston christened his son 'Augustine' at St Leonard, Shoreditch, and Phillips left 'Thirty shilling in gold' to 'my servant Christopher Beeston' in his will of 1605. Robert Pallant might have been another. He had played along-side Richard Burbage and 'Kit' (Beeston?) in 'The Second Part of the Seven Deadly Sins'. Philip Henslowe's 'Diary' shows that on 26 November 1602, less than two weeks after the Bridewell fiasco, Pallant and Beeston assisted with payment for 'The Black Dog of Newgate'.[33] Shortly afterwards, historical events overtook the prosecution and it was seemingly forgotten. With the accession of James I, the Chamberlain's Men were translated to the King's Men, and Worcester's to Queen Anne's Men. They were now unassailable. Yet at the height of this success, plague swept across London, emptying not only playhouses but entire parishes.

George Wilkins, co-author

So far in this chapter, we've seen that details regarding particular individuals in early modern London can shed light on aspects of Shakespeare's world, even if he barely knew them or they him. When we learn of people like East, Baynam, Wilkinson, or Brooke, we gather a little more of the context of Shakespeare's literary characterizations. Perhaps the most extraordinary depiction of London society is given in *Pericles* (published 1609) where a girl of fourteen years is confined to a bawdy house and almost raped. When Shakespeare set about writing *Pericles* with co-writer George Wilkins, he worked from Lawrence Twine's *The Pattern of Painful Adventures*, first printed in 1576. In chapters 13 and 14 of that prose work, Tharsia, daughter of Apollonius and Lucina, is sold to a common bawd who seeks the highest price possible for her virginity. Tharsia's virtue converts all the clients, including the Prince's steward, to godliness. Shakespeare's version of these scenes occurs in the play's fourth act. He brings on stage 'three Bawds', a 'Pander' or pimp, Boult the brothel keeper, and a female bawd or brothel madam, a trio not unlike that of Henry Boyer, Gilbert East, and Black Luce.

Wilkins was a resident of Cow Cross, a lane that lies even today just at the bottom of Turnmill Street. Shakespeare's association with Wilkins went back to at least 1604 when both were living in the house of Christopher Mountjoy in Silver Street. They gave statements in a lawsuit brought by Mountjoy's son-in-law, Stephen Belott, over a withheld dowry. The story of Shakespeare in Silver Street has been told in fascinating detail by Charles Nicholl. Wilkins seems to have been a man of violent temper. There is even a record of him having kicked a pregnant woman in the stomach so hard that she had to be carried home in a chair. This shocking behaviour has led to him being almost entirely ignored by literary critics. But as a writer, he was clearly regarded as a man with potential. The title page of his play *The Miseries of Enforced Marriage* shows that it had been performed by Shakespeare's company in 1607, perhaps in repertory alongside *Pericles*.

Printers also liked Wilkins's work. Three texts—*The Historie of Justine* (1606), *Three Miseries of Barbary* (*c*.1606), and *The Miseries of Enforced Marriage* (1607)—were printed by William Jaggard at his shop in Barbican, just a short walk east from Cow Cross. Jaggard printed the prose tale *Three Miseries of Barbary* for Henry Gosson, the publisher of the 1609 quarto of *Pericles* who once stood bail for Wilkins. It seems that Wilkins enjoyed Jaggard's confidence.[34] Shakespeare similarly had support from stationers. Lukas Erne has shown that his plays outstripped those of his rivals for works reprinted within ten years of their original publication.[35] Valentine Simmes, who reissued Twine's version of the Pericles story in 1609, probably to coincide with the play (and perhaps with Wilkins's prose version of it), saw no less than nine Shakespeare plays into print. Shakespeare and Wilkins's *Pericles* proved so popular that it was reprinted six times prior to 1635. But not one of those editions advertised Wilkins as co-author. By this time, Thomas Heywood and Ben Jonson had started to recycle Shakespeare's work in their own, beginning what has come to be known as the poet's 'mythos'. Playing at Blackfriars and living almost next door at the gatehouse, Shakespeare was already a London phenomenon.

Wilkins is now generally regarded as the author of the first two acts of *Pericles*. He might have added other touches here and there. Staging requirements indicate that he must have collaborated not just with Shakespeare but with the King's Men as a company, for he needed to know that it could produce a stock of decapitated heads or skulls (two at least) for the threats of Antiochus in the opening scene to have any meaning for an audience (1.1.35–41). The company would also need a collection of 'impresas' or insignia for the display of shields and

mottoes in the second act, designs for which Richard Burbage may have
been (perhaps partly) responsible. The tense and unsettling brothel scenes
in the fourth act seem mainly to belong to Shakespeare. Marina,
Pericles's lost daughter, is offered for sale in a bawdy house just like
Tharsia in Twine's tale. The three bawds are looking for 'fresh ones'
for the sex trade, and Marina is just what they need—innocent, pure,
and cultured. She is shown to foreigners who can barely contain
themselves when they see her. Reserved for the better sort, Marina
encounters Lysimachus, governor of Mytilene, who has arrived at the
brothel to view its pleasures. He is especially interested to know how
young she was when she started:

> LYSIMACHUS   Fair one, how long have you been at this trade?
> MARINA   What trade, sir? . . .
> LYSIMACHUS   Did you go to't so young? Were you a gamester at five,
> or at seven?

> (Sc. 19. 71–7)

The governor's questions, and perhaps the manner in which they are
asked, are deeply unsettling. There is nothing like this conversation in
Twine. In fact, Twine's narrative is powerfully moving at this point:
the Prince visits Tharsia to reward her refusal to be debauched with
more gold than she could get through vice, saying that he, after all, has
a daughter at home who might have fallen into a similar plight in other
circumstances. Shakespeare's Lysimachus is an emollient abuser who
only relents at the last minute and begs her to think the best of him
although she has quickly come to know the worst.

Boult was about to rape Marina, but she just managed to talk him
out of it. Others could not be so fortunate. In February 1561, James
Ratcliff stood accused in Bridewell of raping Elizabeth Fettes and
burning her 'in her privy place'. He had 'stopped her mouth and
threatened to kill her if she should cry'. The court noted that the girl
was 'small of stature', about twelve or thirteen years old, and that the
infection had 'not yet healed but grown to a pock to the distraction
[insanity] of the child'. Ratcliff was committed to one of the Counters.
The governors of Christ's Hospital sent John Walker to Bridewell in
October 1575 for raping Katherine More, being 'about xi years of age'. In
1576, Elizabeth Guy, aged eleven, explained to the court that Robert

Archer had repeatedly raped her in a ditch and a field. In her statement, she told the court that, 'she pushed him away & cried when he was doing of it but he wold not away or leave her'. Robert Adams was prosecuted in July 1577 for assaulting Johan Weekes, 'a little girl' of about ten or eleven years. The record of the case states that he set out 'to Ravish her three or four times'. He held a knife to her while he did it, and 'threatened her that if she either told or cried he would stick her'. On 24 May 1598, William Greene was charged with having slept with thirteen-year-old orphan Margaret Swinnerton, to whom Greene claimed to be betrothed. The court did not believe him and he was detained.

These are troubling cases, and it may have been that audiences found Marina's radiant innocence in a brothel-house comic. But there is real tension when the bawds resolve 'she shall be ploughed' (Sc. 19, 170). Boult is about to rape Marina out of what he deems as economic necessity. He asks her, 'What would you have me do? Go to the wars, would you, where a man may serve seven years for the loss of a leg and have not money enough in the end to buy him a wooden one?' (Sc. 19, 195–8). The play makes it clear that poverty, privation, and hunger drive this industry. His lines remind of Pompey's response to a charge of bawdry in *Measure for Measure*: 'Truly, sir, I am a poor man that would live' (2.1.220). These plays show Shakespeare at his most socially engaged. For all their shared interest in faraway maritime adventures, neither Shakespeare nor Wilkins was escapist. Theirs is the only play of its kind to recognize the suffering of some early modern children in garrets and chambers just beyond the playhouse walls.

We have records of Shakespeare's company touring in the provinces, on the road even to places as far removed as Barnstaple, Shrewsbury, Coventry, Cambridge, Maldon, and Dover. In all likelihood, he trav-elled each year (as John Aubrey claimed) to Stratford to see his family. Even in London, it seems, he was itinerant, moving between lodgings and designing performances for different venues—the playhouses, the lawyers' inns, and at Court. This extraordinary energy could only be sustained in collaboration with a wide range of other people. At this historical distance, we perhaps can never exactly know the personal dynamics between Shakespeare and these many collaborators. But if Peter Quince's frustrations with his 'crew of patches, rude mechanicals | That work for bread' (3.2.9–10) are any indication, they may rarely have run smooth.

Art/Authority

For any writer, early modern London was a place of great opportunity but also substantial risk. We saw in Chapter 1 that Thomas Dekker was imprisoned for debt in 1598–9 and later confined to the King's Bench prison in Southwark for another seven years. In autumn 1597, Ben Jonson was thrown into the Marshalsea alongside fellow actors Gabriel Spencer and Robert Shaa for his part in the now-lost play *The Isle of Dogs*, co-written with Thomas Nashe. The following year, Jonson was branded for Spencer's murder. Along with the arrests of Marlowe and Kyd in 1593, these are some of the best-known examples of dramatists coming into conflict with the London authorities. Suppression was a constant threat to the livelihood of any dramatist. Plays were censored, and from their inception the early playhouses were always at risk of closure by the City's leaders. This chapter highlights Shakespeare's awareness of the challenges that civic power presented for both him and his company. It begins with an outline of the hierarchical structure of London society before focusing more closely on plays and poems that seem to connect specifically with questions of civic constraint. The chapter goes on to suggest that Shakespeare resisted these authoritarian pressures sometimes quite directly, as in *Measure for Measure* or *Coriolanus*, or more often indirectly, by repeatedly asserting the priority of art—of poetry, drama, visual art, and music—over politics.

The gilds and livery companies

Peter Quince and the mechanicals of *A Midsummer Night's Dream* each have a trade. Nick Bottom is a weaver, Francis Flute a bellows-mender, Tom Snout a tinker, Snug a joiner, and Robin Starveling a tailor. Frightened away by Bottom with an ass's head, Quince makes a quick reappearance to say just one timorous line: 'Bless thee, Bottom! Bless Thee! Thou art translated' (3.1.111). The word 'translated' is usually glossed as 'transformed' but it also served as an official term for the movement of a labourer from one trade and gild to another. The joke is that Bottom has been demoted, if that were possible, to an absurd and monstrous fool. The records of the Court of Aldermen show that many apprentices in the City were legally 'translated' from one 'profession' to another. While the play transports an audience imaginatively to Athens, London is never far away.

Labour in London was thoroughly regulated through workers' gilds or livery companies. These were quasi-judicial bodies that had evolved through the fourteenth and fifteenth centuries to oversee the work of masters, journeymen, and apprentices in the City. Their responsibilities included collecting quarterly fees, ensuring quality of work, and seeing financial obligations met and entitlements maintained. They also organized city pageants and entertainments. The livery companies kept halls across London, many of them adapted from former feudal mansion houses, and they were run by their own hierarchy of masters, wardens, and officers.[1] They remained subject to the authority of the Lord Mayor and Court of Aldermen who kept lists of companies responsible for supplying members of the nightly watches.[2] Masters were skilled craftsmen 'free' of their trade, qualified to have their own shop and take on apprentices. Journeymen had served their apprenticeship and were entitled to work in their craft for a daily wage. Apprentices were trainees, bound by indentures to a seven-year term at the end of which they would be deemed 'free' of their art.

A 1589 list of stipendiary posts needing to be filled shows the ranked nature of London society. It included the bailiff-wick of Southwark, clerks to the Lord Mayor's Court and Bridge House on the south bank (where corn was stored), Beadle to the Court of Requests, Common Sergeant, Common Crier, Common Pleader, Collector of Scavage (a duty applied to aliens), keeperships of the prisons of Ludgate and Newgate, and the Wood Street, Poultry, and Southwark Counters, Keeperships of Leadenhall, the Guildhall, Bay Hall, the Sessions House, Sergeant and Yeoman of the Chancel, and Yeoman of the Waterside. There was even an 'underwater bailiff' (deputy to the water bailiff).[3] The list illustrates a highly regulated labour force. As Steve Rappaport and Ian Archer have argued, it was this structured system, organized in large part through the livery companies, that helped to maintain a fragile stability in the streets of early modern London.[4]

The gilds and worshipful companies were headed by the 'Great Twelve'—the Mercers (dealers in cloth), Grocers, Drapers, Fishmongers, Goldsmiths, Skinners, Merchant Taylors (tailors), Haberdashers (clothiers), Salters, Ironmongers, Vintners (wine merchants), and Clothworkers—institutions with their own hierarchies, offices, and regulations that kept details of apprentices, journeymen, and freemen on their books. As David Kathman has shown, several early modern actors, including some of Shakespeare's company, were 'free' of their art: John Heminges, for example, belonged to the Grocers' Company, and boy actors Alexander Cooke and Thomas Belt were among ten apprentices bound to him. Cooke retained his association with the Company of Grocers until his death in 1614.[5] E. K. Chambers suggested that Augustine Phillips may have been belonged to the Company of Musicians (eventually chartered in 1604) since he left musical instruments to his 'apprentices' Samuel Gilburne and James Sands in his will.[6]

Being 'translated' under the livery company system did not mean being promoted, and Bottom undergoes his humiliation with a genial, if naïve, optimism. The joke in *A Midsummer Night's Dream* is hardly offensive, but doing what Bottom and his friends were doing—rehearsing a play—was not *work* as the City understood it, and for players to make an ass of a labourer in his vocation would not have impressed its leaders. Shakespeare and his fellow actors were not exactly 'masterless men', because they enjoyed the patronage of the Lord Chamberlain, and later the King, but they stood both figuratively and literally beyond the City's remit and could laugh at its ways from without. To this extent, they represented not a threat but a provocation.

The City rulers

The historic Corporation of London comprised the office of Lord Mayor, sheriffs, aldermen, and the Court of Common Council. There were twenty-six wards in early modern London, and each elected a

Figure 4.1. A section from the Braun and Hogenberg map (1572), showing the City. The City of London's boundary ran from Temple and Holborn Bars in the west, via Barbican and Moorfields to the north, to the Tower in the east. The third-century stone wall, with its gates—Ludgate, Newgate, Aldersgate, Cripplegate, Moorgate, Bishopsgate, and Aldgate—marked a physical, but not a legal, perimeter. Public domain

representative to the Lord Mayor's governing body, the Court of Aldermen, which sat at the Guildhall.[7] Shakespeare refers to aldermen just twice and on both occasions draws attention to the fine rings they wear on their fingers or thumbs (perhaps recalling his own father who was made alderman of Stratford in 1565). The Court of Aldermen in London sat principally as an executive committee formed from the larger Court of Common Council which comprised some 212 persons. Its members belonged to one or other of the livery companies and gilds and elected a mayor annually from the elite group who served on three or four committees. The City's wards were divided into roughly 242 precincts, each notionally at least overseen by a constable (Figure 4.1). According to Stow, writing in 1598, London had around 239 constables. Social and economic activity in London was busy, dealing with practical problems and solutions. Constables' duties included looking into crimes on their patch, calling jurors, selecting members for 'the watch', and arresting vagrants. Assessors served as customs and excise officers, rating imports and exports, plus measures of corn, wine, beer, salt, coal, wood, charcoal and other commodities.

The Court of Aldermen involved itself in all aspects of everyday life, covering ambassadorial visits, care for orphans, disputes over

inheritance, regulation of musicians, fishing in the Thames, punishment of some petty criminals, and oversight of the Bridge House and
watermen. On 8 August 1595, the aldermen appointed 'Thomas
Wood minstrel' as 'Bailiff of the Borough of Southwark' after the
dismissal of Richard Hutton, an armourer.[8] Philip Henslowe and
James Burbage are likely to have welcomed the appointment. But it
wasn't long before Wood himself was in trouble: on 30 April 1598, he
was alleged by Anne Sweno to be the father of her child. We should
not think of Southwark or Shoreditch as wild and lawless: even in its
suburbs and liberties, London was a highly organized city. Its population in 1600 stood at around 200,000, three or four times larger than
the populations of Bristol or Norwich.[9] Given that the playhouses
could accommodate well over a thousand persons at any single performance, and that no other city institution could draw and speak
to such crowds so consistently, it is hardly surprising if the authorities
felt that they had to be regulated, controlled, and, if need be,
altogether removed.

A stream of complaints and restraining orders issued from the Lord
Mayor's office to the Privy Council throughout the later sixteenth
century, all aimed at limiting theatrical activity in the capital. These
complaints gathered pace and strength in times of plague. Assemblies
of large numbers of people, it was claimed, increased the risk of
infection, not to mention instances of crime and licentious behaviour.
But the leading acting companies enjoyed the patronage of the most
highly placed and influential aristocrats in the land, men whose wishes
were difficult to countermand. Writing in 1559, Robert Dudley, Earl
of Leicester, recommended his players to the Earl of Shrewsbury as
'honest men, and such as shall play none other matters (I trust); but
tolerable and convenient'. Leicester's Men, one of the leading companies of strolling players at the time, were in the vanguard of seeking
a London base where they could play more regularly, and in 1571 they
were permitted to perform 'such matters as are allowed' but only 'at
convenient hours & times'. Thereafter, throughout the next decade
they played at court and around the country.[10]

Figures of authority are repeatedly challenged in Shakespeare.
A stark confrontation occurs near the end of *2 Henry IV*, in a short
scene where Mistress Quickly and Doll Tearsheet are dragged off to
prison by beadles. The play was in all likelihood written in late 1597.

The prison scene pitches two ordinary Londoners against men empowered to commit anyone on mere suspicion. The women put up a fight. Quickly and Tearsheet have been rounded up after a fatal broil over a prostitute and now face 'whipping-cheer' at Bridewell. Doll denies any wrongdoing, calls the beadle a 'tripe-visaged rascal', and pleads her belly until a cushion is pulled from under her kirtle. But still she refuses to go quietly, calling him 'blue-bottle rogue' and 'filthy famished correctioner'. The scene ends with the women yelling and cursing: 'Goodman death, goodman bones', 'Thou atomy', 'you thin thing', 'you rascal'. Today, we might find such resistance entertaining, perhaps even heroic, but in 1597 hurling abuse so publicly at an officer of the law was risky comedy. In the following scene, Falstaff is told by Pistol that Doll has been put 'in base durance and contagious prison' by a 'most mechanical and dirty hand' (5.4.34–5). It is hard not to sense genuine disdain for the law's knuckle-dragging henchmen in these words.

The year 1597 was particularly tough for the Lord Chamberlain's Men. They lost James Burbage who died on 2 February, had lost Henry Carey, Lord Hunsdon, the previous year, and suffered the short-lived turbulence of the next Lord Chamberlain, Sir William Brooke, Lord Cobham. Family tragedies also occurred: actor Richard Cowley, a neighbour on Halliwell Street, lost a son (Robert?) on 20 March, and Cuthbert Burbage buried his son James on 15 July. Shakespeare had buried his young son Hamnet the year before.[11] The business of playing also looked precarious. A twenty-one-year lease James Burbage had taken out on the site of the Theatre was in the process of expiring, and the building itself was reportedly in considerable need of repair.[12] On top of all this, opposition to the very existence of the theatres was coming to a head after the *Isle of Dogs* scandal. On 28 July, the Privy Council sent a letter to the London Recorder, William Fleetwood, and Justices of the Peace in Middlesex, giving them notice that no less an authority than the Queen herself wanted the Theatre and Curtain playhouses pulled down and that they should force the owners to comply:

Her Majesty being informed that there are very great disorders committed in the common playhouses, both by lewd matters that are handled on the stages and by resort and confluence of bad people, hath given direction that not only no plays shall be used within London or about the city or in any public place during this time of summer, but that also those play houses that are erected and built only for such purposes shall be plucked down, namely the Curtain and the Theatre near to Shoreditch . . . And likewise that you do send for the owners of the Curtain Theatre or any other common playhouse and enjoin them by virtue hereof forthwith to pluck down quite the stages, galleries and rooms that are made for people to stand in, and so to deface the same as they may not be employed again to such use.[13]

The letter added that the Justices of Surrey should apply the same order to playhouses in Southwark, on Bankside, or anywhere within a three-mile radius of London. When Cuthbert and Richard Burbage came to dismantle the Theatre, partly with the help of carpenter Peter Street, the landowner Giles Allen responded with a protracted lawsuit complaining about the 'outrageous, violent and riotous' manner in which the operation had been carried out. But while the timbers of the Theatre were removed to serve in the construction of the Globe south of the river, no other playhouses were in fact pulled down. In 1600, Charles Howard, Earl of Nottingham and Lord Admiral, issued a warrant approving the plot of ground near Redcross Street for the building of the Fortune theatre, highlighting the Queen's appreciation of the Lord Admiral's playing company, led by Edward Alleyn:

[f]orasmuch as the place standeth very convenient for the ease of people, and that her majesty (in respect of the acceptable service, which my said Servant [Alleyn] and his company have done and presented before her highness to her great liking and contentment as well this last Christmas as at sundry other times) is graciously moved towards them, with a special regard of favour in their proceedings.[14]

The clerk to the London Common Council fired off another letter to the Justices of Middlesex in response reminding them of the earlier directive to 'pluck down' the playhouses, and that should this new theatre be built it would 'not only be an offence and scandal to diverse, but a thing that would greatly displease her majesty'. Yet in a clear demonstration that civic authority could not be constrained by the power of the nobility, the building of the Fortune, a square structure, went ahead.[15]

For all their opposition to playhouses and players, the City authorities had a long-standing and substantial interest in public displays of pageantry. The 'Diary' of Henry Machyn provides plenty of examples of the role of visual culture—arms, banners, flags, escutcheons, and shields—in the rituals, ceremonies, and shows of the City. Throughout the sixteenth century, pageants had traditionally been held to celebrate the election each year of the new Lord Mayor. In early November, the mayor would be sworn in and acclaimed by means of a parade through the streets of London with flags, banners, impresas, and ensignia, all designed to emblazon before the citizens the shared virtues of civic control. The mayor-elect would travel by barge to Westminster to take his oath of office before the monarch's appointed representatives and then process through the City with an entourage of aldermen and other dignitaries, all dressed in splendid livery, attended by artisans and journeymen of various worshipful companies.

Sometimes, these occasions were extraordinarily elaborate, involving exotic costumes, speeches, music, singing, and fireworks. The parade followed a series of stations or performance platforms set up in the streets. Elaborately designed wagons with figures in costume would pass by in a manner akin to the traditional coronation procession of the monarch. It all ended with a feast at the Guildhall and a short service at St Paul's.[16] George Peele, Anthony Munday, Thomas Middleton, John Webster, and Thomas Heywood (and perhaps Ben Jonson) all wrote for Lord Mayor's shows. We tend to think of Peele as a writer of the 1590s, but he was already a well-placed and well-regarded author some years before. One of the signatories to a 1574 refusal of an application by 'one Holmes' to perform interludes within the City was Alderman Wolstan Dixie. When Dixie became Lord Mayor in October 1585, it was Peele who was hired to produce a 'device' to celebrate the occasion. If the City appeared to favour certain writers, Shakespeare was not one of them. So far as we know he was never approached to compose for the Lord Mayor's shows, and he never did. This was probably the City's choice: Shakespeare perhaps belonged too much to Warwickshire and too little to London.

Writing the City

It is somewhat ironic that Shakespeare's most demonstrably 'London' play is one ostensibly set in Vienna. The low-life characters in *Measure for Measure* are largely Shakespeare's own creation and drawn straight from the taverns and bawdy houses of the City. From the start, the processes and hypocrisies of government are starkly exposed. Turning the tables on anti-theatrical denunciations of drama's feigning, the play focuses on 'seeming' or role-playing among the City's elite. Angelo, the most principled and disciplinarian of magistrates, has been appointed to rule as the Duke's deputy but with 'absolute power'. He cracks down on illicit sex in the suburbs, condemning the strumpet's 'double art, vigour and nature' (2.2.184). Yet it is Angelo's nature that proves double. The man whose blood scarce runs in his veins, and whose very urine might turn to congealed ice (3.1.374), thaws out to become as hot-blooded and vigorous a man as any he condemns. Filled with desire for Isabella, sister to the condemned fornicator Claudio, Angelo demands that she sleep with him. The choice for Isabella is effectively her rape or her brother's murder.

Measure for Measure was first printed in the 1623 Folio in a form that seems to have been adapted by Thomas Middleton in or around 1621, some five years after Shakespeare's death. Although the play's references to Hungary have been linked with historical events in 1621, the eastern European setting may derive from the play's main source, George Whetstone's two-part drama *Promos and Cassandra* (1578). Whetstone's work is a rare double-header from the 1570s and dedicated to the Recorder of London (a senior judge), William Fleetwood, whom Whetstone addresses as his 'kinsman'. Set in the fictional city of 'Julio', it is the first Elizabethan play to attempt a developed London-based realism. *Promos and Cassandra* opens with the Lord Mayor, a sheriff, a sword bearer, and 'One with a bunch of keys'. Promos (the Angelo figure) condemns Andrugio to death for getting Polina with child. After Cassandra, Andrugio's sister, pleads for her brother's life, Promos offers a reprieve on condition that she sleep with him. He also offers to marry her. Cassandra reluctantly agrees but determines to bring a complaint to the King. Seeing the gaoler carrying a head she wrongly believes to be Andrugio's, she thinks of committing suicide but instead resolves to seek justice. Interlaced between these more sober scenes are others in which Lamia, the play's courtesan, sings wantonly, and prisoners who rue their crimes are led off to the gallows. Lamia describes herself as 'chief of Lady Pleasure's train', a phrase that sets her alongside Love, Conscience, and Lucre in Robert Wilson's *The Three Ladies of London* (1581). Although Whetstone's play has performance conditions written all over it, there is no evidence that it has ever been staged.

Shakespeare adapted Whetstone by bringing the role of the Duke forward to the play's start, expanding the number of characters to include an analogue to Isabella in Mariana, and forging a potential romance between the Duke and Isabella. Other elements have parallels in Whetstone. Lamia, the courtesan, is introduced in the second scene and later brought into prison in a pattern followed in *Measure for Measure* by Mistress Overdone. Cassandra kneels before Promos, just as Isabella does before Angelo. Cassandra's argument that 'mercy should abate the force of laws' is essentially the argument Isabella presses against Angelo.[17] The King decrees that Promos should marry her and then be executed, a sentence that is subsequently annulled. But in adapting Whetstone's work, Shakespeare omitted virtually all of its London allusions. Whetstone includes a 'Mayors' feast' or pageant and refers specifically to 'Duck Alley', 'St Anne's Cross', 'Cock Lane', and 'Scold's Corner', areas reminiscent of locations around West Smithfield. Duck Lane ran behind St Bartholomew's Hospital and connected Smithfield market to Little Britain and Aldersgate Street. St Anne's Lane and Church were situated nearby at the foot of Aldersgate Street. Cock Lane linked the bottom of Smithfield at Pie Corner with Holborn. Shakespeare erased virtually all the play's London context. Mariana of the 'moated grange', for example, lives beside 'St Luke's' (3.1.266). In London, not a single church was dedicated to St Luke.

'Authority' is not a word that features in Whetstone's play, but Shakespeare uses it five times in *Measure for Measure*. Claudio laments the fact that drink can so easily undo a man: 'Thus can the demigod Authority | Make us pay down for our offence' (1.2.119–20). Lucio explains that the Duke has set Angelo in place to govern 'with the full line of his authority' (1.4.55). The Duke observes the 'celerity' of offences borne in 'high authority' (4.2.112), while Angelo puts his trust in the 'credent bulk' of the 'authority' lent to him (4.4.25). We are left in no doubt, even from the Duke's opening speech, that the play is specifically concerned with civic rule. But crucially what it dramatizes is confrontation with that rule. Isabella challenges Angelo in two powerful exchanges (2.2.29–167 and 2.4.30–170), Lucio, a clown, makes subversive remarks to the disguised Duke (3.1.383–92, 5.1.127–36, 348–52), and the Duke himself plots the overthrow of his own deputy from within the dark corners of a prison ward.

No other Shakespeare play has so many prison scenes, and it is this singularity that links the play to particular events of 1602.

At the play's heart is the comic character of Barnardine, a hung-over prisoner from overseas who insists on sleeping through the day instead of going to the block. Careless, inebriated Barnardine is beyond penitence: he has had the liberty of the prison and effectively made it his home (4.2.130–52). Audiences warm to Barnardine. He may be a reckless drunkard, but when he tells (of all people) the Duke, 'Not a word. If you have anything to say to me, come to my ward, for thence will not I today' (4.3.58–9), it seems that he has control of the prison. He decides whether or not he will go to the block.[18] In the autumn of 1602, Barnardine's attitude was not so implausible. Bridewell Hospital had been turned in 1553 from a former king's palace into a 'house of correction' for the 'setting on work' of vagrant, idle, and poor persons (Figure 4.2). But in 1602, the year of Beeston's trial, it had been turned into a virtual bawdy house. Since March, a small group of private contractors or 'undertakers' had been allowed to run the prison, a step that pitched the institution into a serious crisis.[19]

This experiment in private prison ownership proved a disaster. The 'undertakers' took the best rooms for themselves, demanded favours from some female inmates, allowed prisoners to escape, and generally sought to reduce the number of inmates to minimize their work. The governors quickly drew up a list of 'inconveniences' or complaints against them. In October, the contractors were finally sacked, and control of the prison was given back to the committee of aldermen that had run it in the first place. In a near-revolution at Bridewell, one of London's most feared institutions had become a 'house of ill rule' with prisoners wandering freely, or locking themselves in with others as they chose. An interesting coincidence is the prosecution on 19 September 1601 of Lewin Baradine, a 'stranger' in Southwark. Baradine had tried to sleep with Helen Michell in a garret, telling her that in his country it was a custom to sleep together prior to marriage. He bought his release from the court with a payment of 10 shillings 'towards the relief of the poor of this hospital'. It is not impossible that Shakespeare had heard of this Southwark incident and adapted it for *Measure for Measure*.[20]

Tales of false promises, pregnancy out of wedlock, prostitution, and the needs of children fill the London Bridewell prosecutions. On the

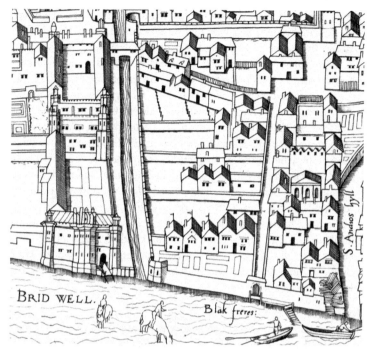

Figure 4.2. Bridewell Hospital as shown on the Copperplate Map (*c.*1553–9). Bridewell Hospital, Wolsey's former palace, was given over to the City by Edward VI by charter in 1553 for the housing and punishment of the vagrant poor and other petty criminals. It was separated from the precinct of Blackfriars by the River Fleet. Courtesy of the Museum of London

same day as the Beeston case (27 October 1602), Mary Houghton (alias Vaughan of Holborn) was brought in by the watch for being 'great with childe'. She protested that 'none but her husband' was the father. The court believed her and set her free. Elizabeth Cartwright dwelling in infamous Turnbull Street, and Agnes Griffin were brought in as 'nightwalkers' and punished. Elizabeth Smith, another 'nightwalker', was sent to St Thomas's Hospital in Southwark 'to be cured of her filthy disease'. On 3 November, Margaret Ashe claimed that John Buckley, a 'dyer' had trapped her in his house and 'had the use of her body', for which she was 'heartily sorry' and 'craved the mercy of God'. The court noted that she was 'very penitent (as it seemeth for her fault)' but ordered that she should be whipped anyway. Rebecca Stiles, a prisoner who had been detained for abandoning her child in the parish of St Andrew's near Puddle Wharf, was similarly whipped before being released. Another woman, Elizabeth Drewe, named John Tey, her master, as the father of her child. He had previously forced her to accuse a cook falsely. She was punished while Tey seems to have escaped prosecution. On 6 November, the constable of Queenhithe brought in Margaret Burley, 'a nightwalker' and 'common harlot'. She was punished and released. Ten days later, Jane White, who had been sent out by her master for 'a penny pot of sack' and was arrested in an alehouse in Smithfield at midnight, was punished as 'a nightwalker'. *Measure for Measure* addresses explicitly these kinds of problems in their urban setting.

Mistress Overdone is brought before Escalus and the Provost just as Elizabeth Cartwright, Agnes Griffin, and Rebecca Stiles had stood before the Bridewell magistrates. Overdone has been a bawd 'of eleven years' continuance' and faces the whip, but like Margaret Ashe, she pleads for mitigation:

> My lord, this is one Lucio's information against me. Mistress Kate Keepdown was with child by him in the Duke's time; he promised her marriage. His child is a year and a quarter old come Philip and Jacob; I have kept it myself; and see how he goes about to abuse me.   (3.1.456–62)

In a court that resembles Bridewell, Mistress Overdone seeks a reduced penalty for the good she claims to have done in discharging the city and parish of Keepdown's child. Her lines refer to the self-help strategies women were often forced to adopt in cases of unplanned or unexpected pregnancy.

The key phrase in Overdone's statement is 'he promised her marriage'. Mawdlyne Hawkins, serving woman, told the court on 16 August 1598 that she was now with child by Robert Welles 'and that he promised to marry her'. Isabell Mosse, servant to a haberdasher in St Peter's Hill, testified on 2 October 1602 that David Jones, a captain's man, 'is the father of her child and that he promised her marriage'. Roger Flambath told the court that Johan [Joan] Crane, an oyster seller, had replied to Thomas Burt openly in the street, 'you promised me marriage once, and if the tiles and windows at your master's could speak they would tell as much'.[21] Many pregnant single women pleaded that they had been promised marriage by a man who played false. In *2 Henry IV*, Mistress Quickly complains that Falstaff had sworn to marry her: 'thou didst swear to me then, as I was washing thy wound, to marry me and make me my lady thy wife' (2.1.92–3). The 'my lady' adds a poignant touch of vanity. Ophelia, in her madness, sings of a discarded lover: 'Quoth she "Before you tumbled me, | You promised me to wed"' (*Hamlet*, 4.5.62–3). Diana, having been wooed by Bertram in *All's Well That Ends Well*, protests before the King, 'Do you know he promised me marriage?' (5.3.257). Even in this short phrase 'he promised her marriage', Shakespeare reminds his audience that the world of the play is also theirs, and so too are its problems.

As *Measure for Measure* makes clear, a city's problems will include corruption in office. Imprisonment in Shakespeare usually represents a kind of ending. We might think of Pinch the schoolmaster in *The Comedy of Errors*, Clarence in the Tower, Richard II in Pontefract Castle, and Malvolio in his 'dark house' as examples. But in *Measure for Measure*, the prison is a place where subversion starts, planned by no less a figure than the Duke. Like Angelo, a number of Bridewell aldermen and officials were implicated in crimes they would have preferred to remain hidden. In 1576, the second son of alderman Sir Owen Hopton was said to visit a bawdy house run by the Dutton brothers in Shoreditch. William Mekyns, a pimp, boasted that 'he could go to Master Winch', an alderman, 'and fetch 3 or 4 crowns of Master Winch when he had need'. The following year, Thomasine Breame, a 'brave girl' and brothel keeper, denied that she had slept with Winch near St Paul's, despite the fact that Henry Boyer, a painter and pimp, had in mind to write to the Earl of Leicester about it. On 21 January 1577, Elizabeth Kirkeman, a prostitute, deposed that Master William Breche, 'the high constable of Clerkenwell', had slept with Mary Dornelly at Gilbert East's house. Humfrey Wynnington, brought in on 21 May 1577 for running a house of 'ill rule' for the servants of 'diverse men of worship', told that Alderman Sir John Rivers' son resorted to 'a young woman' there. Rivers had been Lord Mayor in 1573.

Such City-wide misdemeanours were bound to surface. But crimes occurred at the heart of the Bridewell institution too. On 16 May 1599, the aldermen raised concerns regarding £378 missing from the accounts of Treasurer Thomas Box. The position of 'Treasurer' was the most senior and influential in the institution. Box was allowed to continue in his post until midsummer but was then replaced by Alderman Florence Caldwell. At the same time, the steward and matron, James Harrison and Alice Millett, were dismissed from their posts for sundry 'misdemeanours'. The private 'undertakers' who took over the prison in 1602 simply made things worse.[22] From such cases, we cannot assume that all early modern London was corrupt—far from it. These abuses were discovered and anyone found guilty of a crime, minor or serious, could pay a heavy price. But the hypocrisies of the age were not lost on Shakespeare, and occasionally he would point them out with particular force. Some of the most powerful scenes in *King Lear* are set outside in a rough, exposed landscape. But in these scenes, where the stage is populated by the disabled and destitute—a lunatic, fool, wandering *faux*-demoniac, and a blind man—Lear mixes matter and impertinency in condemning institutions of authority that clearly belonged to London:

> LEAR An the creature run from the cur, there thou
> mightst behold the great image of authority. A dog's
> obeyed in office.
> Thou rascal beadle, hold thy bloody hand!
> Why dost thou lash that whore? Strip thy own back.
> Thou hotly lusts to use her in that kind
> For which thou whip'st her. The usurer hangs the cozener.
> Through tattered clothes great vices do appear;
> Robes and furred gowns hide all. Plate sin with gold,
> And the strong lance of justice hurtless breaks;
> Arm it in rags, a pygmy's straw does pierce it.
> None does offend, none, I say none.
>
> (Folio, 4.5.153–64)

The lines shift imaginatively from a wild, open landscape to the whipping room in Bridewell, where, as Robert Greene put it, Justice Fowler gives poor whores 'the terrible lash'. Lear's words articulate a lacerating condemnation of vices but for the fact that, like Erasmus's Folly, he speaks madness. A censor might easily have struck out these lines, even in their shortened form in the quarto. The speech chimes with sentiments Shakespeare expressed elsewhere in his writing, most notably in the tirades that punctuate the fourth act of *Timon of Athens*. Shakespeare was not afraid of voicing open contempt when confronting abuses of power. Tarquin's threatening statement of intent in *The Rape of Lucrece* has something of Angelo's insidiousness about it. He gives his sensual race the rein: 'Have done,' quoth he. 'My uncontrollèd tide | Turns not, but swells the higher by this let' (ll. 645–6). After the rape, Lucrece inwardly cries out against it: 'Why should the worm intrude the maiden bud? | Or hateful cuckoos hatch in sparrows' nests?' (ll. 848–9). Hamlet's lost mirth may seem to the modern ear like an existential crisis, but it is a young man's response to evident signs of injustice:

> For who would bear the whips and scorns of time,
> Th' oppressor's wrong, the proud man's contumely,
> The pangs of disprized love, the law's delay,
> The insolence of office, and the spurns
> That patient merit of th' unworthy takes.

> (Folio, 3.1.72–6)

These sections from *The Rape of Lucrece* and *Hamlet* are sometimes cited as analogues to the sense of ennui and indignation expressed in Sonnet 66. This world-weary poem comes close to despair in its suggestion that, but for the beloved, the speaker would rather die than live with the wrongs that surround him. It is worth citing the sonnet in full:

> Tired with all these, for restful death I cry:
> As, to behold desert a beggar born,
> And needy nothing trimmed in jollity,
> And purest faith unhappily forsworn,
> And gilded honour shamefully misplaced,
> And maiden virtue rudely strumpeted,
> And right perfection wrongfully disgraced,
> And strength by limping sway disablèd,
> And art made tongue-tied by authority,
> And folly, doctor-like, controlling skill,
> And simple truth miscalled simplicity,
> And captive good attending captain ill.
> Tired with all these, from these would I be gone,
> Save that, to die, I leave my love alone.

The sonnet is very deliberately arranged by a technique known as 'parison', matching word against word either side of a mid-way pause or caesura. Its catalogue of abuses is incrementally built by anaphoric repetitions at the start of each line from the third to the tenth. Merit, or 'desert', seems destined to a life of beggary, fools vaunt themselves in fine clothing, vows are broken, honours showered on the undeserving, the innocent sold as prostitutes, good men disgraced, and the ambitious restrained. Given that the sonnet is written to praise, we might wonder how seriously its apparent death wish can be taken. But for all its rhetorical patterning, there is one line that rings with genuine indignation. Shakespeare writes of 'art made tongue-tied by authority' (l. 9). The phrase, tightened by the word 'made', hints at coercion. As editors of the sonnets have pointed out, the line alludes to the City's desire to restrain poets and close the theatres. In doing so, it goes to the heart of Shakespeare's relationship with London. Against authority, the poem very simply counterposes 'art'. Only in the sonnets is the word 'art' used in its more modern sense of aesthetic practice. In *The Tempest*, one of his later plays, the word denotes a power to enchant an audience, including one's enemies. Shakespeare's response to censorship by authority seems to have been more 'art'. In the twentieth century, Herbert Marcuse argued that the political potential of art lay 'in art itself, in the aesthetic form'. Art's key function is, Marcuse held, to be, in some respect, impervious to ideology.[23] For all its artistry, Sonnet 66 speaks of this opacity or formal resistance to political control. Elsewhere in Shakespeare, we see kinds of authority confronted by myth, magic, and fairy tale. Poetry unties the tongue to assert the priority of art over authority.

Poetry and violence

As Christopher Marlowe's demise and Ben Jonson's killing of Gabriel Spencer both show, early modern London could be a very dangerous place. Sudden quarrels could quickly end in bloodshed. On 31 October 1601, Margaret Ellice deposed that the player Richard Allen had been fatally wounded in Tower Street after 'a falling out about paying the reckoning' in a tavern. The Middlesex County Sessions records, which document many cases of unexpected violent attacks, show that Allen's assailant was John Harrison, a vintner at St Clement Danes.[24] Shakespeare's response to a culture of violence seems to have been the production of dramatic and poetic 'art'. We can trace this response through a handful of examples, starting with one of Shakespeare's early plays, *Titus Andronicus*. This famously bloody play has been known to make audience members faint. Co-authored with George Peele, who was responsible for the first act, the play repeatedly brings art and authority into collision. In few other plays are acts of violence and utterances of poetry brought together so powerfully. Near the play's start, Titus utters a prayer of intense lyricism at the same time as Tamora's son Alarbus is sacrificed offstage:

> In peace and honour rest you here, my sons;
> Rome's readiest champions, repose you here in rest,
> Secure from worldly chances and mishaps.
> Here lurks no treason, here no envy swells,
> Here grow no damnèd drugs, here are no storms,
> No noise, but silence and eternal sleep.
> In peace and honour rest you here, my sons.

(1.1.150–6)

This is Peele rather than Shakespeare—hushed, reverential, and perfectly expressed, but entirely at odds with the violence it accompanies. Shakespeare follows Peele with similar clashes in tone. From the darkness of a pit spattered with Bassianus's 'ragged entrails' Martius calls up to Quintus, reminding him, 'So pale did shine the moon on Pyramus | When he by night lay bathed in maiden blood' (2.3.231–2). Perhaps the starkest example of this dissonance occurs in the play's most aesthetically troubling moment, after Lavinia's rape and mutilation. When Lavinia staggers on stage, hands severed and coughing blood, she is greeted by her uncle Marcus in the most rapt and lyrical classical terms:

> Alas, a crimson river of warm blood,
> Like to a bubbling fountain stirred with wind,
> Doth rise and fall between thy rosèd lips,
> Coming and going with thy honey breath.
> But, sure, some Tereus hath deflowered thee,
> And, lest thou shouldst detect him, cut thy tongue.

(2.4.22–7)

In this moment, violence and art are forced together with striking incongruity: Marcus's words are, to a modern sensibility at least, utterly at odds with the figure of a young woman mutilated and bleeding. The Folio edition of the play added a new scene in which language is once again at odds with action. Titus makes a quip about the fact that he has lost his arm: 'O handle not the theme, to talk of hands | Lest we remember still that we have none' (3.2.29–30). As if to underline this dark comic irony, Marcus kills a fly and Titus condemns him as a murderer (3.2.54). Perhaps an audience is meant to laugh at this scene. But laughter fits uncomfortably in the play. Titus's reaction when he receives his two sons' heads from Saturninus (having severed his arm to redeem them) is to laugh, and Marcus exclaims, 'It fits not with this hour' (3.1.264). Titus replies that he has been driven beyond tears. So many actions in the play 'fit not' with the hour that we might think a deliberate authorial strategy was at work.

Violence and poetry are again forced together when Titus and his followers enter carrying arrows with invocations to the gods tied to them. A stage direction has already signalled the entrance of Lucius with 'a bundle of weapons, and the verses writ upon them'. Poems are here tied to weaponry. Titus gives advice on how to hold and aim a bow correctly and, after a few lines, distributes the arrows among his followers. They draw and shoot. As they do so, they commend each other for how far they have been able to send their messages, as though to Jupiter himself, or so high they might have 'shot off one of Taurus' horns' (4.3.69). The compelling question is how, onstage in Henslowe's Rose theatre, did the players perform this moment?[25] Did they really shoot? Burbage, Shakespeare, and the rest of the company are likely to have been practised archers. Archery training took place in the northern fringes of the City, around Moorfields and Finsbury Fields, adjacent to Shoreditch (Figure 4.3). We know that Richard Burbage kept 'a fowling piece' in his house, and so perhaps a bow.

As Evelyn Tribble points out, the only other Renaissance play to show the live firing of arrows is *Cambyses*, where the king shoots at, and kills, a child. For Tribble, a mimed action would be sufficient to render this event. As for *Titus Andronicus*, she finds it 'wildly improbable' that arrows would have actually been shot onstage. If the actors did, she suggests, they could only have done so 'feebly'.[26] But in *Cambyses*, a stage direction bids Cambyses 'Shoot' (sig. C4^v), and

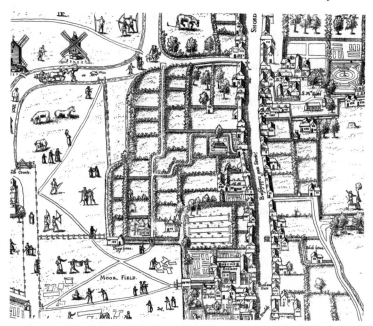

Figure 4.3. Archery practice taking place in Finsbury Fields from the Copperplate Map, courtesy of the Museum of London

since Tribble accepts that real guns were fired in *Henry V*, it may be that some productions did indeed take high risks. A stage direction shows that arrows were indeed shot during performances of *Titus Andronicus*: '*The Emperor brings the arrows in his hand that Titus shot at him*' (4.4.0). Early moderns knew little of occupational safety. A 'View of London from the North' (*c.*1600) shows an archer shooting directly over the heads of travellers, and accidents did happen.[27] Yet, in a theatrical performance, there could be no more vivid way to symbolize the priority of art over authority than to perform the act of shooting poems as if into the free and open sky.

Shortly after *Titus* played at the Rose, the theatres were forced to close as a result of plague. The outbreak occurred in the summer of 1593 and lasted into spring the following year. Church burial records for this period show whole parishes gradually falling sick. It quickly becomes clear that parish officers could barely keep up with the task of collecting and burying the dead. In St Olave's Southwark, on 14 August 1592, Tanaken Winterbeck was slung into a pit alongside her sister. She was the daughter of John Winterbeck, a Dutch thread-dyer whose work might have served weavers and tailors working for the Rose theatre. Only the poetry of her name marks her out amid the long list of fatalities.[28] It was a time that might cause anyone to despair. But in these terrible months Shakespeare turned to poetry to explore ways in which personal resolve might be achieved through art.

Under the patronage of Henry Wriothesley, third Earl of South-ampton, Shakespeare produced *Venus and Adonis* and *The Rape of Lucrece*, published in 1593 and 1594 respectively, both with prose letters of dedication to his patron. There is a remarkable moment in *The Rape of Lucrece* where Shakespeare adopts a technique known as *ekphrasis* (the explication of images through words) to show the transformative power of art. After Tarquin has abused her, the des-pairing Lucrece turns to gaze upon a classical scene woven into a wall hanging. The moment is based upon Book 1 of Virgil's *Aeneid* where Aeneas observes a similar painting. Lucrece notes facial expressions as Greek eyes peer sadly 'through loop-holes', 'blunt rage' rolls 'in Ajax's eye', 'the mild glance that sly Ulysses lent | Showed deep regard and smiling government', grave Nestor's beard 'in speech it seemed ... wagged up and down' (ll. 1398–1406) and in 'despairing Hecuba', the 'painter had anatomized | Time's ruin, beauty's wrack, and grim care's resign' (ll. 1450–1). Lucrece traces the design in detail, and, as she does so, an equivalence is achieved between painting and poetry: 'To pencilled pensiveness, and coloured sorrow; | She lends them words, and she their looks doth borrow' (ll. 1498–9).

Ekphrasis, with its subtle transference from picture to word, works performatively and restores feeling to the raped woman: 'Thus ebbs and flows the current of her sorrow' (l. 1569). The images in this painting have a remedial outcome, some inward benefit, and Lucrece finds herself silently 'Losing her woes in shows of discontent' (l. 1580). Word and image combine to produce emotionally reallocating effects, enabling Lucrece to see anew, or rethink, the consequences of her violation. Far-sighted, she imagines her legacy (ll. 1192–209), seeing now that her suicide will be her fame, her resolve will become Collatine's boast, her shame will be Tarquin's, and her honour will live on among those who 'think no shame' of her (l. 1204). Quiet contemplation of the painting allows complexities of thought and feeling to take shape. Usually, Shakespeare preferred words over silence. Portia describes a potential suitor as 'a proper man's picture, but alas, who can converse with a dumb-show?' (*The Merchant of Venice*, 1.2.70–1). But he could also pull off remarkable reverse-effects, acknowledging the importance of sight and silence. One of his best-known sonnets ends, 'For we which now behold these present days, | Have eyes to wonder, but lack tongues to praise' (106: 13–14). Again, the words have a performative effect, falling short where only the presence of the beloved will do.

In Shakespeare, we find aesthetic creation offering some counterweight to the violence of the age. His most bloody play, *Titus Andronicus*, is followed by a lighthearted, moonlit comedy, *A Midsummer Night's Dream*, and the contrast could hardly be more stark. In this play, Starveling, one of the actors in the 'Pyramus and Thisbe' interlude, observes sagely, 'I believe we must leave the killing out, when all is done' (3.1.13). Had that advice been heeded by Peele and Shakespeare as they sat down to write *Titus Andronicus*, there would have been no play to rehearse. *A Midsummer Night's Dream* answers its bloody precursor by focusing on a world of small, fragile things—cobwebs, mustard seeds, pease blossom, and nodding violets. Elves creep into acorn cups when the fairy King and Queen quarrel (2.1.30–1). In Peter Quince and his fellows, *A Midsummer Night's Dream* stages the precarious position of metropolitan players. The company rehearse 'in the palace wood, a mile without the town', near 'the Duke's oak', a topographical hint at St James's Park, Westminster (Figure 4.4). This is perhaps why Shakespeare calls the delicate plant hit by Cupid's 'bolt' 'a little western flower' (2.1.166). As Bottom discovers from his dream, and Theseus learns from Hippolyta, there is a transformative and 'mending' power in dramatic art.

Another woodland fairy play was John Lyly's *Gallatea*, the first recorded performance of which took place in 1585, about a decade earlier than Shakespeare's play. Lyly's work seems also to have been performed at court on New Year's Day in 1588. As Janet Clare has suggested, *A Midsummer Night's Dream* seems indebted to Lyly's play. She notes a number of shared features, including multiple narratives, the natural and supernatural, fairy and rustic.[29] To these thematic

Figure 4.4. Westminster, as shown on the Braun and Hogenberg map (1572), with deer in St James's Park (far left), the Abbey, Palace, Hall, and Star Chamber, Charing Cross (upper left), and the houses of the nobility stretched westwards along the north side of the Thames. Public domain

resemblances, we can add some verbal parallels. Lyly's Cupid greets a wood-nymph with, 'Fair Nymph, are you strayed from your company by chance, or love you to wander solitarily on purpose?' (1.2.1–2). Shakespeare similarly introduces Puck talking to a fairy: 'How now, spirit! Whither wander you?' (1.2.1–2). Lyly's Rafe, a miller's son, quips with epistrophe, 'Would I were out of these woods' (2.3.2–3) and Demetrius likewise declares, 'here am I, wood within this wood' (2.1.192). Eurota's line to Telusa, 'Why look ye so pale, so sad, so wildly', may anticipate Lysander's to Hermia, 'How now, my love? Why is your cheek so pale?' (*A Midsummer Night's Dream*, 1.1.128). Both Peter, the Alchemist's apprentice, and Theseus refer to the delusions of 'strong imagination' (2.3.146), and Venus and Diana quarrel over the boy Cupid in ways reminiscent of Shakespeare's changeling child: 'I have Cupid, and will keep him' (5.3.47). When Lyly's Cupid complains, 'Love-knots are tied with the eyes, and cannot be undone with hands; made fast with thoughts and cannot be unloosed with fingers...It goeth against my mind to make them loose' (4.2.26–32), his words seem to echo in Helena's: 'Love looks not with the eyes, but with the mind, | And therefore is winged Cupid painted blind' (*A Midsummer Night's Dream*, 1.1.234–5).

The nexus of confused love relationships in *A Midsummer Night's Dream* seems to have been anticipated by the fact that Gallatea and Phillida are both disguised as boys by their fathers: in both plays, four identities become caught up in a woodland maze of confused desire. Together with scattered references in *Gallatea* to dreams, fancies, doting, delights, the moon, a black boy, and an ass, it seems that Shakespeare found in Lyly's art an absorbing demonstration of its transforming power. If the poetry is Shakespeare's, the magic is Lyly's. In *Gallatea*, the mythical world of Neptune, Diana, Venus, and Cupid is matched with homespun miller's sons Robin, Rafe, and Dick, and Peter the black-faced Alchemist's man. In a kind of poetic alchemy, Shakespeare turned these London artisans into Athenian actors. Peter Quince, leader of the bungling players who rehearse outside the City, is a carpenter. In this art imitated life: James Burbage, former leader of Leicester's Men, was also a carpenter. Composing this play, Shakespeare seems to imply that it's outside the City that the richer experience and more imaginative understanding may be discovered.

Poetry and painting

After James Burbage died in 1597, it was left to his eldest son Cuthbert to oversee the transformation of the Theatre into the Globe and make plans for an indoor theatre at Blackfriars. The first we hear of the younger son, Richard, is when he is cited for his involvement in another brawl at the Theatre in 1590. Richard Burbage became the leading actor in the Lord Chamberlain's Men, playing the majority of the principal roles. He seems to have taken after his father in temperament. In 1592, when John Brayne's widow, Margaret, turned up at the Theatre with associates Robert Miles and Nicholas Bishop to demand her share of the gallery takings, Richard and his mother beat them away with a broom staff, shouting 'vehement threats and menacing'. Richard even went so far as to challenge Bishop to a duel, 'scornfully and disdainfully playing with [his] nose'—an almost comical scenario.[30] Besides John Manningham's famous anecdote about 'Rich, the 3d', we have other evidence that Burbage was admired for his arts. John Davies of Hereford's *Microcosmos* (1603) is a long, somewhat rambling poem on matters of philosophy, statecraft, the human body, humours, and complexions. Dedicated to James I, it celebrates a monarchy that promised to unite the 'whole isle of Great Britaine' (sig. A3ʳ). Touching on the question of pride, Davies refers with uncharacteristic directness to Shakespeare and Richard Burbage:

> *Players*, I love ye, and your *Qualitie*,
> As ye are Men, that pass-time not abus'd:
> And some I love for *painting*, *poesie*,
> And say fell *Fortune* cannot be excused,
> That hath for better *uses* you refus'd:
> Wit, Courage, good-shape, good parts, and all good,
> As long as all these *goods* are no worse us'd,
> And though the *stage* doth stain pure gentle blood,
> Yet generous ye are in *mind* and *mood*.[31]

In the margin against the word 'some' in the third of these lines, Davies wrote the initials of his favourite players, 'W.S.' and 'R.B.': William Shakespeare and Richard Burbage. Beside the word 'painting' Davies added another marginal note: 'Simonides saith, that painting is a dumb Poesy, & Poesy a speaking painting' (sig. Ff4). What is striking about this marginalia is that it associates an important sixteenth-century aesthetic debate with Shakespeare and Burbage in particular.

We know that Burbage had skills as a painter. An anonymous funeral elegy written for him after his death in 1619 focuses on his skills of 'limning' or painting, suggesting that Burbage drew the characters he played in a way that seemed true to life. The poem gives some of the leading parts he played and shows an understanding that drama was a multimedia skill requiring both poetic and visual intelligence at once:

> Some skilful limner help me; if not so,
> Some sad tragedian help t' express my woe.
> But O he's gone, that could both best; both limn
> And act my grief; . . .
> And as he could, no man could act so well.
> This part of sorrow for him no man draw
> So truly to the life, this map of woe,

That grief's true picture which his loss hath bred.
He's gone, and with him what a world are dead.
Which he reviv'd, to be revived so
No more: young Hamlet, old Hieronimo,
Kind Lear, the grieved Moor, and more beside,
That liv'd in him, have now forever died.

William Cartwright, a seventeenth-century actor and bookseller, apparently owned over 200 paintings, one of which depicted 'Mr Burbage his head in a gilt frame, a small closet piece'.[32] A painting now in the collection of Dulwich College may be the one referred to, and it is sometimes thought to have been done by Burbage himself. In *Microcosmos*, Davies seems to suggest that 'fell Fortune' has prohibited or hindered the 'better uses' for which the players might have been destined. The stage may be stained with blood after a tragedy, but this could not hide the 'generous' or gentlemanly virtues which both 'W.S.' and R. B.' possess. Not all players have these qualities. Davies writes of 'Apish Actors' who aspire to 'ascend the stage', of their 'base ascent', the elevation of Pride raised up so that 'All men may see her', of the cruelty of 'Fell Fortune', and—in contrast—of Shakespeare and Burbage's 'generous' [i.e. gentlemanly] 'mind and mood' that 'the good by nature loves'.

Shakespeare uses similar language and imagery at the start of *Timon of Athens*, a play co-written with Thomas Middleton, where a painter and a poet demur over the risks of Fortune. The poet carries a book of verse and the painter a canvas depicting 'Feigned Fortune' enthroned upon a hill. These are gifts for Timon in anticipation of patronage or financial reward. The painting shows those who aspire to Fortune's height, 'all, | Whose eyes are on this sovereign lady fixed', and who stand, like the two artists, at 'the base o' th' mount'. The painter feels the humiliating sting of so servile a climb:

> PAINTER   'Tis conceived to scope.
>
> > This throne, this Fortune, and this hill, methinks,
> > With one man beckoned from the rest below,
> > Bowing his head against the sleepy mount
> > To climb his happiness, would be well expressed
> > In our condition.
>
> > (1.1.73–8)

Shakespeare's Poet speaks of Timon's 'good and gracious nature' but also of Fortune's 'shift and change of mood' (l. 85). It may be that some of this language and imagery distantly recollects Davies's poem, but it is significant that the opening scene of *Timon of Athens* should stage a kind of contest between the arts. The Poet bears a sheet with lines written upon it, 'a thing slipped idly from me' as he puts it (1.1.20). Although the Painter boasts the greater excellence of his art over that of his fellow, the Poet in fact greatly appreciates the Painter's picture:

> POET   Admirable. How this grace
> Speaks in his own standing! What a mental power
> This eye shoots forth! How big imagination
> Moves in this lip! To th' dumbness of the gesture
> One might interpret
>
> . . .
>
> It tutors nature; artificial strife
> Lives in these touches, livelier than life.

                                                                    (1.1.30–4)

Shakespeare repeatedly expressed admiration for the abilities of painters to achieve verisimilitude. In *Venus and Adonis*, the narrative pauses for a moment to explain that just as an artist might paint the perfect form of an animal, so Adonis's horse did 'excel a common one, | In shape, in courage, colour, pace and bone' (ll. 294–5). The painting brought on in the opening scene of *Timon of Athens* is a literal embodiment of Sidney's 'speaking picture', transformed to a theatrical property. Ironically, Sidney's claim for the priority of poetry over all other arts becomes the claim Shakespeare's poetry makes for painting. While Shakespeare was central to London's literary activity, as a dramatist, he was very much a part of its visual culture too.

Shakespeare and the *paragone*

The Renaissance had a term for this contest between the arts. It was called the *paragone*, an Italian word meaning 'comparison'. John Florio, in his 1598 *World of Wordes*, defined the word as meaning 'a match, an equal, a proof, a trial, an experience, an equality, a comparison'. The *paragone* traces all the way back to Simonides of

Ceos's idea that painting is dumb poetry and poetry a speaking picture. The idea gained currency in the early sixteenth century from Leonardo da Vinci's short treatise *c.*1500 entitled simply *Paragone*. Leonardo argued for the greater excellence of painting over all sister arts, especially over poetry:

If you call painting dumb poetry, the painter may call poetry blind painting. Consider, then, which is the more grievous defect, to be blind or dumb?[33]

Commentators have attempted to trace the ways in which Leonardo's views filtered into European discourse on the arts throughout the sixteenth century. Clarke Hulse summarizes the consensus: 'This vocabulary is the glue holding the arts together in the Renaissance'. The comparison lies at the heart of Sir Philip Sidney's *Defense of Poesie* (*c.*1582). For Sidney, poetry sets forth nature as a 'rich tapestry', painting virtue 'in her best colours' (111/27). The poet 'doth draw the mind' better than any other artist (115/28–9) and 'pictures what should be' (124/21). In line with Horace's view that a poem is like a painting ('ut pictura poesis'), Sidney unites the two arts in his metaphor of the poem as 'speaking picture'. Davies was not the only English commentator aware of the *paragone*. Sir Edward Hoby, writing in *Politique Discourses* (1586), observed, 'For as Simonides said: painting is dumb Poesy, and a Poesy is a speaking Picture'.

Sidney and Hoby were men who travelled, and both had their portraits painted. In *The Defence of Poesy*, Sidney mentions Simonides (128/31) and refers to Leonardo's lifelong patron, Francis I, 'the great King Francis of France' (131/15–16), who, Vasari tells us, held the dying artist in his arms in 1519.[34] Although Sidney nowhere acknowledges painters or painting in his *Defence*, his argument for the supremacy of poetry is shot through with visual metaphors. We might have expected Shakespeare to share Sidney's preference for poetry, but he repeatedly asserts the priority of painting, especially via moments of silence. In *Lucrece*, Shakespeare uses ekphrasis to unusual effect, in ways that anticipate later dramatic occasions such as the opening scene of *Timon of Athens*, or the awakening of Hermione in *The Winter's Tale*. But it is in the sonnets that we find him repeatedly asserting the priority of visual art.

In the sonnets, some of which are clearly addressed to a young man (1–126), the contest between word and image arises in a plea that the youth should leave a copy of himself, a child, to the world. Pictorial language fills these early poems in the sequence, with the speaker urging the addressee to 'Look in thy glass' and see that 'thine image dies with thee' (3: 1, 14). Yet however often the speaker invokes the figure he loves, that image can never be realized by 'speechless song' (8: 13). All that verse can do is reflect upon 'time's pencil or my pupil pen', neither of which is able to paint the youth's 'inward worth nor outward fair' (16: 6–8, 10–11). Since the beloved's face is 'painted' by nature's 'own hand', it bears an authenticity inimitable by art. The youth is a radiant *nonpareil*, 'a man in hue, all hues in his controlling' (20: 1, 7), and for this reason, the speaker will not bestow upon him false 'painted beauty' (21: 2). Sonnet 24 is predicated upon the power of an image to engrave itself on the tablet of the heart, and it shows Shakespeare's admiration for the 'painter's art'. It is worth quoting the poem in full:

> Mine eye hath played the painter and hath steeled
> Thy beauty's form in table of my heart.
> My body is the frame wherein 'tis held,
> And perspective it is best painter's art;
> For through the painter must you see his skill,
> To find where your true image pictured lies,
> Which in my bosom's shop is hanging still,
> That hath his windows glazèd with thine eyes.
> Now see what good turns eyes for eyes have done:
> Mine eyes have drawn thy shape, and thine for me
> Are windows to my breast, wherethrough the sun
> Delights to peep, to gaze therein on thee.
> Yet eyes this cunning want to grace their art;
> They draw but what they see, know not the heart.

The poem works through intricate and complex metaphors. Echoing St Paul (2 Corinthians 3:3), the poet's heart is inscribed with the image of the beloved, his body a frame, his eye the 'cunning' painter, the lover's eyes 'windows', in a pattern where each reflects the other. But the poem also hints at a touching street scene: the lover gazing into the poet's 'bosom' as though through a 'shop' window and finding his own image there 'hanging still' (24: 7).

We know of few London shops where paintings, engravings, or woodcuts might have been displayed.[35] But it seems, from Sonnet 24, that Shakespeare knew what it was to stand outside one and gaze through its windows. The so-called 'Chandos' painting, passed down through many hands, including Sir William Davenant and Thomas Betterton, perhaps has the best claim to be of Shakespeare. The eighteenth-century antiquarian George Vertue records the story that it had been painted by 'one Taylor', a player and painter and an 'intimate friend' of the poet. Katherine Duncan-Jones has argued that the artist was Joseph Taylor, a reputedly fine actor credited in the First Folio. This possibility was first floated by Edmond Malone. The painting is thought to date from about 1610, fairly late in Shakespeare's literary career. Duncan-Jones argues against the view that Shakespeare retired around this time to Stratford-upon-Avon, citing the painting, his purchase of the Blackfriars gatehouse residence, and his collaborations with Fletcher and Middleton, all of which point to continued activity in London.[36]

One further piece of evidence that Duncan-Jones points to also attests to Shakespeare's awareness of the telling silence of pictures. From the marginalia of Davies' poem we know that he shared an interest in poetry and painting with his co-actor Richard Burbage. That interest was not just theoretical or academic. A record in 1614 shows Shakespeare collaborating with Burbage on the design of an *impresa*, or heraldic design, for the sixth Earl of Rutland, Francis Manners, a Holywell neighbour of the Burbages in Shoreditch. The occasion for which the shield had been made was the King's Accession day tilt on 24 March. A week after the event, Thomas Screvin, Rutland's steward, noted in his *Accounts* the following: 'Item, 31 March to Mr Shakespeare in gold about my Lords impreso, xliiij^s; to Richard Burbage for painting and making it, in gold xliiij^s. – iiij^{li}. Viij^s.'

The entry returns Shakespeare to the northern suburb in which, according to John Aubrey, he began his career. Manners was thirty-six years old at this time. On 8 February 1601, he had marched with his elder brother through the streets with Essex's faction, and was subsequently imprisoned and fined. Under James, this young man's rashness was forgotten. But Rutland would not have forgotten Shakespeare and Burbage's part in those events. It seems such tournament items could be lucrative work. Sir Henry Wotton noted in his *Letters* that some of the emblems at this tilt were intriguing, their symbolism 'so dark, that their meaning is not yet understood'.[37] Given the high level of reward, it is probable that Burbage and Shakespeare had collaborated on similar projects before, and Davies's reference to them in connection with 'painting, poesie' perhaps suggests as much. Their collaboration in all likelihood lies behind the tilting scenes in *Pericles* where the design of *impresas* takes centre stage (Sc. 6). Versed in the agency of images, it cannot have been by accident that Shakespeare changed the name of the king of Pentapolis in that play from Artestrates or Altistrates to 'the good Simonides'.

Politics, art, and music

Shakespeare returned to the question of authority in *Coriolanus* where the Roman tribunes are blamed for a lack of corn. Failed harvests, hunger, and discontent weigh on this play. Caius Martius, celebrated as 'Coriolanus' after his heroic defeat of the Volsces at the city of Corioli, is a man renowned not just for his military prowess but also for his pride and disdain towards the plebeians, the 'many-headed' 'monster' of the Roman multitude (2.3.12–16). The elite in this play—the tribunes and consuls—depend for their position on the *vox populi*, the voice of the people. When Caius Martius is compelled by Roman custom to beg the people's favour, he can barely bring himself to do it, and the crowd turns against him. He cares little for popular acclaim.

Shakespeare took this story in large part from Thomas North's 1579 translation of Plutarch's *Lives* (itself from the 1559 French version by Jacques Amyot). The play should not, therefore, be read simply as an allegory of early-seventeenth-century political events. Attempts to see in Coriolanus a depiction of the Earl of Essex, or the tribunes as Members of Parliament, are likely to be only partially successful.[38] Yet this is a play in which the word 'city' features more times than in any other Shakespeare play and where allusion is made to 'courts and cities' reminiscent of the social and political divide between Westminster and London. Coriolanus mocks the hungry populace as 'worshipful mutiners' (1.1.250), a phrase that links with 'citizens' (1.1.13–14) and 'apron-men' (4.6.100), as if to signal a metropolitan context for the play's relentless disputes about power and legitimacy. Critical to these disputes is the availability or lack of corn. The Volsces have plenty of it: the Romans little.

Coriolanus is a play probably belonging to 1608, fairly late in Shakespeare's writing career. Since 1574, the authorities had taken responsibility for the distribution of grain throughout the City. Four years later, the Common Council allocated responsibility for meal provision to a committee of twenty-four officers, drawn from the great twelve worshipful companies. But grain stocks were poorly managed around 1600. The gilds tended not to buy in corn when harvests were plentiful and stores rapidly diminished without a reserve. *Coriolanus* opens with starving citizens in an ugly mood, resolving to kill Caius Martius and 'have corn at our own price' (1.1.10). When Coriolanus stands condemned by his fellow Romans, one of the chief complaints against him is that 'When corn was given them gratis, you repined' (3.1.44). Coriolanus reiterates his grievance that grain was distributed freely: 'Whoever gave that counsel to give forth | The corn o' th' storehouse gratis... nourished disobedience, fed the ruin of the state... This kind of service | Did not deserve corn gratis' (3.1.116–21).

As Peter Holland's edition of the play points out, poor harvests in the mid-1590s led to serious popular protest throughout the Midlands. State papers indicate that grain shortages were particularly acute in 1608. Sir Richard Knightley wrote to Sir Robert Osborne and others on 29 May 1608 that 'the price of corn daily increases by not being brought to market, and mutinies ensue'. Urgent requests were issued from around the country to allow the passage of barley, even as far as Cornwall, 'for relief of the poor there'. On 9 August, George Margitts, at Fenchurch Street, wrote to Sir Robert Cecil regarding a proposal by a 'merchant stranger' to 'prevent dearth of corn'. On 25 September, the Earl of Southampton sent a letter to Cecil concerned at the 'great scarcity of corn'. He requested a supply of grain from Sandwich to the city of Southampton, urging that corn be imported 'from foreign parts'. A memorandum for November calculated quantities of wheat and rye brought in over the previous two months, and in early December a proclamation was issued to brewers and alehouse keepers that they should not make their beer too strong, leaving enough barley spare for making bread.

These shortages came after years of largely unregulated corn exports. Even as late as Christmas 1607, the government was issuing licences to 'transport out of the realm such foreign corn as they have imported'. Again in March 1608, an order allowed 'all merchants to export corn free of duty, if not sold within a reasonable time'. By April, it was imperative that these exports were 'stayed'.[39] Shakespeare took

Coriolanus' complaint against corn being given out 'gratis' from Plutarch. But, in 1608, the story had a pressing significance for his audience. London was hungry. Plutarch tells us that Coriolanus was killed when a group of tribunes and senators fell upon him in the marketplace. Shakespeare has Coriolanus return to his old enemy Aufidius having brokered a peace with Rome yet torn between loyalty to his family and city and to his new ally. His death is sudden and shocking. A mob surround him, hooting, crowing, and chanting. Lear in his madness had raved at nothings, shouting, 'Kill, kill, kill, kill, kill, kill' (4.5.183). Shakespeare revived the chant for Coriolanus' end, a clamour any Londoner might have heard as a condemned man was carted off to Tyburn: 'Kill, kill, kill, kill, kill him!' (5.6.130).

Coriolanus is a work to berattle the common stages. Depicting a man ill at ease with his city, and filled with aggression, it seems almost out of place for Shakespeare's later period of writing when he seems so interested in myth and magic, art and strange sounds. The only music in *Coriolanus* is the martial sound of drums and trumpets. A very different kind of music occurs in *The Winter's Tale*, *Cymbeline*, and *The Tempest*, works written after 1608. Leontes, in *The Winter's Tale*, finds 'much content' in the 'singularities' (that is, curious or rare objects) of the royal gallery through which he and Paulina pass on their way to see the statue of Hermione (5.3.11–12). Paulina's comments on the lifelike nature of the statue echo the poet's words to the painter in *Timon of Athens* about the way 'imagination moves in this lip' (*Timon*, 1.1.34–5). Leontes sees a kind of 'magic' in what he believes to be a stone carving of his dead wife and declares himself 'mocked with art' (5.3.38, 67). Just before Paulina brings the 'statue' to life, Shakespeare gives her words that are the precondition of any art at all, whether painting or drama: 'It is required | You do awake your faith' (5.3.94–5). Music plays as Hermione steps down from her plinth, and the magic that seems to have awakened her to new life is declared 'an art | Lawful as eating' (5.3.110–11). Art once again answers force. Leontes' violent, murderous instincts are transformed and followed with the restoration of a family.

In 1608 the King's Men finally achieved their goal of securing an indoor playhouse at Blackfriars, in addition to the open-air Globe at Bankside. Blackfriars stood just east of the feared Bridewell Hospital, separated from it by the infamous River Fleet that stretched north from the Thames, under Holborn Bridge, and up to Clerkenwell. As an old Dominican priory set within a 'liberty', Blackfriars was an area of London technically free from the jurisdiction of the Lord Mayor (Figure 4.2). Suppressed in 1538, the priory was split into several holdings. In 1596, James Burbage paid £600 for rooms in the old priory. After his death in 1597, the rooms passed to Richard Burbage, who leased them out to Henry Evans and Nathaniel Giles, again for performances by the Children of the Chapel. In *Hamlet*, Rosencrantz famously speaks of the popularity of these 'little eyases' (2.2.340–5). By late 1608, the King's Men were ready to move in and use the theatre for themselves.

But they had been blocked from this move ever since Burbage's purchase in 1596. A number of highly placed persons lived in the Blackfriars precinct including Lords Cobham and Hunsdon, Lady Mary Kingston, and the fiery dowager Elizabeth Russell, Countess of Salisbury.[40] In November 1596, Lady Russell's name headed a petition by the inhabitants of Blackfriars to the Privy Council, protesting against Burbage's plans to turn the buildings into 'a common playhouse'.[41] Among the signatories was Richard Field, the printer of Shakespeare's *Venus and Adonis* and *The Rape of Lucrece*, and fellow Stratfordian. Field kept his printer's shop in Blackfriars, and he may simply have bowed under pressure from more powerful neighbours. Yet despite that pressure, in August 1608 Richard Burbage issued leases and shares in the Blackfriars playhouse to his brother Cuthbert, Henry Condell, Thomas Evans, John Heminges, William Shakespeare, and William Sly. The following year, the Blackfriars theatre was fully functioning for the King's Men.

Shakespeare's later plays have often been regarded as illustrating a turn towards what has been called romance, to the otherworldly and the mythical. *Cymbeline* is one of the most strikingly lyrical of these plays. It has at its heart the story of a dispersed family—something also seen in *Pericles*, *The Winter's Tale*, and *The Tempest*—and the possibility of its restitution. Murderous instincts are again on display, especially in the Queen and Cloten, her blockheaded son. Away from the court, in the wilds of Milford Haven in Wales, Innogen finds a place of safety with Guiderius, Arviragus, and their guardian Belarius, an exiled counsellor and military hero. The two sons now have assumed names, Polydore and Cadwal respectively. Pursuing

Innogen (who has disguised herself as a young man, Fidele), Cloten is encountered by Guiderius, slain, and beheaded. The old heads stored in the property box of the theatre company—required for Cade, Lord Say, and his son-in-law, Titus's sons, Tereus in *2 Seven Deadly Sins*, failed suitors in *Pericles*, and Macbeth—are needed one last time. The play builds to scenes of intense emotional power as Innogen-Fidele lies motionless, having drunk a potion that simulates death. Believing Fidele lost, Arviragus plays funereal music offstage, as though in the darkness of the cave. A stage direction bids 'Solemn music' play, and, as if taken by surprise, Belarius remarks upon it:

> My ingenious instrument!
> Hark Polydore, it sounds. But what occasion
> Hath Cadwal now to give it motion? Hark!
>
> (4.2.187–9)

Shortly afterwards, the trio speak (Polydore argues that he cannot sing) their haunting funeral song 'Fear no more the heat o' th' sun', an obsequy of profound feeling. The acoustics of an indoor theatre are likely to have been sonorous, resonant, and intimate compared with those of the Globe. We do not know what kind of instrument it was that Cadwal was said to have used. That it was 'ingenious' suggests an innovation, perhaps one worked by some new or complex mechanism. It is also intriguing that Cadwal gives it 'motion', as though it had moving parts. If we are to enquire into what sort of instrument it might have been, it may be useful to turn to one of the most comprehensive catalogues of musical instruments produced in the era.

The German musicologist Michael Praetorius provides, in the second volume of his *Syntagnum Musicum* (1620), illustrations of instruments driven by the operation of bellows. The first engraving in the appendix to this volume, separately titled as 'Theatrum instrumentorum', shows an instrument consisting of a keyboard and upright pipes of different lengths driven by two foot-operated bellows (see Figure 4.5). In an accompanying note to the illustration, Praetorius writes: 'Old Positive with pipes and three different registers: so that there are three strange voices with a two feet, or one and a half feet, or a one foot sound'.[42] As the *OED* suggests, the word 'Positive' (n. †6), refers to a small wind-driven organ sometimes placed or positioned (hence the name) at the foot of a larger instrument. The earliest

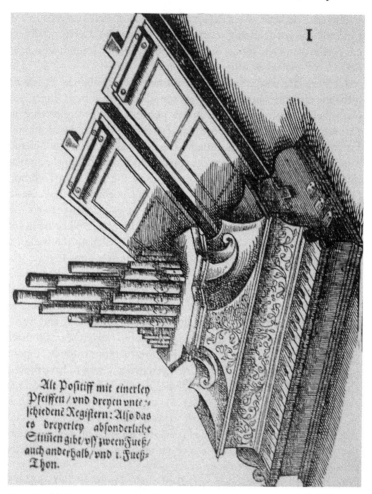

Figure 4.5. An 'old Positive' organ, from Michael Praetorius' *Syntagnum Musicum* (1620), and perhaps the kind of 'ingenious instrument' used at the Blackfriars theatre. Public domain

English example cited for this usage is 1728, but the word clearly goes back in European languages to around 1600. Thomas Platter notes that he saw 'small positive organs' at the Palace of Whitehall.[43] It may well be that Belarius's 'ingenious instrument', an unlikely item in a

Welsh cave perhaps, was a device of this kind sourced by the company from the continent. Being relatively portable, it could adapt to different performance situations, including those at court. It might also have been accompanied by other instruments.

In these late plays, Shakespeare pushed the possibilities of his art into new territories in which strange sounds produced by an 'ingenious instrument' accompany the wonders performed. The appearance in *Cymbeline* of the ghosts of Posthumus's family who plead with Jupiter for an end to his miseries initiates a dream sequence where 'Solemn music' plays once again before the apparitions suddenly vanish. Similar musical effects are created in *Pericles* when the physician Cerimon orders linen, a log fire, and music to warm the encoffined Thaisa to life: 'The rough and woeful music that we have, | Cause it to sound, beseech you. | The viol once more' (Q 1609, 3.2.86–8). They are heard again in *The Tempest* where Juno, Iris, and Ceres bless the wedding masque, and stage directions call for a banquet or visions that vanish, with more 'Solemn and strange music' (3.3.18; 5.1.57). Praetorius's 'Positive' is aptly described as providing 'strange voices'. Solemn and strange music points to performance conditions rather different to those like *Coriolanus* that require martial flourishes, drums, and trumpets. Whatever Belarius's 'ingenious instrument' was, it seems to have gone hand in hand with the acquisition of a more intimate indoor playing space at Blackfriars. This new venue is thought to have proved almost twice as profitable as the Globe. By the 1630s, it had become the main house for the King's Men. At a time when playwrights such as Middleton, Jonson, and Marston were busy with London-based city comedy, Shakespeare at Blackfriars was opening up new imaginative worlds far removed from the pressures of local interests and City constraints.

In March 1613, Shakespeare at last bought a property in London, a 'dwelling house or tenement' in the old Blackfriars priory which partly extended over a 'great gate'.[44] The chief playwright of the King's Men now owned property just beside the forbidding walls of Bridewell, an institution run by men intent on ridding the City of playhouses altogether. But for as long as plays were required at the royal court, the companies would survive. Called upon to perform for the wedding festivities in 1613 of Princess Elizabeth and Prince Frederick, Elector Palatine of the Rhine, Shakespeare's company staged fourteen plays, among them *The Winter's Tale* and *The Tempest*. Shakespeare's art was popular with powers greater than the City, and it now occupied the centre of London's literary culture.

In this contest between the theatres and London's authorities, it is worth considering the position of Peter Street, an expert carpenter who had worked for the Burbages. In following his trade, Street inhabited both of these conflicting worlds—the community of poets, dramatists, actors, and theatre owners, and the governors whose task it was to police the City, punish wrongdoing, and put an end to the ungodly activity of playing. The Burbages had long planned to acquire an indoor theatre at Blackfriars, a goal they achieved in 1608. Should anything happen to the Globe, they retained a space north of the river where they could play all year round. Five years later, the catastrophe happened. On 29 June 1613 (St Peter's Day), fire achieved what the City authorities had failed to do for all these years—by putting an end to a playhouse. Sparks from a cannon shot set fire to the thatch during a performance of *All is True* (*Henry VIII*), and the Globe famously burned to the ground. The King's Men now faced a major setback.

The company immediately set about rebuilding the theatre. But their move to Blackfriars in 1608 must have seemed fortuitous. Peter Street had constructed the first Globe from the timbers of the old Shoreditch theatre and also worked for Henslowe in building the Fortune playhouse on the corner of Whitecross Street and Goulding Lane in 1600. Yet at the same time, he was working for the London Bridewell authorities and given six weeks to 'make a frame in the middle yard' of Bridewell on 9 April that year. Henslowe continued to make payments to him in May and dined with him in July and August. On 4 August 1600, Street was again engaged to carry out work at Bridewell and thereafter became its principal carpenter. He is likely to have been asked to convert rooms for the Burbages' indoor stage at Blackfriars, but if so, he did not live to see that project through. When he died in Blackfriars in 1609, he had become so respected a figure just over the Fleet ditch at Bridewell that he had—since 7 March 1601—sat as a magistrate at many of its hearings, rubbing shoulders with those who had fought constantly to see the structures he had put up razed to the ground.

Diversity

Early modern London was a diverse, cosmopolitan city. As Antonio says in *The Merchant of Venice*, 'the trade and profit of the city | Consisteth of all nations' (3.3.30-1). Ships from across the world docked along the Thames at Billingsgate, Wapping, and Rotherhithe, bearing not only exotic goods—wines, spices, fabrics, even bears—but also many kinds of people.[1] This diversity could easily cause friction. Tensions concerning overseas workers undercutting native crafts simmered in the City.[2] There was no escaping the fact that living in London meant dwelling alongside very different groups of people who had their own interests to pursue. Encounters with strangers, visitors, and new-comers, with all the complications that entailed, seem to be every-where in Shakespeare. Repeatedly, an audience is presented with the perspective of an outsider in what amounts to a drama of exclusion. Uniquely, he even coined a new verb for the process: the banished Cordelia is, Lear declares, 'strangered with our oath' (1.1.193). This chapter focuses on cultural exclusion and assimilation in the plays. Necessarily drawing on selected examples, it argues that these prob-lems are rooted in the audience's awareness of inequities in their own London world. Specifically, what Antonio called 'the trade and profit of the City' was structured by local civic tensions generated by class and gender, but especially by ethnicity. Shakespeare's diverse worlds, filled with strangers, may seem to promise a means to escape these conditions, but in fact they create their own alienating effects by making that awareness even more acute.

The diverse nature of London was not missed by overseas visitors to the City. Visiting London in the mid-1570s, L. Grenade recorded that at the Royal Exchange, situated on the fork of Cornhill and

Figure 5.1. The Royal Exchange and Bucklersbury, from the 'Agas' map (*c*.1561–70), with the Royal Exchange (right) on the fork of Threadneedle Street and Cornhill, and a 'grasshopper' weather vane to represent Sir Thomas Gresham's crest. Nearby are St Mary Woolchurch ('Woll chur'), St Christopher le Stocks (tower north of 'Woll chur'), Bucklersbury, and the site of the Poultry 'Compter' just east of Old Jewry (far left). Reproduced by kind permission of British History Online

Threadneedle Street, merchants of different nationalities would gather in their own areas among the alleys and galleries. The institution was built as a commercial centre by Thomas Gresham and opened by the Queen on 23 January 1571 (Figure 5.1). The lower gallery, called New Venice, was set beneath ground level and lined with shops. Merchants strolled in the middle gallery which was 'paved with squares of black and white marble intermixed'. A central courtyard allowed space for an estimated 4,000 merchants. The highest gallery was the most lavish, with a circle of 150 stalls mainly selling cloth and textiles.[3] This was Shylock's Rialto to any theatre spectator who knew the Exchange. But the English did not make life easy for merchant-strangers. Writing in 1597, André Herault, Monsieur de Maisse, Henry IV's Ambassador Extraordinary, observed that the English monopolized trade: 'Everything that comes from the Levant and of Venice is in their hands ... They traffic also in Poland, Muscovy and as far as Persia'. In London, he notes, they levy a double duty on merchants from overseas. Strangers in the City, he reports, are harassed and 'perpetually troubled' if they try to engage in trade independently.[4]

Some strangers visited the theatres. Thomas Platter, a Swiss traveller who lodged in Mark Lane near the Tower in 1599, recorded seeing a performance while in the suburb of Bishopsgate—almost certainly at the Curtain. The play he saw seems to have been a comedy in which an Englishman outwitted his rivals, including a German who had won a maiden in a 'tussle'. The Englishman stole the woman away from a tent while the German and his servant were in a drunken slumber.[5] Another visitor, an 'Almain', or German, had 300 crowns stolen from him in 1598 at a performance of Jonson's *Every Man in his Humour* by the Lord Chamberlain's Men, again in all likelihood at the Curtain.[6] The Venetian ambassador, Foscarini, visited the Curtain in August 1613 and found the audience clamouring 'Friars, Friars!' because they wanted to see a play they called 'Friars'.[7] Perhaps the best-known foreign visitor to attend the theatres was Johannes de Witt, who gave a brief description of the playhouses and sketched the Swan playhouse in 1596.[8]

Strangers in the City

The international dimension of Shakespeare's work is immediately striking, yet it seems he never travelled abroad. His understanding of alien experience must have been drawn from closer to home. For this reason, it is worth exploring the historical circumstances in which early modern immigrants in London found themselves. How many were there? Where did they live? In what kinds of trade did they engage? How were they received, and to what extent were they able to assimilate? And perhaps over and above all this, how are contemporary anxieties about aliens addressed in Shakespeare's writing? Thanks to continuing research by a number of scholars, it is possible to go some way towards answering these questions.

Estimates regarding the total number of persons from overseas settling in the metropolis can only be gauged approximately, although annual 'Returns of Strangers' provide a basis for a statistical count.[9] Laura Yungblut suggests that there were about 3,000 aliens in London in 1500, rising to 4,000–5,000 by the middle of the century.[10] Newcomers in Elizabeth's reign were predominantly Huguenots displaced by Spanish persecution from France and the Low Countries. Some of these were merchants, but others were artisans, textile workers, musicians, and painters.[11] Nigel Goose points out that the influx of aliens occurred against a backdrop of an expanding population and economy. He follows a scholarly consensus in thinking that London grew in population from 50,000 in 1500 to 80,000 in 1550, 200,000 in 1600, and just under 400,000 by the mid-seventeenth century.[12] The founding of the Dutch and French 'stranger' churches under Edward VI is one sign of this increase in immigrants. A 1562 survey of strangers in London counted 4,534 men, women, and children in the City, liberties, and suburbs. Jacob Selwood argues that the overall population of London grew mainly because of English rather than continental migrants, seeking work as apprentices or servants. He suggests that by 1572, strangers in London numbered around 6,500, and by 1593 that figure had risen slightly to over 7,000. Thereafter, in the early seventeenth century, there would be a decline in the number of overseas aliens, perhaps to fewer than 4,000 in the City and suburbs by the 1630s.[13]

Given that, on these figures, aliens comprised less than 5 per cent of London's population at any one time, the kaleidoscope of cultures we find in the plays is noteworthy. Shakespeare seems fascinated by alien experience: a Sicilian arriving in Ephesus in *The Comedy of Errors*, an African soldier fighting for the Venetian state in *Othello*, and Caliban in *The Tempest* who ends up as the sole possessor of a remote island in the poet's imagination. It seems that many strangers settled in London's peripheral wards, especially Farringdon Within, Cripplegate, Bishopsgate, Aldersgate, and Bridge Without (Southwark).[14] At least two generations of the musical Venetian family of Anthony, Alvise, Jasper, and John Bassano resided in and around Bishopsgate and Norton Folgate near Shoreditch.[15] Elsewhere, the burial register of St Olave's church, Hart Street, located just north of Tower Hill, includes a notable number of strangers, especially Africans: 'Isabell a blackamore' (6 June 1588), 'a man blackamore lay in the street' (21 June 1588), 'John Looprino stranger' (6 July 1590), 'Grace a nigro out of Doctor Hector's' (13 July 1590), 'Frauncisco a nigro', 'Philip Lucatello, Mr Innocent's son' (25 February 1590/1), 'Peter Marley a blacamore' (9 November 1594), 'George a Blackamore out of Mrs Barker's' (23 January 1595/6), 'Madelen a blackeamore out of Bernard's house' (25 November 1598).[16] In the early seventeenth century, French, Dutch, and Italians become very much more prominent in these records. Augustine Bassano, Alvise's eldest son, was buried at St Olave, Hart Street, London, on 24 October 1604. Living in Bishopsgate, in Southwark, or in Aldersgate with a Huguenot tire-maker, Shakespeare was surrounded by non-Londoners whose traces survive in the records.

Trade was transnational. Along the Thames, especially at the northside docks of Queenhithe and Billingsgate, ships like the *Bonaventure* or the *Swift-Sure* would put in and depart laden with all kinds of goods. A single document, undated but probably from 1595, gives a detailed list of the various materials sold and bought:

The principal exports are cloths, Manchester cottons, hides, leather, wheat, etc, salt, fish, ordnance, butter and cheese, whale oils, cutlery, alum, wines, and silks. The imports, oranges and lemons, timber, pitch and rosin, wines, flax and hemp, furs, cordage, linen, silks, currants, sugars, saltpetre, dates, molasses, sweet oils, spices, large onions, woad, wax, pitch, cross-bows, and sword blades, prunes, tar, gold, silver, pearls, hides, salt beef etc. The places traded with are Galicia, St Jean de Luz, Nerva, Rye, and Revel, the Levant, Barbary, Andalusia, Lisbon, St Michael and Terceira, the Canaries, St Nicholas, Russia, Bilboa, Bordeaux, Rochelle, West Indies, Brazil, Ireland etc.[17]

It is no exaggeration to say that Elizabethan commerce was global. The privateer Thomas Cavendish picked up three Japanese boys on his voyage to the South Seas in 1593.[18] Under James, this expeditionary spirit continued. In June 1604, a licence was issued to Sir Edward Michelborne to 'discover the countries of Cathay, China, Japan, Corea and Cambaya, and to trade there'.[19] This far-reaching exploration left traces in London: 'Oryente Paves straunger' was interred at St Mary Woolnoth on 31 October 1570, and on 8 December 1592, a 'Master Orient of Whitehorse street' was buried in the parish of St Dunstan and All Saints, Stepney.[20]

The question of how far aliens were able to assimilate has prompted different views. Some, like Laura Yungblut and Lien Luu, have characterized the English as broadly xenophobic. Yungblut writes, 'At least according to extant sources, the English, especially Londoners, actively disliked foreigners'. Anti-alien sentiment would intensify in periods of economic stress.[21] The famous 'Ill' or 'Evil May Day' of 1517 is perhaps the best-known example of popular uprising against the presence of strangers in London. On the eve of 1 May, a group of apprentices defied the curfew, broke open Newgate prison, and attacked the homes of aliens and strangers in the City. These disturbances went on well into the night, but by the morning, around 300 young men had been arrested and thirteen were hanged. It was an event that lived long in the memory and provided the opening scene to the manuscript play *The Booke of Sir Thomas Moore* to which Shakespeare may have contributed some 165 lines in Scene 6. Yet neither the play nor the event itself should be taken at face value as a sure sign of persistent antipathy towards strangers.

A number of historians—among them Steve Rappaport, Ian Archer, and Joe Ward—have expressed reservations about whether early modern Londoners should be described as broadly xenophobic. Archer points not just to a lack of violence against aliens but also to evidence of peaceful coexistence. He argues that English attitudes were 'rather more ambiguous and the reception rather less unwelcoming' than has sometimes been suggested. Rappaport accepts that tensions often arose but usually from a sense that aliens could avoid rules that native artisans were expected to observe. Ward has suggested that the term 'xenophobia' is too strong and that the characterization of attitudes towards aliens in Thomas Dekker's *The Shoemaker's Holiday* shows considerable sympathy for aliens in some quarters.[22] For Nigel Goose, English attitudes towards strangers were 'diverse and ambivalent' but sometimes even admiring. He finds little or no evidence of violent attacks against aliens in the sixteenth century after 'Evil May Day' and raises the possibility that England may in fact have represented a 'veritable oasis of tolerance' at the time.[23] Similarly, Andrew Pettegree has counselled against regarding that day's violence as evidence of a sustained hostility towards London aliens throughout the sixteenth century. 'Evil May Day' may have been notorious because it was rare.[24] Even so, one cannot help but suspect that, for many aliens, the reality was likely to have been mixed at best.

The merchant of London: Sir Horatio Palavicino

People of some nationalities or ethnicities seem to have been able to assimilate more effectively than others. We find evidence of some Italians fairly securely integrated into London life. The most prominent of these was Sir Horatio Palavicino, an Anglophile who settled in

London and was granted letters of denization in 1585. Palavicino's London circle included Walsingham, Burghley, and Sir Edward Stafford, but also his uncle Alessandro and Italian friends Prospero and Benedict Spinola, Acerbo Velutelli, and Hippolito Buonamonte. Born in Genoa and related by marriage to the Spinola family, Palavicino ran a virtual monopoly on stocks of alum, a necessary ingredient in the process of dyeing cloth. He was also at the centre of a merchant network that made him an invaluable provider of intelligence to the English. He was knighted in 1587. When the Armada threatened the following year, he raced to the south coast in order to participate in the defensive campaign.[25] So useful was he that he was repeatedly involved in military and diplomatic negotiations in France and Germany.

In public, Palavicino was a merchant-banker so wealthy that Elizabethan government could rely on him for emergency funding if needed. But he was also keen to integrate in his private affairs. On 19 January 1576, Gregorius Legrande, a 'stranger', was arraigned for concealing 'much whoredom' in his house. In particular, 'diverse Italians' had got children by his serving-maids. He was bound to appear again by the sum of £40. One of the infants put out to nurse with a midwife, Mistress Angelles, had been conceived by 'Oratio Pallavasina', who got his servant, 'Gregorie Defrancko', to make suitable arrangements and stand as its godfather.[26] On 16 March 1578, Gilbert Pereman, former servant to 'Oratio Palafasyne', was interrogated concerning his master's activities. He had served his master for two years and initially, he declared, resisted Palavicino's instructions to procure 'harlots'. He was, he testified, 'innocent and unacquainted' with such matters. Palavicino was fond of taking his 'recreation' at Barking with a friend named Christopher Demonte, and Pereman was asked to arrange 'wine and good cheer' for them and to send along a couple of serving-women. In the event, the women apparently had the good sense not to turn up.

Pereman claimed to have first become aware of his master's prefer-ences a year before this hearing, when Palavicino 'committed whore-dom' with one 'Jenetta a Venetian woman which lieth about Ludgate' in Pereman's house in St Nicholas's Lane and again at Palavicino's in Mincing Lane. Pereman had been instructed to bring home a 'maiden which had not been dealt withal before', but he was unable to find one.

Contradicting his earlier testimony, he explained that about two years previously he had heard of a young woman named 'Sibell' rumoured to be a virgin, and so brought her to the Red Bull in Thames Street and then to his master's house in Mincing Lane, where she stayed overnight. About five or six years previously, he deposed, Palavicino had got a child by the wife of one Robert Thomas, who, in exchange for money, also let him sleep with his daughter. Palavicino's friends, 'one Bonefacio Fusio and his wife', were staying at his house, and knew, Pereman explained, of their host's interest in young prostitutes.[27]

One of the wealthiest men in England, Palavicino sought to integrate himself into London life at every level. In this he was joined by his uncle, Alessandro. William Mekyns, a pimp who carried clients to several bawdy houses, testified in July 1576 that he brought 'Alexander Palavasyne' to Worcester House to sleep with Thomasine Breame, reputed to be a 'brave girl'. She enjoyed a number of wealthy clients, among them a Master Courtney, steward to Henry Carey, Lord Hunsdon. Mekyns also took 'Palavasyne' to the house of John and Jane Fuller, who kept 'Katherine a little wench' just outside Cripplegate. Palavicino had an inclination for younger girls: 'the said Alexander hath diverse other young wenches between Aldgate and Whitechapel of xiii & xiiii years old as the said Alex himself reported to an apothecary'.[28] One of the highest-earning prostitutes in early modern London, Anne Levens, worked from a variety of different houses. In her prosecution of December 1576, she lists twenty-two separate addresses at which she met wealthy clients. At Mistress Esgrigge's in Whitefriars, she lay with 'Alexander Palavasyne'. Two days after Levens's examination, 'Little Kathryn Jones' confessed to prostitution at Jane Fuller's house, where she had been frequented especially by 'Palavasyne' and the French ambassador's steward, one Captain Augustine.[29] The uncle and nephew seem to have been joined in these activities by their friends.

Mekyns declared further that 'Acerbo Velutelly is a notorious whoremonger'. On 25 February 1578, Elizabeth Jackson claimed that her child had been fathered by 'Acerbo Velutelly' two and a half years earlier at his house in Newington. She had been betrothed to a waterman named Apryse, but (probably) pregnant and afraid, 'she ran away when the wedding dinner was provided'. A year later, Morrice Willliams confessed that Mistress Samwaye had been fetched from the Minories (just north of Tower Hill) to Acerbo Velutelli's house in Hart Street, close to Crutched Friars, where she stayed for two days. Anne Levens admitted that her very first client had been one 'Cyprian Velotelli', probably Acerbo's brother, who used her in a garden by Crutched Friars around 28 October 1573 ('Simon and Jude's days'). Cyprian paid twenty nobles to Anne's brother Christopher for the introduction. In the years following, Christopher Levens moved to Bankside and, perhaps with his sister, became one of its wealthiest residents.[30]

Naturalization could occur through marriage, although this seems to have been a fairly rare and difficult process, largely affected by wealth or class. Mekyns mentioned that one 'Polito', a stranger, 'kept' Mistress Whalley at his garden in Tower Hill. Polito (sometimes written as 'Hippolito') was prosecuted and quickly confessed, securing both a pardon and his freedom by offering to pay £5 'to the poor' of the hospital. A note taken two years later indicates that Polito had gone overseas and Whalley fled to the country, but they now both requested to be allowed to return and live separately 'in honest manner'.[31] The following month 'Oratio Franhate merchant stranger' appealed again for clemency: 'that Pollito Bonamontey merchant stranger and Katheren Whalley wife of John Whalley of Bishopsgate Street might not be troubled further for complaints heretofore made against them'. Hippolito was now married, was acculturated, and had vowed 'a new life'. With an eye to the money, the court accepted a payment of £5 'to clothe the poor' and agreed. At the lower end of the social scale, prostitute Alice Farewell had fallen for an unnamed stranger: at the house of Mistress Fowkes, she slept with an Italian 'whom she called her Love, who gave her a ring of gold, a pair of shoes and a pair of slippers, which now she hath on her feet'.[32]

Class and money determine the inequities in these exchanges. The court also heard that a 'Master Jeronomey an Italian dwelling in Lombard Street' spent the night with Mary Digbye, who shared her proceeds with her landlady, Mistress Bramwells (alias Cesar). Digbye confessed to having also slept with one 'Martine Frederigo' and other gentlemen. Grenade describes Lombard Street as lined with 'more than 20 goldsmiths' shops touching, and next to each other. There are also hosiers, drapers, mercers, booksellers, apothecaries, haberdashers etc'.[33] Lombard Street would have been Shylock's London address and had indeed been home to one Adrian Tubal, buried on 4 October 1562 at St Mary Woolnoth. It was also the locality in which the dramatist Thomas Kyd grew up: 'Jeronomey' is the Anglicized version of Kyd's protagonist's name, Hieronimo, jocularly quoted by Shakespeare, Jonson, and Marston. Another Italian, Jacomo Devielmo, is recorded in the local burial register as having died in Frederigo's house on 17 April 1604, and Frederigo himself was interred as a respectable citizen four years later 'in the South Isle of the Choir close to the 4 & 9 pews' on 15 April 1608.

Reading Italy as London: *The Taming of the Shrew* and the Spinola family

Of all Shakespeare's plays, *The Taming of the Shrew* seems his most Italian. It makes more references to Italian locations than any other of his works, and it even has a character speak lines in the Italian language (1.2.24–6). Lucentio's first speech mentions Padua, Lombardy, Florence, and Pisa. Elsewhere the play alludes to Naples, Venice, Mantua, Bergamo, Genoa, and Verona. One of the play's main sources, George Gascoigne's *Supposes* (1566), is a play based on Ariosto's Italian prose tale *I Suppositi* (1509). Gascoigne tells the story of a master and servant, Erostrato and Dulippo, who swap roles in order to allow the master to continue a love affair with Polynesta, daughter of Damon, and at the same time deter a rival suitor, Cleander. As part of this ruse, the servant engages a Sienese merchant to play the role of Erostrato's supposed father who will guarantee Polynesta's jointure. Shakespeare took from Gascoigne's work the Italian names of Petruccio and Litio.[34] It is possible that he may also have partly modelled Kate after the 'old hag' or 'crooked crone' Psyteria in Gascoigne. The title page of *Supposes* tells us that it was 'a Comedie written in the Italian tongue by Ariosto, English by George Gascoygne of Grayes Inne Esquire and there presented 1566'. In this connection, *The Taming of the Shrew* sits alongside *The Comedy of Errors*, an Italianate play of mistaken identities performed at Gray's Inn in 1594. The kind of Italy Shakespeare had in mind in *The Taming of the Shrew* was clearly one tailored for a London audience.

There are different aspects to the London context for *The Taming of the Shrew*. First, it is generally agreed that it is one of Shakespeare's earliest plays. But we do not know exactly when it was written. *The Taming of a Shrew*, an anonymous play set in Athens that clearly bears strong resemblances to Shakespeare's, may give some indication of a latest date or 'terminus ad quem'. This work was entered into the Stationers' Register on 2 May 1594 and printed in quarto that year by Peter Short. Just over a month later, on 11 June 1594, Philip Henslowe recorded the Admiral's and Chamberlain's Men as having played 'The tamynge of A Shrowe' at Newington Butts. Geoffrey Bullough regarded *A Shrew* as an earlier version of the play which Shakespeare then rewrote.[35] What troubles this view is the fact that, as Samuel Hickson pointed out in the nineteenth century, *A Shrew* reproduces lines verbatim from Marlowe's *Tamburlaine* and *Dr Faustus*. Additionally, it fills out Kate's final speech with lines from Joshua Sylvester's translation of Guillaume Du Bartas's *La Sepmaine ou creation du Monde* (printed in 1611).[36] On the whole, *A Shrew* seems to be a kind of reconstruction by memory and pastiche.

Taken together, *A Shrew* seems something of a patchwork text, drawing mainly on Shakespeare and where necessary on Marlowe and others. Whether or not the text printed by Short matches the play performed at Newington Butts, it seems not to have been the version Ben Jonson knew, or perhaps saw, since he plays on a line from *The Shrew* ('Let's be no stoics nor no stocks, I pray', 1.1.31) in *Bartholomew Fair*, after Justice Overdo has been set in the stocks:

> QUARLOUS   What's here! a Stoick i' the Stocks? the Fool is
> turn'd Philosopher.
>
> (4.6.91–2)

Historical readings of *The Shrew* have tended to focus unsurprisingly on the play's notorious gender inequalities. Linda E. Boose has argued that Kate's bodily subjugation in the final scene re-enacts both her words and 'ceremonial directions' of early modern marriage treatises. For Boose, these ritual actions were ultimately guaranteed by the potential humiliations represented by cucking stools and implements such as 'scolds' bridles' designed both to shame and compel a woman into subservience.[37] There is plenty of evidence that the 'shrew' was a current stereotype in London at the time.

Examples of 'shrewish' women in early modern London highlight the kinds of punishment routinely used against them. Anne Wood was bought into Bridewell on 31 August 1559 for publicly condemning Bridewell prison in the street before a gathered crowd. The fact that she drew attention seems to have worsened her punishment: '[Wood]...is a common harlot and now brought in chiefly for railing most unhonestly and slanderously upon this house and governors thereof openly in the street in the hearing of 500 persons and therefore she was well whipped and punished and committed to the Labour of the house the said date and year'. Wood had clearly gained quite an audience for her grievances. In 1562, Agnes Wicke, a former prisoner at Bridewell, was 'now brought into the same at the commandment of M[aste]r Taylor for slandering and railing on honest men and women the 8 of April for which she was well whipped the same day and delliv[ere]d by court then holden'. '[S]cold Joane' was detained on 17 July 1561 'for that she ys a runagates & rayler and one that disturbeth the hole towne by her evell lyving'.[38] Although Joane's punishment is not stated, she is likely to have suffered a severe whipping. Given these historical examples, London audiences may have responded to Petruccio's actions in either of two ways: his subjugation of Kate may have struck some as symptomatic of these brutal inequalities; others may have deemed it almost mild by comparison.

There is a second dimension to the London context of the play that also has a bearing on its composition. If *A Shrew* is a patched-up reconstruction of *The Shrew*, then we have a latest date from the Stationers' Register of May 1594. It may also be possible to point to an earliest date. In 3.2, Petruccio delays coming to his wedding, a sign Kate takes as humiliation and one that Boose reads as another shaming tactic.[39] But there may be another historical aspect to this episode which has a less ideological bearing on the play. Petruccio's eventual arrival on horseback is comically described by Biondello, one of his hapless serving men. The groom is wearing 'a new hat and an old jerkin, a pair of old breeches thrice turned, a pair of boots that have been candle-cases, one buckled, another laced, an old rusty sword ta'en out of the town-armoury, with a broken hilt, and chapeless [without a sheath]' (3.2.42–8).

These items are the 'household stuff' of the playing company. They are props that need sourcing and to be made ready for Petruccio's appearance on stage. The rest of the description pictures Petruccio's horse—lame in the hips, diseased, ulcerated, marked by swellings and sores, terminally afflicted with tumours, eaten within by intestinal worms, with a dislocated shoulder and knock-kneed in the forelegs. 'Who comes with him?' asks Baptista. Biondello replies, 'O sir, his lackey, for all the world caparisoned like the horse' (ll. 48–61, 63–8).

The word 'caparisoned' means tricked out or dressed. It is relatively rare, but we find it also in George Peele's *Polyhymnia*, an account of the accession day tilts of 1590, printed that year by Richard Jones. The tilts were jousting tournaments held on 17 November at the Palace of Whitehall to celebrate the anniversary of the Queen's accession to the throne. They had been devised by Sir Henry Lee, Elizabeth's champion, and, as *Polyhymnia* makes clear, the 1590 event was his last. Peele's text consists of a series of orations describing each pair of jousting courtiers as they enter the lists, mounted on ornately prepared steeds. Sir Henry Lee, Elizabeth's champion, enters 'in rich embroidery, | And costly fair caparison, charg'd with crowns' (sig. A2^v). As Katherine Duncan-Jones has pointed out, Peele seems to pun on Shakespeare's name in his play *Edward I* (*c.*1593): 'Shake thy speres in honour of his name'.[40] When, in *Polyhymnia*, Masters Thomas Sidney and Robert Alexander take the field, Peele uses a very similar phrase, suggesting that Sir Philip Sidney's younger brother has lived to behold 'many a shaken spear' (B2^v).

The possibility that this might be a veiled allusion to Shakespeare is strengthened if Petruccio's entrance on his courser was indeed a satirical response. The link is uncertain but not entirely implausible. It is now broadly accepted that Peele collaborated with Shakespeare around this time on *Titus Andronicus*, and it seems probable that his sister Isabella married a Matthew Shakespeare.[41] If, in Petruccio's decay, Shakespeare had in mind a comical antithesis to the grandeur of mounted knights as described by Peele in *Polyhymnia*, then *The Taming of the Shrew* postdates the day the tilts took place. Although this still allows no precise date for the play, it does narrow the range to between 17 November 1590 and 2 May 1594 when it was entered into the Stationers' Register by Peter Short, and adds to the connections between Peele and Shakespeare as two collaborating London writers.

A third dimension lends weight to the idea that we might read Italy as London in *The Taming of the Shrew*. It remains possible that, in naming the father in the play Baptista Minola, Shakespeare may have deliberately played on the reputation of a prominent Italian merchant in London, Baptista Spinola, a close associate of Sir Horatio Palavicino. Both are named by Sir Vincent Skinner, officer of the Exchequer, in a letter to Cecil about state finances in 1599, as lenders to the state.[42] This hypothesis becomes all the more intriguing for the fact that Hortensio Spinola, who termed himself 'a poor gentleman', was asked by his son Frederico to spy out the fortifications at the major ports along the coast from Torbay to Harwich. In 1599, Hortensio was subject to repeated interrogation by the Privy Council about his son's actions and plans. From another letter to Cecil,[43] we learn that Frederico was a merchant 'left very rich by his father', an observation that chimes with Petruccio's claim about himself in the play (2.1.115–16).

The Spinola family had been living and working in London for some time. Benedict Spinola was perhaps the most famous member of this merchant family, becoming naturalized in 1552 and rising to become a leading trader in wool and wines. He lived all his life in the parish of St Gabriel, Fenchurch, joined by his nephews Hannibal and Ascaneo Spinola. Robert Dudley, Earl of Leicester, admired him as 'my dear friend and the best Italian I know in England' and through him acquired tapestries and hangings.[44] In February 1578, Elizabeth I was recorded as owing over £5,000 to Spinola and over £16,000 to Horatio Palavicino. These Italians were bankrolling the English state.[45]

But Spinola was part of the more local London economy too. In January 1577, he was named in testimony by William Mekyns as a 'cashere' who two years previously had 'had the use of Mistress Mewtas at Bermondsey Street'. He had given her forty shillings and a gold ring which she pawned for twelve shillings. She returned the compliment with the gift of a pair of gloves. On another occasion, he slept with one Mary Patman in his chamber and at the Ship at Temple Bar. The record of the case states, 'He promised her a gown of clothes and Giles Keys brought it, and about a year past he lay with Mary Patman at the Ship at Temple Bar'. Mekyns added in a further statement that Spinola's serving-man had previously enjoyed the favours of one

Elizabeth Cooper at the house of a notorious brothel owner, Mistress Esgrigge, in Whitefriars at a cost of ten shillings.[46] In other testimony, we learn that Rose Flower, a notorious prostitute also mentioned in the *Gesta Grayorum*, kept a bawdy house in Shoreditch 'in a lane by Master Spinaloes garden'. These details may seem a long way from Shakespeare's play, but they show that there were visitors with cash in the City seeking to acquire women by less honourable means. In 1580, Spinola died of plague and was buried in the choir of St Gabriel, and by the early 1590s little damage could be done to his reputation by representing Baptista Minola and Signior Hortensio on the stage.

Shakespeare is likely to have played in the houses of great lords throughout his career but perhaps especially when he was starting out as an actor-writer and moving between locations. *The Taming of the Shrew* is set up as an extended vision in a lord's manor house, but it turns out to be a prototype of what will later emerge as city comedy. Baptista the 'cashere' was long gone, but his family remained: at almost the same time as Katherine Minola married her Petruccio offstage at the Curtain, Theatre, or Newington Butts, another Spinola family member, Mary, married Edward Revington in the church of St Christopher le Stocks on Threadneedle Street on 27 August 1592, in what was probably a quieter ceremony.[47]

African London: Will Kemp and 'Reasonable blackamore'

People of different ethnicities probably encountered varying levels of toleration or hostility in early modern London. It remains probable that, had he stayed in Stratford, Shakespeare might never have met anyone from Italy, the Netherlands, Spain, or Africa. But walking by wharves and jetties on the Thames, he would have seen ships unloaded by people from any number of faraway places. Shakespeare was clearly fascinated by Italy, but he also seems to have had a keen interest in the stories of dark-skinned people, an interest that grows in complexity throughout his works. In creating black characters, Shakespeare was following Marlowe, Kyd, Peele, and perhaps also Lyly whose character Clitus in *Campaspe* has the appearance of one 'born in the east' (1.1.23).[48] In an article on *Othello*, Ian Smith has asked, 'In the absence of Africans to play certain roles, how was blackness staged in the early modern English theater?' Challenging traditional views, he argues that fabrics, textiles, and leather were sometimes used in the depiction of black characters and cites an example of cloth being wrapped around the actors' limbs for the purpose. The use of black textile as a signifier of racial otherness seems also, he suggests, to have extended, in *Othello*, to the famous handkerchief.[49] All the same, contemporary illustrations—for example the 1615 title page of *The Spanish Tragedy*, or the Henry Peacham drawing of a scene from *Titus Andronicus*—suggest that face paint was sometimes used for characters of dark skin.

Occasionally, Shakespeare's early comedies seem to make light of racial otherness. Under magical influence, Lysander spurns Hermia, calling her 'Ethiope' and 'tawny Tartar' (3.2.257, 264). Yet Rosaline in *Love's Labour's Lost* is adored by Biron for her 'ebony' beauty (4.3.245-6), and a company of 'blackamoors' graces the long, final scene of the play 'with music' (5.2.156). It is possible that the character of Sir Thurio, in *The Two Gentlemen of Verona*, was played as dark-skinned. He bluntly tells Proteus, 'My face is black'. Proteus replies with a comment that might well be salacious: 'the old saying is "Black men are pearls in beauteous ladies' eyes"' (5.2.10–12). It is a lyrical phrase and anticipates associations of blackness with the rare, strange, and visually alluring in Shakespeare's Sonnets 127, 130, and 132.

From surviving documents known as 'plots', we know of other characters who were probably staged as dark-skinned. The 'plot' or 'platt' of 'The Second Part of the Seven Deadly Sins' shows that Augustine Phillips played the Assyrian king Sardanapalus. The 'plot' of *Frederick & Basilea* has an actor of the Admiral's company named Griffen playing the part of 'Athanasia Moore'. The 'plott' of Peele's *The Battle of Alcazar* indicates that Edward Alleyn played Muly Mahamett, Anthony Jeffes played his son, and Samuel Rowley, Thomas Hunt, and Will Cartwright took the parts of moors.[50] It is possible that Shakespeare may have imagined other of his characters as dark-skinned. Philo speaks of the African queen Cleopatra as a 'gipsy' and a woman with a 'tawny front' (1.1.6, 9), and Cleopatra calls herself 'black and wrinkled deep in time' (1.5.28–9). When Cleopatra becomes caught up in distractions of grief, she imagines angling in the Nile and wishes that every 'tawny-finned' fish she brings up might be an Antony (2.5.12). The Amazons who play lutes and dance in *Timon of Athens* (1.2.127) may also have been tanned: the 'black-amoors' who appear 'with music' in *Love's Labour's Lost* (5.2.157) almost certainly were.

Few plays have generated more controversy over race than *The Merchant of Venice*. This is a highly charged play that refashions Marlowe's extraordinary comic tragedy *The Jew of Malta* and fills the stage with strangers. At times, the play can seem unpalatable to modern tastes. Graziano is a bullying, sneering racist, and despite the Prince of Morocco's plea, 'Mislike me not for my complexion' (2.1.1), Portia eventually dismisses him saying, 'Let all of his complexion choose me so' (2.7.79). Like Marlowe's Barabas, Shylock loses his daughter and his ducats, and his humiliation is complete when, in the dénouement, he is forced to convert to Christianity and silenced. But earlier in the play, Shylock makes his famous and eloquent appeal to a shared humanity: 'If you prick us, do we not bleed? If you tickle us, do we not laugh? If you poison us, do we not die?' (3.1.59–62). In the sonnets, Shakespeare is yet more radical, identifying his brown-skinned love with a new aesthetic: 'Now is black beauty's successive heir' (Sonnet 127: 3). To a modern sensibility, the line is little short of breathtaking for the future it imagines.

Black Elizabethans living in early modern London are unlikely to have seen their lives as material for epic drama or light entertainment. So far as we can tell, most of them seem to have belonged to the lower levels of society, the 'common sort', employed as servants in well-to-do white households. We find glimpses of some of them from prosecutions at Bridewell Hospital. Jane Trosse, a notorious prostitute, had in her entourage one Myles, 'a little black fellow' who was 'Master Osborne's man'. Bawdy-house owner Rose Brown was said to receive 'diverse serving men blackamores and other persons [who] resort to her house'. Some black servants seem to have been regarded as an exotic accessory for a wealthy household. The wedding of Elizabeth Carey, Lord Hunsdon's daughter, to Thomas Berkeley in 1596 has been suggested as a possible occasion for the earliest performance of *A Midsummer Night's Dream*. In 1600, Berkeley set off on a grand tour of the continent and left his wife Elizabeth to run their household affairs in Clerkenwell. Elizabeth had a reputation for severity, and in January 1601 she sent her serving girl, Augustina Patra, into Bridewell for punishment: 'Augustina Patra a blackamore servant to the Lady Berkeley sent in by her warrant was punished for running away diverse times'. Henry Lee, possibly son to Sir Henry Lee, commissioner of the Ditchley portrait of Elizabeth I, fathered a child named Anne Blackcoller in Clerkenwell. It was buried on 9 July 1565. If these cases are indicative of black children associated with aristocratic households, it might be that Shakespeare's inclusion of an Indian changeling boy in *A Midsummer Night's Dream* was prompted by just such a child.

Black people were neither a common nor a rare sight in early modern London.[51] Two years after Patra's appearance, Roger Holgate, servant to Thomas Browne, a hat maker, confessed to having 'committed with his fellow a blackamoor in the house the abominable sin of whoredom'. Since he had made her pregnant, he was punished and required to put in sureties to 'discharge the City and parish of the child and children'. On 19 March 1606, another young black woman named Mary, living in the house of a Master Conradus and probably a merchant's servant, testified that 'one John Edwards' who boarded there had slept with her twice and she was now big with his child. Young black men and women would have arrived in London from trading ships docked in ports around the country. Paul Bayning was one of London's leading merchants and a prominent citizen. He kept three black serving-maids in his household. In 1601, he had a black girl named Julian christened as 'Mary' in 1601, and in his will he left £5 for 'instructing Anthony my Negro in the principles of the Christian faith and religion when he shall be fit to be baptised'. In 1608, 'Abell a Blackamore', described as 'servant to Master Paul Bannyng', was kept at work at Bridewell Hospital until a further hearing. Ten days later, he was whipped and detained 'for stubbornness being incorrigible'. Other black people appearing at Bridewell included 'Phillip Moore a Negro', who once sold brooms in Southwark but was caught begging in May 1605, and Mary Dane or Darne 'a Negro', 'Rachell Moore a Blackamore' and 'John a Blackamore', whose occupations are not recorded. These lives, and others like them, mark the origins of black Britain. Sadly, we know no more of these people's stories, but the impression given is of young black men and women lately arrived in London and bound to forms of service.[52]

The case of 'Reasonable' (or possibly 'John Reason') is slightly different. He had a trade as a silkweaver and possibly worked, so Imtiaz Habib has argued, in making costumes for the theatre industry on Bankside.[53] The parish of St Olave's, Tooley Street, lay on the south bank of the Thames, just to the east of St Saviour's and London Bridge. Its parish registers reveal a busy community of clothworkers, especially felt-mongers, dyers, and silk-weavers. St Olave's harboured just the kinds of specialists in fine fabrics needed for making costumes for the playhouses. We find traces of Reasonable's family living in or near the parish. An entry for 19 February 1587 gives the christening of 'Edward the son of Resonabell blackman silkweaver'. Two further entries indicate burials at a time when the plague outbreak was intense. On 13 October 1592, a burial is recorded: 'Jaine daughter of Resonable blackmor'. Three days later, another burial is noted: 'Edmund [probably Edward] son of Resonabell blackmor'. The name 'widow Blackmore' occurs twice in the token books for Boroughside, in 1595 with marginalia indicating 'a woman brought abed', and again in 1596 on 'The west side of the street', the same location as Reasonable, but this time deleted. It is possible that Reasonable or 'Reason' had died, leaving his wife alone—a woman is listed as 'Widow Blackmore' in the token books residing at the Eagle and Child in 1595.[54]

Although Shakespeare occasionally wrote into his plays foreigners like Don Armado and Dr Caius, he seems to have deliberately scattered references to strangers into *The Merchant of Venice*. Of these, Shylock is clearly the most prominent, but others include the Neapolitan prince (1.2.37), the County Palatine (1.2.44), the French Monsieur Le Bon (1.2.52), the English Falconbridge (1.2.63), a Scottish lord (1.2.74), the young nephew of the Duke of Saxony (1.2.81), the Prince of Morocco with his 'three or four Followers' (2.1.0), the Prince of Aragon 'and his train' (SD, 2.9.3-4), and Tubal, a fellow Jew (SD 3.1.69-70). All are outsiders and held up for mockery to varying degrees. Reasonable's widow, if we allow these surmises, may have been another such outsider.

If we grant that a black family named 'Reasonable' (perhaps also 'Reason') lived in Southwark, as the evidence seems to suggest, then a fleeting interchange between Lorenzo and Lancelot the Clown in *The Merchant of Venice* carries added implication. After Jessica has fled her father's house with her new husband Lorenzo, Lancelot the Clown makes a mildly bawdy joke about the religious conflict her marriage with a Christian must entail: 'the sins of the father are to be laid upon the children' (3.5.1–2). Lorenzo returns the accusation, remarking that Lancelot has sins of his own on which to dwell:

LORENZO I shall answer that better to the commonwealth than you can the getting up of the Negro's belly. The Moor is with child by you Lancelot.

LANCELOT It is much that the Moor should be more than reason, but if she be less than an honest woman, she is indeed more than I took her for.

(3.5.35–40)

This passage seems puzzling.[55] Editors have found it odd that this apparently extraneous detail should appear in the text. To give just three examples, in 1926 John Dover Wilson asked, 'Who was the black woman referred to in this passage? Clearly, she has nothing to do with the play as it stands. Was she a character in an earlier version, e.g. a member of Morocco's train? Or was she some real figure, a London notoriety familiar to the audience for whom this dialogue was written?' John Russell Brown, in the second Arden edition, acknowledged the difficulty: 'This passage has not been explained; it might be an outcrop of a lost source, or a topical allusion. Perhaps it was introduced for the sake of the elaborate pun on Moor/more'. John Drakakis, editor for the third Arden series, again notes its incongruity: 'an allegation that is never explained, since there is no "negro" woman in the Jew's household ... It is puzzling that a non-Christian should be present in a Venetian (i.e. Christian) household'.[56] No hint of implicit or unconscious racism is to be imputed to editors doing their best to make sense of the passage for readers. Russell Brown is representative in glossing 'reason' as implying 'reasonable'. In other words, the female 'Moor' was compliant, and now grown large, 'more than' she should be. An unsettling possibility remains. Perhaps she was reluctant, and so the clown 'took her'. Lancelot insouciantly laughs the allegation off, but the scene openly ascribes to him a whipping offence.

The actor playing Lancelot was very probably Will Kemp, who transferred to Worcester's company in 1599, a move followed three years later by Beeston who had a rape charge hanging over him all through the summer of 1602. What makes the notion that Kemp might have bedded Reasonable's widow all the more possible is that he lived very close by. The Southwark token books that record the Reasonable family residing on the south side of the Thames show William Kemp living in 'Samson's Rents' in the parish of St Saviour's.[57] This in itself points to no more than the fact that Kemp was a near neighbour and may have known of the family or Reasonable's wife. But it lends to Lancelot's literary proximity with the negress a near historical analogue by locating Kemp directly in Widow Blackmore's vicinity. It is generally agreed that *The Merchant of Venice* was written around 1595, and Russell Brown's edition supplies the clearest evidence for this supposition.[58] Often excised from performance, these troubling lines look like a contemporary allusion. Lorenzo's precise attitude towards Lancelot is hard to determine, as is Shakespeare's: but more importantly, so too was that of his audience.

French connections

Thomas Nashe, in *Pierce Penniless, his Supplication to the Devil*, tells the story of a French nobleman who, arriving in England, expected to be waited upon as he would in France. On his way to the privy one night, he gave one English lord a candle, another his girdle, and another the paper. But the Englishmen, 'not acquainted with this new kind of gracing', left him with the items he needed at the privy door. This was a deed the nobleman, 'considering what inestimable kindness he extended to them...took very heinously'.[59] If a writer wanted to please an audience at the Curtain or Theatre, he only had to make fun of the French. France was both England's nearest international neighbour and one of its fiercest rivals. Hostilities towards France had not ceased after the Field of Cloth of Gold in 1520, a summit that at last brought a truce between Henry VIII and France. English Catholics like Charles Arundell sought refuge in Paris and from there plotted the assassination of Elizabeth.[60] Already predisposed to deride the French, Shakespeare's audiences were unlikely to warm to his depictions of Queen Margaret and Joan La Pucelle in the Henry VI plays. Margaret joins with the perfidious Duke of Suffolk, and Joan goes through extraordinary contortions of repentance, defiance, and confessions of witchcraft and fornication.

William Haughton's *Englishmen for My Money, or A Woman will have her Will* (1598) pandered to popular conceptions of the French as laughing-stocks. The play quotes phrases from Shakespeare and shows that Haughton was one of Shakespeare's earliest readers. Pisaro, a wealthy, vaguely Jewish, Portuguese merchant, wishes to educate his three daughters, marry them to foreigners, and keep them from their English suitors, Harvey, Heigham, and Walgrave. He hires foreign tutors skilled in languages and music, including the Frenchman Delion whom he intends for Mathea. Delion speaks with a heavy patois, and is only too keen to enjoy Pisaro's food and daughters (1.3.20–2). But Mathea mocks his approaches and refuses to speak 'this gibberish, | Or the pig's language' (2.1.97–8). By a series of ruses, he and an Italian and a Dutchman are outwitted by the young English men. The play transposes aspects of *The Taming of the Shrew* to a London setting, making allusion to several City locations, including the Exchange, Fenchurch Street, Crutched Friars, the Spital, Bishops-gate, and the cross in Cheapside.

Popular English perceptions of the French as 'lecherous, or at least overheated' (Charles Nicholl's phrase) would not have been moderated by contemporary prosecutions. On 9 April 1561, Adrian Petite, a French servant, was imprisoned at Bridewell for being 'a filthy bugger' and desiring a boy.[61] On 17 December 1576, prostitute Kathryn Jones confessed that the French ambassador's man had 'thuse of her body' on three or four occasions.[62] This was Captain Augustine who also 'kept' Alice Furres at Black Luce's brothel in Clerkenwell. Anne Levens confessed that she had slept with 'one Mandurant', a French gentle-man, in Mrs Clarke's house on Tower Hill. Mandurant had 'thuse of her body diverse and many times in many places' and paid generously, giving some thirty or forty pounds for her services.[63] On 27 January 1603/4, Alice Haynes reported that a prostitute named 'French Meg' worked at a bawdy house in Holborn.

Shakespeare's Dr Caius, in *The Merry Wives of Windsor*, is the play's clown and, like Haughton's Delion, speaks with a heavy French accent. His favourite verbal tic, 'By gar' ('by God'), is one that an actor might easily mispronounce as something close to the English word 'bugger'. But, jealous, fiery, and absurd as he is, he is another of

Shakespeare's comic creations that we warm to, especially as the Welshman Evans and he set aside their differences 'in friendship'. His brief appearance at the end of 3.3 is made only to enable a scatological joke: 'if there be one or two, I shall make-a the turd' (3.3.225). His reference to the Duke of Germany at 4.5.81 has been taken as a topical allusion to Frederick, Duke of Württemberg, who failed in 1597 to attend his investiture to the Order of the Garter.[64]

Dr Caius may have proved a model for Haughton's Delion, but overall Shakespeare's play has little of the contempt and jingoism found in *Englishmen for My Money*. There is something rather absurd and yet touching in the fact that, after the Host of the Garter has misdirected Caius and Evans for their duel, they resolve to be friends. This amity is worth noting. Charles Nicholl has usefully explored Shakespeare's French connections through his association with Richard Field, a fellow Stratfordian who had married Jacqueline, widow of a French Huguenot printer, Thomas Vautrollier. The early comedy *Love's Labour's Lost* is set in the southern French court of Navarre and evokes for the stage the intellectual academy convened by Henri IV of Navarre. Nicholl additionally notes the Warwickshire origins of John Eliot, a Francophile, one of whose books Shakespeare used for *Henry V*.[65] He shows that, living on Silver Street with a French Huguenot family in the heart of London, Shakespeare was unlikely to have shared the xenophobia of a writer like Haughton. His French characters are enlisted into a comedy of verbal mistakes of the kind Shakespeare repeatedly used to make an English audience laugh.

Politically, the country's relations with France were a good deal more serious. It is worth remembering that, at the time that the play was performed, Elizabeth's official title was Queen of England, Scotland, France, and Ireland. But with Elizabeth's age and frailty increasing, future French action held sobering implications. The English had reason to fear France in 1599. By August, there were rumours that English priests in Paris were encouraging Henry IV of France to claim the English throne for himself. Elizabeth was sixty-six, and James, King of Scotland, was regarded as unlikely to accede.[66] In October, rumour had it that Elizabeth was willing to give Arbella Stuart in marriage to the French king and declare him her successor.[67] A book was even reported to have been written in defence of the French claim.[68] France was, of course, home to the notorious Catholic seminaries of Douai and Reims and the country from which Jesuit priests usually entered into England. But it was also home to many Huguenot Protestants caught up in waves of persecution. Henry IV had been baptized into the Catholic faith but was raised as a Huguenot by his mother and only just escaped assassination in the St Bartholomew's Day massacre of 1572. While he reverted to the old faith, religious persecution forced many Huguenots to seek asylum in England.

Shakespeare's most sustained representation of the French comes in *Henry V*, a play that celebrates the famous English victory at Agincourt in 1415. For this play, Shakespeare drew upon *The Famous Victories of Henry V* (printed 1598) and possibly other plays about Agincourt that are now lost. The French begin their role in *Henry V* with an insult, offering the young king tennis balls to keep him distracted from the serious events of international politics. This insult triggers Henry's invasion. We first encounter the French directly in 2.4 where King Charles VI of France and the Constable warn the young Dauphin not to imagine the English king a fool. Shakespeare uses the French in 3.5 to narrate the progress of Henry's invasion. These are serious scenes, and when the French Herald Montjoy encounters the English king, the parley has a rhetorical dignity that lends credit to both sides.

In the long night before battle, the French are depicted as nervous, wakeful, and given to petty disputes over whose horse is the finest (3.7). King Henry spends the night disguised, walking among his troops and hearing powerful debates about the right of the king to lead poor men to war. The high seriousness of these scenes is undercut partly by a sequence of absurd exchanges among the English— involving Bardolph, Nym, Pistol, Fluellen, and Williams. Critics since Hazlitt have noted the uneven nature of this play, the high-flown rhetoric of rallying speeches contrasted with scenes of buffoonery among the lowest ranks of the English army.

Pistol's capture of the French soldier, Le Fer, produces tense, darkly comic exchanges, with a boy acting as intermediary and translator (4.4). Throughout the scene, Pistol repeatedly threatens to cut his prisoner's throat: 'Couper la gorge' (4.4.36). His French comes from John Eliot's *Ortho-epia Gallica*, or *Eliot's Fruits for the French* (1593).[69] But after the attack on the boys of the luggage train, it is the king who gives the order that all the French captives should be slaughtered: 'Then every soldier kill his prisoners' (4.6.37). At this point in the play, the quarto reiterates Pistol's gloating threat, '*Coup' la gorge*' (4.6.39). Yet amid these sometimes harrowing scenes, Shakespeare devises a lighthearted interlude in which the French princess Catherine, Henry's future wife, takes an English lesson with her elderly waiting-woman Alice. The scene dwells on the humour of words misunderstood. Catherine takes delight in naming parts of the body in French and English only to mistake the words 'foot' and 'gown' for the French 'foutre' (to fuck) and 'con' (cunt). Ironically, this is common bawdry only for the most educated audience member. The verbal play is moderated into something more serious, diplomatic, and poignant in the final scene where King Harry's courtship of Catherine seals a truce between the two powers. There is nothing in the least jingoistic about this later sequence of exchanges, and it comes to a close with Henry's extraordinarily touching line, 'You have witchcraft in your lips, Kate' (5.2.274).

'The Book of Sir Thomas More'

How, then, might we better understand Shakespeare's works in relation to these culturally mixed social conditions? There is no single way to answer such a question, but we can begin to make some assessment from particular examples. Perhaps the most relevant place to start is with Shakespeare's contribution to a play about 'Evil May Day'. There is now a scholarly consensus that he was responsible for 165 lines added to a play titled 'The Book of Sir Thomas More', a work that never made it to performance or print, perhaps owing to censorship of the script by Edmund Tilney, Master of the Revels. *Sir Thomas More* was a collaborative work, originally drafted and copied by Anthony Munday (perhaps with Henry Chettle) and subsequently added to by Chettle, Thomas Heywood, Thomas Dekker, and, it now appears, Shakespeare. The fact that Munday, Heywood, and Dekker were all writers hired to pen speeches for the Lord Mayor's pageants indicates that they were held in some regard by the City. But their play of *Sir Thomas More* depicted a capital ill at ease with itself, especially concerning the incendiary question of immigrants.

It is worth pointing out that, as a collection of dramatic documents, *Sir Thomas More* presents many complex textual challenges. Munday appears to have first drafted this play in the early 1590s and then made a fair copy. After these 'fair sheets' had been rejected by the Master of the Revels, it seems to have been set aside until after Elizabeth's death in 1603. Probably at this point, additions were made, in different hands, by Henry Chettle, Thomas Heywood, (probably) William Shakespeare, and Thomas Dekker. These respective contributions have, since W. W. Greg's edition for the Malone Society in 1904, been labelled Hands A, B, D, and E. Hand C appears to have been a scribe and annotator whose work included transcriptions of lines by Dekker and (possibly) Shakespeare. As John Jowett explains, Hand C acted as a kind of 'project manager' for the whole enterprise, supervising the revision and transcribing rather than composing material.[70] The second addition has attracted the most attention since a section of it seems to be in Shakespeare's hand. Jowett, whose Arden edition of the play offers the most thorough consideration of the evidence for this attribution, finds much of it strong and 'some of it decisive'.[71] The three pages of Hand D's writing on folios 8a, 9b, and 9a appear to provide unique evidence of Shakespeare in the process of composition.

The play's plot, once sorted out in a responsible edition, remains impressively coherent given the manuscript's many deletions, amendments, and revisions. It begins with a slice of action depicting the events of 'Evil' or 'Ill' May Day, with London citizens threatening to attack the homes of foreigners in revenge for perceived abuses. Senior London magistrates, including the Mayor and Recorder, convene at the Sessions House where a cut-purse is due to be hanged. More, as Sheriff of London, plays a prank on one of the magistrates, Justice Suresby, and arranges for the thief to steal his purse and teach him a lesson—that wealthy men should not carry money ostentatiously and thereby entice a desperate man to commit a potentially capital offence. John Lincoln, one of the rioters, is later hanged, while the others win a late reprieve through More's intervention. More, now promoted to High Chancellor, wittily plays the role of an actor but gradually comes under pressure to support the monarch in his break with Rome. Unable to countenance this change, and finally at peace with himself, he goes to his execution with resigned dignity.

This was contentious material. Not only was More a Catholic and here represented sympathetically but the play is set firmly in London with an immediacy and potential for impact. Tilney, as censor, objected to the opening scene with Doll Williamson, 'a lusty woman' (Sc. 1.0), and her husband, whipping up hostility against foreigners. At the head of the manuscript, he wrote, 'Leave out the insurrection wholly and the cause thereof, and begin with Sir Thomas More at the Mayor's sessions, with a report afterwards of his good service done being Sheriff of London upon a mutiny against the Lombards—only by a short report and not otherwise, at your own perils'.[72] Tilney also objected to the lines 'the displeased commons of the City' (Sc. 3.8) and 'the city is in an uproar, and the mayor | Is threatened if he come out of his house' (Sc. 3.74–5). Against the first eight lines of Scene 3, he wrote tersely, 'Mend this'. Beside another twenty-five lines, he put 'All alter' (Sc. 10.79–104). The text in fact only mentions 'Lombards' once: it seems to be Tilney who has in mind that the strangers in the play are either from Lombardy, Italy, or Lombard Street, London. As Jowett points out, Tilney was also acting as a facilitator in urging these conditions. He might have suppressed the play entirely but chose not to.

The text makes reference to a number of locations in the City, including St Mary's Spital, Cheapside, Moorfields, Ludgate, Newgate, Cornhill, Chelsea, and St Martin's in the Fields. We have a vivid sense of specific events and practices—public sermons at the Spital (St Mary's Hospital), the sheriff's court at the Guildhall, strangers' houses in St Martin's, carts collecting condemned prisoners at the stairs of Newgate, and the gibbet set up in Cheap. Hand D's addition returns the play to the characters with which it began, Doll Williamson, her husband, and indignant neighbours. But crucially, it puts into More's mouth a passionate appeal for toleration and an understanding of the situation of immigrants. He asks the unruly crowd to consider what they will have achieved with strangers forcibly removed from the City, 'plodding to th' ports and coasts for transportation' (l. 86). The crowd would have proved merely 'How insolence and strong hand should prevail', and when they are old and weak, 'other ruffians . . . would shark on you' (ll. 91, 94–6). If banished for insurrection, what country, More goes on to ask, would give them refuge? They too would be strangers, spurned like dogs. This intolerance Shakespeare describes via More as 'mountainish inhumanity' (l. 155).

An identification with those who feel excluded extends throughout Shakespeare's writing. At the start of one of his last plays, *Henry VIII* (or *All is True*), the Prologue gives notice that some scenes may 'draw the eye to flow...[and] let fall a tear' (0.4–6). In this work, Shakespeare (in collaboration with John Fletcher) focuses on the plight of Queen Katherine, Henry's Spanish-born wife. By the start of the second act, the process of Henry's divorce is under way and a sense of exclusion is already palpable. In two scenes penned by Shakespeare, Katherine feels reduced to the status of an alien, a person lacking the rights any other native citizen might enjoy. The 'Old Lady' who accompanies the young Anne Boleyn pities Katherine: 'Alas, poor lady! | She's a stranger now again' (2.3.17–18). In the next scene, Katherine enters the court to plead, with great dignity, that she has always proved a loyal and lawful wife to the King. Yet she is distressingly aware of her new circumstance: 'I am a most poor woman, and a stranger, | Born out of your dominions, having here no judge indifferent' (2.4.13–15). At the time these lines were written, James I had repeatedly sought to marry off one of his children in a Spanish match. In 1613, Don Diego Sarmiento de Acuña, 1st Count of Gondomar, arrived in England to begin negotiations for just such a marriage. That background could only have lent Katherine's words added poignancy.

Shakespeare tends to give his alien characters a history—brief and oblique, but a history nonetheless: Aaron's countryman 'Muliteus' and his family (*Titus Andronicus*, 4.2.150–5), Titania's 'vot'ress' on the Indian shore watching ships set sail, swimming in the sea and gathering 'trifles' (*A Midsummer Night's Dream*, 2.1.123–37), the Prince of Morocco's battles in Persia (*The Merchant of Venice*, 2.2.24–31), Othello's travels among the 'Anthropophagi' (*Othello*, 1.3.127–45), and Desdemona's maid 'Barbary' (4.3.25–32). These micro-narratives have an effect. They acknowledge the lives of strangers and endow them with a value, if only as a transitory memory or sign of life lost. It is hard to avoid the conclusion that, by means of such fragments, Shakespeare wanted his art to recognize the lives of others.

Repeatedly, Shakespeare asked his audiences to see from the point of view of those who have been 'strangered'. And if we wonder why this might be, it is worth remembering that Shakespeare too was an outsider, one of those 'foreign born' immigrants, drawn to London from the countryside. Unlike his contemporaries, Ben Jonson, Thomas Dekker, Thomas Middleton, and Anthony Munday, he did not really belong in the City. Powerful as the international dimension of his writing was, a homeward instinct is also strong in the plays. London made Shakespeare a phenomenon, but Stratford made the man. He was, in the end, as Orlando puts it in *As You Like It*, unalterably 'forest-born' (5.4.30).

Conclusion

So much of early modern life remains unknown to us. There are many details we would very much like to learn more about and many uncertainties to be resolved. Yet at the same time, documents, sources, and traces of that life have survived. The material stuff of early modern life is intelligible to us through artefacts and papers that tell us about their time. Frustratingly, they can only tell us so much. Sometimes, historical imagination has to fill in the gaps, respecting at the same time important gradations of plausibility. On the whole, it is impossible to be rosy-eyed about this era. Everyday experience could be horrifying. Margery Smyth was arrested on 21 July 1599 after the child she had 'delivered in the street' was found there, dead. Ellen Skelton, arrested as a vagrant in 1607, had given birth in the street, was found lunatic, and committed to Bedlam. Other records show how fragile life could often be. Burial registers show 'Jone who died in the Fleet privy', 'a stranger that died in the streets', 'Russell taken up in the streets', or 'a woman out of the fields (unknown)'.[1] If there is a conclusion to be drawn about Shakespeare's life in London, it is that most of it will certainly never be told. Shakespeareans learn to live with incompleteness. Life was easily lost, in sudden quarrels, accidents, or through disease. Sometimes, only scraps remain.

Lost

Occasionally, we might think Shakespeare's plots far-fetched and unrealistic. The play *All's Well That Ends Well* is rarely regarded as an exemplar of verisimilitude. Helen pursues Bertram in disguise, intent on making their marriage good, even though he has rejected her entirely. The story derives ultimately from Boccaccio, perhaps via a French version, and was retold by William Painter in *The Palace of Pleasure* (Novella 38). Yet in London, it might have had a certain resonance, especially for women in the audience. Just five short lines in the Bridewell prosecutions tell of the extraordinary circumstances of Francis Hudson:

23 October 1606 in the afternoon

Frances Hudson vagrant being with child by John Goulser Dutchman and as she sayeth is gone away by sea. And afterwards she put herself in man's apparel and so would have followed him. She was punished by order of Court and kept.[2]

These few words record a biography. Hudson may have understood that, for her part, she was betrothed to Goulser by promise or 'hand-fast'. From the court's point of view, her transgressions included vagrancy, fornication with a stranger, pregnancy out of wedlock, cross-dressing, and attempting to cross borders by subterfuge. This is the substance of *All's Well That Ends Well*. With no regard for the child she carried, Hudson was whipped and detained. Mariana in the play warns Diana of men who seduce women and lead them to ruin: 'Beware of them, Diana: their promises, enticements, oaths, tokens, and all these engines of lust' (3.5.18–19). On 23 January 1605, Amey Bennet, a serving-maid, testified that a Frenchman, John de Lane, dwelling with his master in the Minories (just north of Tower Hill), was the father of the child she now carried. He gave her 'two rings the one was a gold gemoll and the other was a diamond and promised her marriage, which said rings (as this examinate saith) the said John took from her again after he had had his desire of this examinate's body and would not restore them again'.[3] Like de Lane, Bertram promised marriage to Diana, daughter to the Widow Capilet, and sought to buy her maidenhead by giving her his ring. Helen manages to turn Bertram's strategies against him by means of a bed-trick. At the end of the play, she 'feels her young one kick' (5.3.304). Helen's story, unlikely as it may seem, goes some way towards evening out the balance when weighed against a tale like Hudson's.

Birth and loss feature strikingly in *The Winter's Tale*. Shakespeare had employed similar motifs before—a mother dying in child-birth, a thrown-off wife accused of infidelity and believed dead, a lost daughter recovered and a family restored—in *A Midsummer Night's Dream*,

Much Ado about Nothing, and *Pericles*. Having fathered an infant daughter by a wife he regards as an adulteress, King Leontes rejects all sight of it: 'This brat is none of mine' (2.3.93). Unsure of whether to burn the child or let it live, he allows Antigonus to remove it:

> We enjoin thee,
> As thou art liegeman to us, that thou carry
> This female bastard hence, and that thou bear it
> To some remote and desert place, quite out
> Of our dominions; and that there thou leave it…
>
> (2.3.173–7)

The 'poor babe' Antigonus eventually abandons, wrapped in a mantle, with a box containing some gold coins and letters, is the company's first use of a stage infant since Aaron's black-faced babe in *Titus Andronicus*. In performance, the child was probably either a wooden doll wrapped in cloth or just a bundle. Before leaving the child, Antigonus dreams of Hermione instructing him to call the child 'Perdita' ('she who is lost'). The dream ends as Hermione departs: 'And so, with shrieks, | She melted into air' (3.3.35–6).

From the point of view of a contemporary London audience, Leontes has instructed Antigonus to commit a crime. In London, the offence of 'laying a child' in the street, or at a door, was deemed especially serious: it separated an infant from its parents, placed a heavy burden on whoever found it, and drained already hard-stretched parish coffers in maintaining it. In his all-consuming jealousy, Leontes rejects the idea that Perdita was ever his. The audience knows that he has no basis for this notion but watches him persist in it. Without taking the play as an exact analogue for social relations in London, the king's denial that his daughter is his, happened to be, like Bertram's denial of Helen, a not uncommon feature of London life.

There is one especially notable case of this kind that involved Francis Bacon, author and senior barrister of Gray's Inn. Katherine Floyd (or 'Flood') claimed on 3 December 1600 that a Master Hughes was the father of her child and that he had given her 'a gold hoop ring' which she'd pawned for twelve shillings. She had carried the child to his chamber at Gray's Inn and told him that if he did not provide for it, she would 'go to Master Bacon & the rest of the gentlemen of the house & complain of him'. On 10 December, Anne Morrice testified that for all she knew anyone might be the father, including Bacon, but that Hughes was not.

Floyd explained that she had frequented Bacon's chamber, and he had given her five shillings and a blanket 'with billament [ornamental] laces'. A Master Muscott had sent her 'a whistle & a silver chain & two bells'. She had been instructed that 'so long as she laid her child to Master Hughes she should not want anything'. In Floyd's view, 'it was Master Bacon's desire to have Master Hughes ousted out of Gray's Inn'. Bacon had been at Gray's Inn since 1576. There is no admission record for 'Muscott', but he appears to have been Simon Muskett whose son entered Gray's Inn on 9 March 1609. Thomas Hughes, admitted to Gray's Inn in 1580, had written most of a drama entitled *The Misfortunes of Arthur, Reduced into Tragical Notes by T.H.*, performed at Greenwich Palace by the Inn's members on 8 February 1588. Although Hughes continued at the Gray's Inn, rising to Dean of the Chapel in 1618, his career seems to have been chequered, and it is clear that, by 1600, he and Bacon had severely fallen out.[4] There is some likelihood that Floyd herself did not know who the father was. Naming men seems to have been an effective way of procuring money. The problem for Bacon and Muskett was that by the end of 1600, everyone seemed to know about it.

For whatever reason—perhaps as a result of rape, poverty, or plain incapacity—some women felt unable to keep their child. On 11 September 1574, Mabel Wilkinson stood charged with 'laying a child at the door of Thomas Copland', who she claimed was the father. Joan Thewe abandoned a child in November 1598 in the church porch in Lombard Street. She had planned to leave it at the gate of Lady Ramsey but, being interrupted, left it on the church bench instead. She had been paid to leave it there, she claimed. On 9 January 1607, Elizabeth Carr was prosecuted for 'unnaturally leaving of her child of the age of one month in Barnard's Inn in Holborn and departed from it in the night time'.[5] Sometimes, and in what must have been desperate circumstances, women would seek to abort a child or kill it at birth. Effectively, this is what Leontes plans in the abandonment of his daughter.

Care for orphans went to the heart of London's civic and religious culture. In this respect, a last case is worth noting. On 31 August 1612, in the parish of St Helen's Bishopsgate, Richard Atkinson, a boxmaker, was busy shovelling ash into a wheelbarrow, presumably to use it as fertilizer. Digging in to the pile with his spade, he retrieved a baby which had been almost 'stifled' from being left in the heap. He gathered neighbours and rushed it to the church for baptism in case it died. There they christened the child 'Job Raked from the Ashes', after the mournful character of the Old Testament. The register entry is unusually informative:

Job Raked out of the Ashes being born upon Monday being the last of August, about viii of the clock in the morning, was then presently laid upon a dunghill of seacole ashes in the lane going to Sir John Spencer's back gate, was christened the first day of September, then next following, which child so laid and covered over with the same ashes was within an hour after found out by Richard Atkinson, boxmaker, coming thither to shovel up the same dunghill into a wheelbarrow, and by that time he had taken up two shovels of the same ashes, he espied the child almost stifled therewith. The godfathers and godmother were these, viz., Mr Nicholas Spering merchant, John Harvey of the parish & Anne Maunder alias Bedwell, the wife of Andrew Bedwell dwelling at the upper end of Goulding Lane, Anno Domini.

There is no miraculous end to this story as in *The Winter's Tale*. The parish burial register lists for 2 September: 'Job Raked out of the Ashes'. He died in Atkinson's house at about 5 o'clock in the morning and was buried 'in a coffin in the very corner towards Widow Parnell's door the same afternoon' (Figure C.1). A 'printed memory' of him was hung in the church porch, and further details about his discovery and death were inserted by Anthony Munday into the third edition of Stow's *Survey of London* (1633).[6] Job's was one of the shortest and least significant of London lives, but it clearly had impact at the time and signals that Shakespeare's dramas of children lost and found were likely to have proved demanding for some in contemporary audiences.

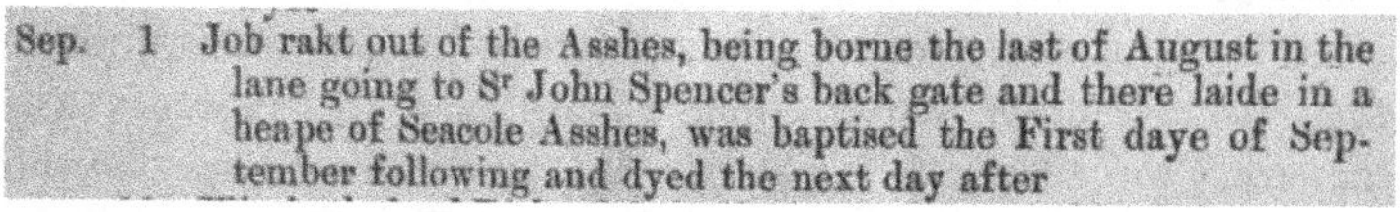

Sep. 1   Job rakt out of the Asshes, being borne the last of August in the lane going to Sʳ John Spencer's back gate and there laide in a heape of Seacole Asshes, was baptised the First daye of September following and dyed the next day after

Figure C.1. Transcription from St Helen's, Bishopsgate, Composite register: the baptismal entry for 'Job rakt out of the Ashes' on 1 September 1612. From W. Bruce Bannerman (ed.), *The Registers of St. Helen's, Bishopsgate, London* (London: 1904), p. 14. Public domain

Job's mother does not seem to have wanted her child to be a foundling, a Perdita restored to its family. But we cannot know, for, like Hermione in Antigonus's dream, she too melted as if into air.

Found

By way of conclusion, we return to one of Shakespeare's latest plays, *All is True* (*Henry VIII*), written in collaboration with John Fletcher. This work deals with the events of Henry's divorce from Katherine of Aragon, the fall of Cardinal Wolsey, the King's secret marriage to Anne Boleyn, and the baptism of Elizabeth, his child by that marriage. The play makes mention of several London locations, including the Tower, St Lawrence Pountney, Blackfriars, Westminster Abbey, York Place, Paris Garden, St Paul's, Moorfields, the Strand, Tower Hill, and the Marshalsea prison in Southwark. But the London topicality in *Henry VIII* seems to be down to Fletcher's part in writing 1.3–4, 2.1–2., 3.1, the latter half of 3.2, 4.1–2, and 5.2–4. The two writers seem to have collaborated in quite distinct ways, taking sole responsibility for particular scenes, dividing the third act, for example, between them. Working in this manner, Shakespeare once more seems to position himself at a remove from the metropolitan setting of the play.

The penultimate scene, often cut from performance, focuses on the jostling crowds gathered to witness the christening of the baby Princess Elizabeth. The scene is set in a crowded entrance to the court at Westminster. In all likelihood by Fletcher, it is designed to lighten the mood before the more solemn and stately final scene in which Cranmer baptizes England's future queen. It is also the most crowd-pleasing scene, where the audience gets to watch onstage spectators outdo them for rowdiness and vulgarity. Politically, the play is highly nuanced. Henry's pangs of conscience over the legitimacy of his marriage to Katherine are made very clear, yet Fletcher's writing steers close to other, less spiritual, motives. When the Lord Chamberlain suggests to Suffolk that the king's marriage to his brother's wife 'has crept too near his conscience', he elicits a blunt reply: 'No, his conscience has crept too near another lady' (2.2.16-18).

The play picks up on a powerful word associated with the reign of Henry VIII—that of 'reformation'. Sir Thomas Lovell draws attention to a new proclamation posted on the 'Court Gate' (the principal entrance to Wolsey's palace at York Place, just between Charing

Cross and the Thames) for the 'reformation of our travelled gallants |
That fill the court with quarrels, talk and tailors' (1.3.19–20). Young
men return from the continent with too much of the French court
about them, including its 'diseases' (1.3.36). Later, when Cranmer is
interrogated by members of the Privy Council, the word is again used,
this time by way of criticizing Cranmer's 'new opinions' or Protest-
antism (5.2.51). By 1613, the term 'reformation' had long denoted the
seismic change in national politics and religion brought about by
Henry's separation from Katherine and Rome and his marriage to
Anne. An entire epoch of prior belief had been, in many cases literally,
whitewashed.

But after Perdita, Elizabeth. In the final scene, when Cranmer
makes a famous prophecy over the infant princess, the sense of a
future gained is powerfully felt. This future is one through which
many in the audience, including Shakespeare, had already lived—a
future now already past. A divided perspective is achieved. When
the Globe Theatre burned down in 1613, it too was lost. The play of
Henry VIII had just started. Fifty or so lines into the fourth scene, a
discharged cannon accidentally set the thatched roof alight and the
entire building was destroyed. Ballads were written about the event.
Ben Jonson cynically suggested that a 'burned' or infected Bridewell
prostitute, Katherine Arden, might have been responsible. John
Chamberlain described the catastrophe in a letter to Sir Ralph
Winwood.[7] Chamberlain was then sixty years of age, old enough
to remember Elizabeth's coronation and to have heard the stories of
Henry's reign from his own family. The following year, the playhouse was rebuilt, more sumptuously than before, and a new future
thereby gained. But this time, not for Shakespeare: his part was
done.

Most of Shakespeare's London life will never be known to us. How
much of it was lost in the 1666 Fire of London, or to kindling in a cold
winter, is impossible to measure. Unlike Marlowe, Kyd, Peele, and
(probably) Nashe, Shakespeare survived London's many hazards and
took advantage of its opportunities. In Shoreditch, Bishopsgate,
Southwark, Blackfriars, and other London localities, he found communities that wanted to create, join, and somehow connect with the
worlds—of France, Verona, Venice, Troy, Antioch, Sicily, Athens,
or other distant shores—reimagined in his writing. These other
Londoners enabled the success he achieved, sometimes at substantial

personal cost. Their stories are also hidden with his. However removed the action of a play might seem to be, local realities were rarely far away. Occasionally they surfaced onstage, for example in a quip about a black girl's compliance, a garrulous hostess and a fat knight, a young woman denounced as a whore, a bungling constable, or a lost child. These were elements of the City's vitality. Shakespeare's plays had life in London, and so we find London life in the plays.

INTRODUCTION

1. Quotations are cited from R. W. Van Fossen (ed.), *Eastward Ho* (Manchester and New York: Manchester University Press, 1979). I have used Ann Thompson and Neil Taylor (eds), *Hamlet* (London: Thomson Learning, 2006) for comparison.

2. LMA, St Botolph Bishopsgate, Composite register, 1558–1628, P69/BOT4/A/001/MS04515, 23 May 1578. 'Ester de Boyes' and 'Jayne de Boyes' were buried on 17 and 26 April, in the same year.

3. Sweno (BCB 4. 13^v). Cuffe and Jasper (BCB4. 61^{r-v}, 67^r, 71^v). Roger and Mary Elsinore (BCB 4. 87^v). Mary Berry (BCB 5. 66^r). Stow explains that Pilcock Lane was located near St Nicholas Shambles, east of Newgate. See Charles Kingsford (ed.), *John Stow, Survey of London* (Oxford: Clarendon Press, 1908), 2 vols, i. 316–19.

4. Paul Griffiths, *Lost Londons: Change, Crime and Control in the Capital City, 1550–1660* (Cambridge and New York: Cambridge University Press, 2008), 38–42.

5. Ibid., 51–4, 70–6. For population figures, see chapter 4, n. 8, and chapter 5, n. 13.

6. Ibid., 22.

7. Eleanor Hubbard, *City Women: Money, Sex, and the Social Order in Early Modern London* (Oxford and New York: Oxford University Press, 2012), 26–7, 53, 189–234.

8. Ibid., 107–8.

9. William Ingram, *The Business of Playing: The Beginnings of the Adult Professional Theatre in Elizabethan London* (Ithaca, NY and London: Cornell University Press, 1992), 18–25.

10. Lukas Erne, *Shakespeare and the Book Trade* (Cambridge and New York: Cambridge University Press, 2013), 130–85. David Kathman, 'Grocers, Goldsmiths, and Drapers: Freemen and Apprentices in the Elizabethan Theater', *Shakespeare Quarterly*, 55.1 (2004), 1–49, and 'Henry Condell and His London Relatives', *Shakespeare Quarterly* 63, 1 (2012), 108–15. Charles Nicholl, *The Lodger: Shakespeare on Silver Street* (London: Allen Lane, 2007). James Shapiro, *1599: A Year in the Life of William Shakespeare* (London: Faber, 2005), and *1606: Shakespeare and the Year of Lear* (London: Faber, 2016).

11. The cases involving Fawkenor, Kyd, and Breame are found in the Bridewell Court of Governors' Minute Book (hereafter BCB) volume 3, held at the Museum of the Mind, Bethlem Royal Hospital, Beckenham, Kent. The Bridewell books are digitally available at the Bethlem Museum of the Mind website: Fawkenor, BCB 4. 140^v; Kyd BCB 2. 250^v–255^v and 3. 315^r; Breame 3. 28^v. Also, my *Shakespeare Among the Courtesans: Prostitution, Literature and Drama, 1500–1650* (Farnham and Burlington, VT: Ashgate, 2012) 97–108.

12. A good starting point would be Vanessa Harding's guide to the literature on the subject, 'Early Modern London 1550–1700', *The London Journal* 20, 2 (1995), 34–45, and Ian Archer, 'The Government of London, 1500–1650', *The London Journal* 26, 1 (2001), 19–28. My own chapter, 'Crime', in Andrew Hadfield, Matthew Dimmock, and Abigail Shinn (eds), *The Ashgate Research Companion to Popular Culture in Early Modern England* (Farnham and Burlington, VT: Ashgate, 2014), 193–206, discusses instances and statistics of City crime, including a survey of 800 prosecutions from the Middlesex County Sessions, 1549–1609.

CHAPTER 1

1. F. E. Halliday, *A Shakespeare Companion, 1564–1964* (London: Duckworth & Co., 1964), 59. For a full-length study of the dispute, see Nicholl, *The Lodger.*

2. E. K. Chambers, *William Shakespeare: A Study of Facts and Problems* (Oxford: Clarendon Press, 1930), 2 vols, ii. 215, 221.

3. Gary Taylor, 'Thomas Middleton: Lives and Afterlives', in Gary Taylor and John Lavagnino, with MacD. P. Jackson, John Jowett, Valerie Wayne, and Adrian Weiss (eds), *Thomas Middleton: The Collected Works* (Oxford and New York: Oxford University Press, 2007), 25–58, esp. 44–9. Also, 'Middleton, Thomas (bap. 1580, d. 1627)', *Oxford Dictionary of National Biography* (Oxford: Oxford University Press, 2004); online edn, May 2008 <http://www.oxforddnb.com/view/article/18682>.

4. Paul S. Seaver, 'Middleton's London', in Gary Taylor and John Lavagnino et al., *Thomas Middleton: The Collected Works*, 59–73, 73. For Middleton and London, see also David M. Bergeron, 'Thomas Middleton, Thomas Middleton in London 1613', in S. P. Cerasano (ed.), *Medieval and Renaissance Drama in England*, vol. 27 (Madison, NJ: Fairleigh Dickinson University Press, 2014), 17–39.

5. Thomas Dekker, *The Seven Deadly Sinnes* (London: 1606), A3^v; *A Rod for Runaways* (London: 1625), B^v. For Dekker's (possible) father, see London Metropolitan Archives (hereafter LMA), St Leonard, Shoreditch, Burials 1558–1654, P91/LEN/A/012/MS07499, 4 October 1599.

6. John Twyning, 'Dekker, Thomas (*c*.1572–1632)', *Oxford Dictionary of National Biography* (Oxford: Oxford University Press, 2004); online edn, January 2008 <http://www.oxforddnb.com/view/article/7428>.

7. John L. McMullan, *The Canting Crew: London's Criminal Underworld, 1500–1700* (New Brunswick, NJ: Rutgers University Press, 1984).

8. R. A. Foakes (ed.), *Henslowe's Diary* (Cambridge and New York: Cambridge University Press, 2002), 86.

9. See Foakes, *Henslowe's Diary*, 122. E. D. Pendry (ed.), *Thomas Dekker* (London: Edward Arnold, 1967) 172–308. Stanley Wells, 'Thomas Dekker and London', in *Shakespeare & Co.* (London: Penguin, 2006), 106–28.

10. E. K. Chambers, *The Elizabethan Stage* (Oxford: Clarendon, 1923), 4 vols, iii. 347–8.

11. David Kathman, 'Heywood, Thomas (*c*.1573–1641)', *Oxford Dictionary of National Biography* (Oxford: Oxford University Press, 2004), <http://www.oxforddnb.com/view/article/13190>.

12. Fran C. Chalfant, *Ben Jonson's London: A Jacobean Placename Dictionary* (Athens, Georgia: University of Georgia Press, 1978). Jonathan Haynes, *The Social Relations of Ben Jonson's Theatre* (Cambridge and New York: Cambridge University Press, 1992). Janet Dillon, *Theatre, Court and City, 1595–1610* (Cambridge and New York: Cambridge University Press, 2008), 109–36. James D. Mardock, *Our Scene is London: Ben Jonson's City and the Space of the Author* (Abingdon and New York: Routledge, 2008).

13. Ian Donaldson, *Ben Jonson, A Life* (Oxford and New York: Oxford University Press, 2011), 22. For Deaf John and Whetstone, 'Literary Traces in Bridewell and Bethlem, 1602–24', *The Review of English Studies* 56, 225 (2005), 380–85.

14. David Riggs, 'Ben Jonson', in Paul Edmondson and Stanley Wells (eds), *The Shakespeare Circle: An Alternative Biography* (Cambridge and New York: Cambridge University Press, 2015), 186–98.

15. H. R. Woudhuysen (ed.), *Love's Labour's Lost* (London: A&C Black, 1998), 76–83.

16. See Richard Savage (trans.), *The Registers of Stratford-on-Avon, Baptisms 1558–1652* (London: The Parish Register Society, 1897).

17. According to John Aubrey, 'There was at this time another Butcher's son in this Towne that was held not at all inferior to him [Shakespeare] for a natural witt, his acquaintance and coetanean, but dyed young', in Oliver Lawson Dick (ed.), *Aubrey's Brief Lives* (Harmondsworth: Penguin, 1982), 334. I am grateful to Martin Wiggins for reminding me of this observation.

18. David Fallow, 'His father John Shakespeare', in Edmondson and Wells (eds), *The Shakespeare Circle*, 30. For Elizabeth Hall, see Harriet Joseph, *Shakespeare's Son-in-Law: John Hall, Man and Physician* (1976), 32.

19. For Humphrey Brace[r], see The National Archives (hereafter TNA), Kew, Prob/11/79; for Alice Smith (previously named 'Chitla' or Chidlow, presumably by a previous marriage), see TNA Prob/11/68. For Quiney's letter and the 1592 Stratford list of recusants, see S. Schoenbaum, *William Shakespeare: A Compact Documentary Life* (Oxford and New York: Oxford University Press, 1977), 238–9, 41–2.

20. Chambers, *William Shakespeare*, ii. 101–6.

21. Thomas Clark (BCB 2. 196^r); Roger Quiney (BCB 3. 143^r).

22. E. Fripp, *Master Richard Quyny, Bailiff of Stratford-upon-Avon and Friend of William Shakespeare* (Oxford: Oxford University Press, 1924), 201. Chambers, *Elizabethan Stage*, iv. 104.

23. John Stow, *A Survey of London, reprinted from the text of 1603*, int. C. L. Kingsford (Oxford: Clarendon Press, 1908), 2 vols, i. 206, ii. 330.

24. Harriet Joseph, *Shakespeare's Son-in-Law*, 101–2.

25. For Matthew Shakespeare, see Salkeld, *Shakespeare Among the Courtesans*, 142–5.

26. Andy Kesson, 'His Fellow Dramatists and Early Collaborators', in Edmondson and Wells (eds), *The Shakespeare Circle*, 235–47, 239.

27. Jacob Selwood, *Diversity and Difference in Early Modern London* (Farnham and Burlington, VT: Ashgate, 2010), 3, 66–7.

CHAPTER 2

1. There was also a 'Long Lane' in Southwark, leading east–west between St Margaret's Hill and Bermondsey Street. See the 1542 map reproduced in William Rendle, *Old Southwark and its People* (London: Drewett, 1878).

2. Ben Weinreb and Christopher Hibbert, *The London Encyclopaedia* (London: Macmillan, 1983), 803.

3. It is currently held at the Museum of London for petrological analysis.

4. C. L. Kingsford (ed.), *A Survey of London, by John Stow, Reprinted from the text of 1603* (Oxford: Clarendon Press, 1908), 2 vols, i. 25.

5. Ibid., i. 336.

6. See John D. Cox and Eric Rasmussen (eds), *King Henry VI, Part 3* (London: Bloomsbury, 2001), 5–6; Edward Burns (ed.), *King Henry VI, Part 1* (London: A&C Black, 2000), 1–4.

7. See Hugh Craig and Arthur Kinney (eds), *Shakespeare, Computers and the Mystery of Authorship* (Cambridge and New York: Cambridge University Press, 2009), 54.

8. For poetic eulogies of London, see Lawrence Manley, *London in the Age of Shakespeare* (London and Sydney: Croom Helm, 1986), 49–74.

9. Julian Bowsher, *Shakespeare's London Theatreland: Archaeology, History and Drama* (London: Museum of London Archaeology, 2012), esp. 89–96.

10. Kingsford, *Survey*, i. xcviii.

11. Ibid., xv–xvi.

12. Ibid., ii. 65 (Bridge House); i. 1 (Livy).

13. Ibid., lx.

14. Craig and Kinney, *Shakespeare, Computers and the Mystery of Authorship*, 78–99. MacDonald P. Jackson, *Determining the Shakespeare Canon: 'Arden of Faversham' and 'A Lover's Complaint'* (Oxford and New York: Oxford University Press, 2015), 104–28.

15. J. G. Nichols (ed.), *The Diary of Henry Machyn, Citizen and Merchant-Taylor of London, 1550–1563* (London: Camden Society, 1848). For 'maying' (20, 137), fairs (207–8), the Middle Temple (275), 'misrule' (13, 28), banquet (237), hanging (4), the bear-bite and fallen horse-rider (78, 139), thrown infant (301), Lady Jane Grey (35), Mary Tudor (38–40), Wyatt's rebellion (53–4, 60), the comet (101), lightning (259–60), the death of Mary and coronation of Elizabeth (178, 181–6).

16. Nicholl, *The Lodger*, 39.

17. Kingsford, *Survey*, i. 93, ii. 73–5.

18. See Holger Schott Syme, 'Post-Curtain Theatre History', online blog article at <http://www.dispositio.net/archives/2262> (accessed 20 June 2016).

19. Glynne Wickham (ed.), *English Professional Theatre, 1530 to 1660* (Cambridge and New York: Cambridge University Press, 2000), 408.

20. Derek Keene and Ian W. Archer (eds), *The Singularities of London, 1578 by L. Grenade* (London: London Topographical Society, 2014) 78–82.

21. Wickham, *English Professional Theatre, 1530 to 1660*, 334–5.

22. Ibid., 349.

23. Andrew Gurr, *Playgoing in Shakespeare's London* (Cambridge and New York: Cambridge University Press, 2004), 84.

24. Ibid., 415; Chambers, *Elizabethan Stage*, ii. 400.

25. E. A. J. Honigmann and Susan Brock (eds), *Playhouse Wills, 1558–1642* (Manchester and New York: Manchester University Press, 1993): 'youse' (69), 'saint lennards' (70), 'beleeve' (81). R. A. Foakes, *Henslowe's Diary* (Cambridge and New York: Cambridge University Press, 2002), 26–7.

26. TNA C14/226/11 (Pt 1).

27. LMA, St Leonard Shoreditch, Register of Burials, 1558–1654, P91/LEN/A/012/MS07499.

28. Warren (BCB 5. 68ᵛ), Price and Havis (BCB 5. 217ʳ). For thefts, see J. C. Jeaffreson, *Middlesex County Sessions Records* (London: GLC, 1974), vols i and ii. See Hill (i. 17l), Dolling (i. 189), Manson and West (i. 232), Cuthbert and Richard Burbage (ii. 108–9). For Burbage's will, see E. A. J. Honigmann and Susan Brock (eds), *Playhouse Wills, 1558–1642* (Manchester and New York: Manchester University Press, 1993), 113–14.

29. Alan H. Nelson, 'George Buc, William Shakespeare, and the Folger *George a Greene*', *Shakespeare Quarterly* 48 (Spring 1998), 74–83. Lukas Erne, *Shakespeare and the Book Trade* (Cambridge and New York: Cambridge University Press, 2013), 200.

30. Hannah Crawforth, Sarah Dustagheer, and Jennifer Young, *Shakespeare in London* (London and New York: Bloomsbury, 2014), 184–5. Jean Howard writes, 'we know that many brothels were still located there', in *Theatre of a City: The Places of London Comedy, 1598–1642* (Philadelphia: University of Pennsylvania Press, 2007), 122.

31. Paul Griffiths finds cases mainly of theft in Southwark in *Lost Londons: Change, Crime and Control in the Capital City, 1550–1660* (Cambridge and New York: Cambridge University Press, 2008), 90–1.

32. Kingsford, *Survey*, ii. 52.

33. See Bowsher, *Shakespeare's London Theatreland*, 75, 82.

34. LMA, The Repertories of the Court of Aldermen, 23, 585ᵛ. The watermen's petition is transcribed in Chambers, *The Elizabethan Stage*, iv. 312.

35. Kingsford, *Survey*, ii. 55.

36. References to Stow's *Survey* in this paragraph are taken from Kingsford, *Survey*, 52–7.

37. Kingsford, *Survey*, 61 (Marshalsea murder). Nichols, *Machyn's Diary*, 269. For Essex, see Mary Anne Everett Green (ed.), *Calendar of State Papers, Domestic, 1598–1601* (London: Longmans Green and Co, 1869), 590. Legate (BCB 5.68ʳ). For Bankes, see LMA, P92/Geo, St George, the Martyr, Southwark, composite register (28 June 1610).

38. Chambers, *William Shakespeare*, ii. 88.

39. Ibid., 90.

40. St Saviour's Vestry Minutes, 1582–1628, LMA, P92/SAV/450 (31 October 1605), 390.

41. Bullough, *Narrative and Dramatic Sources*, iii. 329, lines 1309–13.

42. Mary Anne Everett Green (ed.), *Calendar of State Papers, Domestic, 1591–4* (London: Longmans, Green, Reader and Dyer, 1867) 484, 707; Robert Lemon (ed.), *Calendar of State Papers, Domestic, 1581–90* (London: Longman, Green, Longman, Roberts, and Green, 1865), 361.

43. J. F. Merritt, *The Social World of Early Modern Westminster: Abbey, Court and Community 1525–1640* (Manchester and New York: Manchester University Press, 2005), 225–56.

44. Bullough, *Narrative and Dramatic Sources*, iii. 414.
45. *A Full Description of the Manner of Executing the Sentence Upon Titus Oats for Perjury* (London, 1685).
46. Lawrence Manley, *Literature and Culture in Early Modern London* (Cambridge and New York: Cambridge University Press, 1995) 84–112.
47. Lawrence Manley (ed.), *London in the Age of Shakespeare: An Anthology* (London and Sydney: Croom Helm, 1986) 49–74.

CHAPTER 3

1. Glynne Wickham, Herbert Berry, and William Ingram (eds), *English Professional Theatre, 1530–1660* (Cambridge and New York: Cambridge University Press, 2000), 63.
2. Ibid., 361.
3. Mary Edmond, 'Burbage, James (c.1531–97)', *Oxford Dictionary of National Biography* (Oxford: Oxford University Press, 2004); online edn, January 2008 <http://www.oxforddnb.com/view/article/3950>, accessed 29 April 2016.
4. Wickham et al., *English Professional Theatre*, 345–46. Chambers, *The Elizabethan Stage*, iv. 277, 282, and 298. Also, J. C. Jeaffreson, *Middlesex County Sessions* (Greater London Council, 1972, 1886), ii. xlvii–xlviii.
5. On the date of this document, see David Kathman, 'Reconsidering *The Seven Deadly Sins*', *Early Theatre* 7, 1 (2004), 13–44. It is reproduced in Tarnya Cooper et al., *Searching For Shakespeare, with essays by Marcia Pointon, James Shapiro and Stanley Wells* (London: National Portrait Gallery, 2006), 102–3.
6. Kathman, 'Reconsidering *The Seven Deadly Sins*'. See also Andrew Gurr, 'The Work of Elizabethan Plotters and *2 The Seven Deadly Sins*', *Early Theatre* 10, 1 (2007), 67–87, and Kathman's reply, '*The Seven Deadly Sins* and Theatrical Apprenticeship', *Early Theatre* 14, 1 (2011), 121–39.
7. Honigmann and Brock, *Playhouse Wills*, 142, 69, 125; LMA, St Leonard Shoreditch, Register of burials, 1558—1654, P91/LEN/A/012/MS07499, 17 November 1604.
8. 'Horseshoe Alley' is clearly marked on both the 1738–47 map by John Rocque and the 1792–1813 map by Richard Horwood and William Faden.
9. R. Foakes (ed.), *Henslowe's Diary* (Cambridge and New York: Cambridge University Press, 2002), 249.
10. For further details and references concerning 'Black Luce' and her associates, see my *Shakespeare Among the Courtesans*, 128–50.
11. For Elizabeth Evans, see ibid., 1–4.
12. S. Schoenbaum, *William Shakespeare: A Compact Documentary Life* (Oxford and New York: Oxford University Press, 1977), 255–6.

13. Chambers, *William Shakespeare*, ii. 88.
14. Anne Smith (BCB 3. 220ᵛ), Elizabeth Everys (BCB 3. 374ʳ), Margaret Browne (BCB 4. 23ᵛ), Noxon (BCB 4. 343ʳ), Flower and Hill (BCB 4. 373ʳ). For Alleyn's list of his estate, *Memorandum-Book of Edward Alleyn, 1594–1616*, MSS 8, Dulwich College, 42ʳ⁻ᵛ, 43ᵛ–44ᵛ, available online at the Henslowe-Alleyn Digitisation Project. Lena Cowen Orlin provides a fuller discussion of the case against Underhill in *Locating Privacy in Tudor London* (Oxford and New York: Oxford University Press, 2007), 177–8.
15. For the case against Holden, see BCB 4.84ʳ-90ʳ (10–13 June 1599). The statements in this case are unusually detailed, especially in their accounts of the preparation of food.
16. BCB 4. 373ʳ (30 April 1603).
17. Lawrence Manley and Sally Beth MacLean, *Lord Strange's Men and Their Plays* (New Haven and London: Yale University Press, 2014), 47–8. Manley and MacLean note the possibility that Alleyn may have played the roles of Cade in *2 Henry VI* and Warwick in *3 Henry VI* (112).
18. Warner, *Catalogue of the Manuscripts and Muniments of Alleyn's College of God's Gift at Dulwich* (London: Longmans, Green and Co., 1881), 167, 174.
19. Ibid., 166–8. On Buckett, see Edward Town, 'A Biographical Dictionary of London Painters, 1547–1625', *Walpole Society*, 76 (2014), 1–235, 44–7.
20. Katherine Duncan-Jones (ed.), *Shakespeare's Sonnets* (London: Thomson Learning, 1997), 7–8.
21. Paul Edmondson and Stanley Wells, *Shakespeare's Sonnets* (Oxford and New York: Oxford University Press, 2004), 4. Arthur Freeman and Janet Ing Freeman, *John Payne Collier: Scholarship and Forgery in the Nineteenth Century* (New Haven and London: Yale University Press, 2004), ii. 1142. Alan H. Nelson, 'Letter from Thomas Bowker to Edward Alleyn About a Dog, with Numerous Notes on the Verso by Alleyn of Payments, Including for a Book of Shakespeare's Sonnets, June 19, 1609', available online at the Shakespeare Documented website. Lena Cowen Orlin includes it in a list of contemporary Shakespeare documents in 'Anne by Indirection', *Shakespeare Quarterly* 65, 4 (2014), 421–54, 452, item 71.
22. Roslyn Knutson, *Playing Companies and Commerce in Shakespeare's Time* (Cambridge and New York: Cambridge University Press, 2001), 10.
23. Nungezer, *Dictionary of Actors*, 143.
24. For James and Fuller, see Chambers, *William Shakespeare*, ii. 242, 244. David Scott Kastan (ed.), *Henry IV Part 1* (London: Thomson Learning, 2002), 54–6.
25. Wickham (BCB 3. 176ʳ). Dorrett (BCB 4. 433ʳ). Earl of Oxford's man ('Sharlocke') (BCB 3. 134ᵛ).

26. These details may be found at BCB 4.8^r–10^r.

27. See the entry by J. E. Mousley in P. W. Hasler, *The History of Parliament: The House of Commons, 1558–1603* (London: HMSO, 1981), 3 vols, i. 497. Mousley renders the word 'geast' as 'jest'.

28. For the case involving Wilkinson, Partridge, and Allen, see BCB 4.8^r–10^r. For Brooke's duel with Lucas, see D. McKeen, *A Memory of Honour: The Life of William Brooke, Lord Cobham*, 2 vols (1986), ii 439–40. Also John Roche Dasent (ed.), *Acts of the Privy Council of England New Series Vol. XXVIII, A. D. 1597–8* (London: Eyre and Spottiswoode, 1904), 198, 205. Brooke's will contains the codicil added 24 December 1597, TNA Prob 11/90/644.

29. On Essex's relationships with the Cobham sons, see Paul E. J. Hammer, *The Polarisation of Elizabethan Politics: The Political Career of Robert Devereux, 2nd Earl of Essex, 1585–97* (Cambridge and New York: Cambridge University Press, 1999), 358.

30. F. E. Halliday, *A Shakespeare Companion, 1564–1964* (London: Duckworth & Co., 1964), 107. Francis Bacon, *A Declaration of the Treasons of the Late Earl of Essex and his Complices* (London, 1601), sig. E4^v.

31. On the question of whether the Essex 'following' constituted a faction, see Hammer, *The Polarisation of Elizabethan Politics*, 356–7. For Achilles as Essex, see David Bevington (ed.), *Troilus and Cressida* (London: Thomson Learning, 2001), 11–18.

32. For a full transcription of the Beeston case, see my 'Theatrical References from the Court of Governors' Minute Books for London's Bridewell and Bethlem Hospitals', *Malone Society Collections XVI* (Manchester and New York: Manchester University Press, 2011), 47–64, 57–9.

33. Beeston's address for Augustine's christening is given as 'Halliwell Street', LMA, St Leonard Shoreditch, *Burials 1558–1654*, P91/LEN/A/012/MS07499 (17 November 1604). Phillips's will is reproduced in Chambers, *Elizabethan Stage*, ii. 73, and Honigmann and Brock, *Playhouse Wills*, 72–5. For Beeston and Pallant's assistance with *The Black Dog of Newgate*, see Foakes, *Henslowe's Diary*, 220. On Worcester's Men at the Rose, see Foakes, 225–6.

34. Duncan Salkeld, 'His Collaborator George Wilkins', in Paul Edmondson and Stanley Wells (eds), *The Shakespeare Circle: An Alternative Biography* (Cambridge and New York: Cambridge University Press, 2015), 289–96.

35. On the Mountjoy–Belott dispute, see Nicholl, *The Lodger*, and David Kathman, 'Living with the Mountjoys', in Edmondson and Wells, *The Shakespeare Circle*, 174–85. Lukas Erne, *Shakespeare and the Book Trade* (Cambridge and New York: Cambridge University Press, 2013), 53.

CHAPTER 4

1. George Unwin, *The Gilds and Companies of London* (London: Frank Cass, 1963), 176–7, 227–31. There are many 'histories' of individual livery companies. As exemplars, see Alfred Plummer, *The London Weavers' Company 1600–970* (London: Routledge, 2005), Penelope Hunting, *A History of the Drapers' Company* (London: Drapers' Company, 1989), W. A. D. Englefield, *The History of the Painter-Stainers Company of London* (Hazell, Watson & Viney, 1950), and Matthew Davies and Ann Saunders, *The History of the Merchant Taylors' Company* (London: Maney, 2004).

2. Unwin, *The Gilds and Companies of London*, 371.

3. *The Repertories of the Court of Aldermen*, 22, 90^r (6 August 1589).

4. Steve Rappaport, *Worlds Within Worlds: Structures of Life in Sixteenth-Century London* (Cambridge and New York: Cambridge University Press, 1989), 17–18. Ian Archer, *The Pursuit of Stability: Social Relations in Early Modern London* (Cambridge and New York: Cambridge University Press, 1992).

5. David Kathman, 'Grocers, Goldsmiths, and Drapers: Freemen and Apprentices in the Elizabethan Theater', *Shakespeare Quarterly* 55, 1 (2004), 1–49. Cooke's will is in Honigmann and Brock, *Playhouse Wills, 1558–1642* (Manchester and New York: Manchester University Press, 1993), 95.

6. Chambers, *William Shakespeare*, ii. 85. For Phillips's will, Chambers, *The Elizabethan Stage*, ii. 73, and Honigmann and Brock, *Playhouse Wills*, 72–5.

7. On the government of early modern London, see F. F. Foster, *The Politics of Stability: A Portrait of the Rulers in Elizabethan London* (London: Royal Historical Society, 1977). See also Caroline Barron, 'The Government of London: The Formative Phase, 1300–1500', *The London Journal* 26, 1 (2001), 9–18 and Ian Archer, 'The Government of London, 1500–1650', *The London Journal* 26, 1 (2001), 19–28. A. B. Beaven's *The Aldermen of the City of London* (London: Corporation of London, 1908) remains a useful resource.

8. For numbers of constables, F. F. Foster, *The Politics of Stability: A Portrait of the Rulers in Elizabethan London* (London: Royal Historical Society, 1977), 30. For Thomas Wood, Repertories of the Court of Aldermen, Rep 23, 429^v.

9. On comparative population figures, see Roger Finlay, *Population and Metropolis: The Demography of London, 1580–1650* (Cambridge and

New York: Cambridge University Press, 1981), 7, and Selwood, *Diversity and Difference*, 20–3. Also, Vanessa Harding, 'The Population of London, 1550–1700: A Review of the Published Evidence', *The London Journal* 15 (1990), 111–28, and 'Early Modern London 1550–1700', *The London Journal* 20 (1995), 34–45. As Harding argues in the first of these articles, 'Probably the most valuable insight . . . into . . . demographic change in [London], will come from detailed study of localities' (124).

10. Chambers, *Elizabethan Stage*, iv. 264, 268.
11. LMA, St Leonard Shoreditch, Register of burials, 1558–1654, P91/LEN/A/012/MS07499.
12. On decay of the Theatre and surrounding buildings, Glynne Wickham, Herbert Berry, and William Ingram (eds), *English Professional Theatre, 1530–1660* (Cambridge and New York: Cambridge University Press, 2000), 382–3.
13. Wickham, *English Professional Theatre, 1530–1660*, 100.
14. Ibid., 537–8.
15. Chambers, *Elizabethan Stage*, iv. 326.
16. Tracey Hill, *Pageantry and Power: A Cultural History of the Early Modern Lord Mayor's Show, 1585–1639* (Manchester and New York: Manchester University Press, 2013), 138.
17. G. Bullough (ed.), *Narrative and Dramatic Sources of Shakespeare* (London: Routledge and Kegan Paul, 1958), ii. 459.
18. Although Barnardine is said to have been 'Bohemian born', the editors of the Oxford *Thomas Middleton: The Collected Works* accept him as original to Shakespeare's text.
19. See BCB 4. 284^r.
20. For the undertakers' resignations, see BCB 4. 324^v-325^r (16 October 1602). For Baradine's attempt at rape, see BCB 4.262^r. For his release, see BCB 4. 265^r.
21. BCB 4. 327^v (Cartwright and Griffin); BCB 4. 329^v (Ashe, Stiles, Drewe, and Tey); BCB 4. 330^r (Burley); BCB 4. 332^v (White); BCB 4. 36^r (Hawkins); BCB 4. 322^r (Mosse); BCB 5. 46^v (Crane).
22. The Dutton brothers were actors in the Queen's Men and based at the Bell, 'beyond Shoreditch' (BCB 3. 120^v). It is important to distinguish this tavern from the Bell, Gracechurch Street, Bishopsgate. BCB 3. 187^v (Mekyns and Winch). BCB 3. 296^r (Breame and Winch). BCB 3. 280^r (Kirkeman). BCB 3. 222^r (Wynnington). BCB 4. 83^r, 86^r (Box). For abuses against prisoners, see BCB 4. 316^r–317^v, and my *Shakespeare Among the Courtesans*, 125.
23. Herbert Marcuse, *The Aesthetic Dimension* (Boston: Beacon Press, 1978), ix.

24. BCB 4.270v; William Le Hardy (ed.), *County of Middlesex, Calendar to the Sessions Records, 1612–14* (London: Westminster Guildhall, 1935), 13.

25. In Lucy Bailey's 2006 production of the play at the Globe Theatre (revived in 2014), the Andronici drew their bows but quickly hid the arrows behind their backs in semi-comic playfulness.

26. Evelyn Tribble, 'Where Are the Archers in Shakespeare?' *ELH*, 82, 3 (Fall 2015), 789–814, 803.

27. When, in 1566, Francis Ellman practised archery near Whitechapel, he and his fellows shouted to William Barnes 'to beware of the danger and avoid the arrow', but it struck Barnes's head, from which wound he 'languished' four days and died. See J. C. Jeaffreson (ed.), *Middlesex County Sessions*, vol. 1 (London: GLC, 1972), 58.

28. Tanaken Winterbecke, LMA, St Olave, Bermondsey, Composite Register: Burials March 1583–December 1627, P71/OLA/009, 14 August 1592. See also Paul Slack, *The Impact of Plague in Tudor and Stuart England* (Oxford and New York: Clarendon Press, 1985), 144–72.

29. Janet Clare, *Shakespeare's Stage Traffic: Imitation, Borrowing and Competition in Renaissance Theatre* (Cambridge and New York: Cambridge University Press, 2014), 121.

30. Wickham et al., *English Professional Theatre*, 360–61.

31. John Davies of Hereford, *Microcosmos* (Oxford, 1603), 215.

32. For the funeral elegy on Burbage, see Wickham et al., *English Professional Theatre*, 181–2. On the painting of Burbage, see Tarnya Cooper et al., *Searching for Shakespeare*, 133.

33. John Florio, *A World of Wordes, Or Most copious, and exact dictionarie in Italian and English* (London: 1598), 257. Jean Paul Richter and Irma A. Richter (eds), *The Literary Works of Leonardo da Vinci, Compiled and Edited from the Original Manuscripts* (London and New York: Oxford University Press, 1939), 2 vols, i, 201.

34. For Hulse, see Leatrice Mendelsohn, *Paragoni: Benedetto Varchi''s Due Lezzioni and Cinquecento Art Theory* (Ann Arbor, MI: UMI Research Press, 1982), 37. See also Hulse, *The Rule of Art*, 117. For Hoby, Jean Hagstrum, *The Sister Arts: The Tradition of Literary Pictorialism and English Poetry from Dryden to Gray* (Chicago: University of Chicago Press, 1958), 58. For Francis I, see George Bull (trans. and sel.), *Giorgio Vasari: The Lives of the Artists* (Harmondsworth: Penguin Books, 1965), 270.

35. Painter-Stainers John Beaumont and Arthur Cutler had shops in Wood Street, Thomas Cappe kept his shop on the ground floor of his house in Old Jewry, Cornelius Ketel worked from a 'messuage' that had formerly

been part of Crosby Place in Bishopsgate, Randolph May was a neighbour to the Burbages in Shoreditch, and Robert Peake kept his workshop
in Newgate. See Edward Town, 'A Biographical Dictionary of London
Painters, 1547–1625', *The Walpole Society* (2014), 33, 51, 121, 141,
and 152.

36. Katherine Duncan-Jones, *Portraits of Shakespeare* (Oxford: Bodleian
Library, 2015), 77–91. See also Tarnya Cooper et al., *Searching for
Shakespeare*, 54–6.

37. Screvin's note and Wotton's observation are reproduced in Chambers,
William Shakespeare, ii. 153.

38. W. Gordon Zeefeld, 'Coriolanus and Jacobean Politics', in *The Modern
Language Review* 57 (1962), 321–37. Also Peter Holland (ed.), *Coriolanus* (London and New York: Bloomsbury, 2013), 99–102.

39. For City responsibility for corn, see F. F. Foster, *The Politics of Stability*,
46. For the gilds' purchase of corn, see Norman Gras, *The Evolution of the
English Corn Market, from the Twelfth to the Eighteenth Century* (Cambridge, MA: Harvard University Press, 1915), 84. On the Midlands
protests, see Peter Holland (ed.), *Coriolanus* (London and New York:
Bloomsbury, 2013) 56–68. Quotations from the state papers are from
Mary Anne Everett Green (ed.), *Calendar of State Papers, Domestic Series,
1603–10* (London: Longman, Brown, Green, Longmans and Roberts,
1857), 35, 391, 418, 421, 451, 458, 471, 474.

40. Chris Laoutaris, *Shakespeare and the Countess: The Battle That Gave Birth
to the Globe* (London: Penguin, Random House, 2014).

41. Chambers, *Elizabethan Stage*, iv. 320.

42. Michael Praetorius, *Syntagnum Musicum*, vol. ii, 239.

43. P. Razell (ed.), *The Journals of Two Travellers in Elizabethan and Early
Stuart England* (London: Caliban Books, 1995), 26.

44. S. Schoenbaum, *William Shakespeare: A Compact Documentary Life*
(Oxford and New York: Oxford University Press, 1977), 273.

CHAPTER 5

1. On trade routes and merchants, see R. Davis, *English Overseas Trade
1500–1700* (London: 1973), and B. Dietz, 'Overseas Trade and Metropolitan Growth', in Lee Beier and Roger Finlay (eds), *The Making of the
Metropolis: London 1500–1700* (London and New York: Longman,
1986), 115–40.

2. Steve Rappaport, *Worlds Within Worlds: Structures of Life in Sixteenth-
Century London* (Cambridge and New York: Cambridge University Press,
1989), 18.

3. L. Grenade, *The Singularities of London* (London: London Topographical Society, 2014), 114–17, 172–3.
4. G. B. Harrison and R. A. Jones (eds), *De Maisse, A Journal . . .* (London: The Nonsuch Press, 1931), 46–7.
5. P. Razzell (ed.), *The Journals of Two Travellers in Elizabethan and Early Stuart England* (London: Caliban Books, 1995), 27.
6. Mary Anne Everett Green (ed.), *Calendar of State Papers, Domestic, Elizabeth I, 1598–1601* (London: Longmans, Green, and Co., 1869), 97.
7. Andrew Gurr, *Playgoing in Shakespeare's London* (Cambridge and New York: Cambridge University Press, 2004), 84.
8. De Witt's sketch survives in a copy made by his friend Arend van Buchell.
9. Andrew Pettegree, *Foreign Protestant Communities in Sixteenth-Century London* (Oxford: Clarendon Press, 1986), 17; Selwood, *Diversity and Difference*, 26.
10. Laura Yungblut, *Strangers Settled Here Among Us: Policies, Perceptions and the Presence of Aliens in Elizabethan England* (London and New York: Routledge, 1996), 12.
11. Ibid., 14–15.
12. Nigel Goose, 'Immigrants in Tudor and Early Stuart England', in Nigel Goose and Lien Luu (eds), *Immigrants in Tudor and Early Stuart England* (Brighton: Sussex Academic Press, 2005), 10–13. See Chapter 4, n. 8.
13. Ibid., 25.
14. Yungblut, *Strangers Settled Here Among Us*, 25ff.
15. David Lasocki, 'Bassano, Alvise (d. 1554)', *Oxford Dictionary of National Biography* (Oxford: Oxford University Press, 2004) <http://www.oxforddnb.com/view/article/70535>.
16. LMA, St Olave Hart Street, Composite register, P69/OLA1/A/001/MS28867.
17. Mary Anne Everett Green (ed.), *Calendar of State Papers, Domestic, Elizabeth I 1595–7* (London: Longmans, Green, and Co., 1869), 152.
18. Mary Anne Everett Green (ed.), *Calendar of State Papers, Domestic, Elizabeth I 1591–4* (London: 1867), 356.
19. Mary Anne Everett Green (ed.), *Calendar of State Papers, Domestic, James I, 1603–10* (London: 1857), 121.
20. LMA, St Mary Woolnoth, Composite register, 1558–1641, P69/MRY15/A/001/MS07635); St Dunstan and All Saints, Stepney, Burials, September 1568–July 1603, P93/DUN/274.
21. Yungblut, *Strangers Settled Here Among Us*, 9, 39.
22. Nigel Goose, '"Xenophobia" in Elizabethan and Early Stuart England: An Epithet Too Far?', in Goose and Luu (eds), *Immigrants in Tudor and Early Stuart England*, 111.

23. Ibid., 129.

24. On 'Evil May Day', see Susan Brigden, *London and the Reformation* (Oxford: Clarendon Press, 1989), 129–33. Selwood, *Diversity and Difference*, 53–6; Pettegree, *Foreign Protestant Communities*, 14, 282.

25. Ian W. Archer, 'Palavicino, Sir Horatio (c.1540–1600)', *Oxford Dictionary of National Biography* (Oxford: Oxford University Press, 2004); online edn, January 2008 <http://www.oxforddnb.com/view/article/21153>. Michael Wyatt, *The Italian Encounter with Tudor England: A Cultural Politics of Translation* (Cambridge and New York: Cambridge University Press, 2012) gives brief discussion of Palavicino's military and political responsibilities, 144–5.

26. BCB, 2.235ʳ–236ʳ. The Legrande deposition is interleaved with minutes post-dating 29 February 1575/6.

27. For Pereman's examination, see BCB 377ʳ⁻ᵛ. Also, Ian Archer, *The Pursuit of Stability: Social Relations in Elizabethan London* (Cambridge and New York: Cambridge University Press, 1991), 232.

28. BCB 3.33ʳ.

29. BCB 3.101ᵛ.

30. BCB 3.30ʳ, 316ᵛ. See also my 'Much Ado About Italians in Renaissance London', in Michele Marrapodi (ed.), *Shakespeare and the Italian Renaissance: Appropriation, Transformation, Opposition* (Farnham and Burlington, VT: Ashgate, 2014), 305–16. For Christopher Levens living on Bankside, see Warner, *Catalogue*, 30.

31. BCB 3.138ʳ, 316ᵛ.

32. BCB 4.429ᵛ–431ᵛ (27 January 1603/4).

33. Grenade, *The Singularities of London*, 111–12.

34. Geoffery Bullough, *Narrative and Dramatic Sources of Shakespeare* (London: Routledge and Kegan Paul, 1958), i. 66–8.

35. R. A. Foakes, *Henslowe's Diary*, 22. Bullough, *Narrative and Dramatic Sources*, i. 58.

36. Barbara Hodgdon (ed.), *The Taming of the Shrew* (London and New York: Bloomsbury, 2010), 397–8.

37. Lynda E. Boose, 'Scolding Brides and Bridling Scolds: Taming the Woman's Unruly Member', *Shakespeare Quarterly* 42 (Summer 1991), 179–213.

38. BCB 1.145ʳ, 207ᵛ.

39. Boose, 'Scolding Brides', 193.

40. Katherine Duncan-Jones, *Upstart Crow to Sweet Swan, 1593–1623* (London and New York: Methuen, 2011), 107.

41. Salkeld, *Shakespeare Among the Courtesans*, 142–5.

42. Mary Anne Everett Green, *Calendar of State Papers (Domestic) 1598–1601* (London: Longmans, Green & Co., 1869), 342.

43. Ibid., 174, 178, 311.

44. John Bennell, 'Spinola, Benedict (1519/20–1580)', *Oxford Dictionary of National Biography* (Oxford: Oxford University Press, 2004) online edn, January 2008 <http://www.oxforddnb.com/view/article/52156>. See BCB 3.141ᵛ (2 January 1576/7).

45. 'Cecil Papers: February 1578', in *Calendar of the Cecil Papers in Hatfield House: Volume 2, 1572–82* (London, 1888), pp. 172–3.

46. BCB 3.141ᵛ (2 January 1576/7).

47. LMA, St Christopher Le Stocks, Composite Register, 1557–1653, P69/CRI/A/001/MS04421.

48. G. K. Hunter and David Bevington (eds), *Campaspe and Sappho and Phao* (Manchester and New York: Manchester University Press, 1991), 55.

49. Ian Smith, 'Othello's Black Handkerchief,' *Shakespeare Quarterly* 64, 1 (Spring 2013), 9–10. See also Robert Hornback, 'Emblems of Folly in the First *Othello*: Renaissance Blackface, Moor's Coat and "Muckender"', *Comparative Drama* 35, 1 (2001), 69–99. Significant studies of blackness in *Othello* include Martin Orkin, '*Othello* and the "Plain Face" of Racism', *Shakespeare Quarterly* 38, 2 (1987), 166–88, Jack D'Amico, *The Moor in English Renaissance Drama* (Tampa, Florida: 1991), Kim F. Hall, *Things of Darkness: Economies of Race and Gender in Early Modern England* (Ithaca, NY: Cornell University Press, 1995), and '*Othello* and the Problem of Blackness', in Richard Dutton and Jean Howard (eds), *A Companion to Shakespeare's Works: The Tragedies* (Oxford: Blackwell, 2003), 357–74.

50. These 'plotts' are reproduced in T. J. King, *Casting Shakespeare's Plays: London Actors and Their Roles* (Cambridge and New York: Cambridge University Press, 1992), 258–63.

51. See Roslyn Knutson, 'A Caliban in St. Mildred Poultry', in *Shakespeare and Cultural Traditions: The Selected Proceedings of the International Shakespeare Association World Congress Tokyo 1991* (Newark: University of Delaware Press, 1991), 110–26. Imtiaz Habib, *Black Lives in the English Archives* (Aldershot: Ashgate, 2000). David Dabydeen, John Gilmore, and Cecily Jones (eds), *The Oxford Companion to Black British History* (Oxford and New York: Oxford University Press, 2007), 144–6. Matthew Steggle, 'New Directions: Othello, the Moor of London: Shakespeare's Black Britons', in Robert C. Evans (ed.), *Othello: A Critical Reader* (London: Bloomsbury, 2015), 103–24. Miranda Kaufmann, *Black Tudors: African Lives in Renaissance England* (London: Oneworld, 2017).

52. For details of these and other black early moderns, see Duncan Salkeld, 'Alienating Laughter in *The Merchant of Venice*: A Reply to Imtiaz Habib', *Shakespeare* (May 2013), 14–22. See also Habib's *Black Lives in the*

English Archives and Kaufmann, *Black Tudors*. Kaufmann names 'John Reason' as 'Reasonable Blackman', a change she defends as 'the most modern composite of the variations in which he is recorded' (private communication).

53. Imtiaz Habib, 'The Resonables of Boroughside, Southwark: An Elizabethan Black Family Near the Rose Theatre', *Shakespeare* 11, 2 (2015), 1–13. It is possible, though not certain, that Reasonable may be identified with 'John Reason' in the same parish, although Kaufmann disputes this identification.
54. See Salkeld, 'Alienating Laughter in *The Merchant of Venice*, 14–22.
55. I owe my interest in this passage to a conversation with Lesley C. Dunn of Vassar College, USA at the SAA conference, Bellevue, 2011.
56. John Dover Wilson (ed.), *The Merchant of Venice* (Cambridge: Cambridge University Press, 1926, reprinted 1953), 158. John Russell Brown (ed.), *The Merchant of Venice* (London: Methuen, 1955), 99. John Drakakis (ed.), *The Merchant of Venice* (London: A&C Black, 2010), 327.
57. See LMA P92/SAV/242 for 'William Kempe' living at 'Samson's rents', St Saviour's, Southwark. See also Edwin Nungezer, *A Dictionary of Actors*, 220.
58. Russell Brown, xxi–xxvii.
59. R. B. McKerrow (ed.), *The Works of Thomas Nashe* (London: A. H. Bullen, rpt. 1958), 5 vols, i. 177.
60. Mary Anne Everett Green (ed.), *Calendar of State Papers, Domestic Series, of the Reigns of Elizabeth and James I, Addenda, 1580–1625* (London: HMSO, 1872), 157, 190.
61. Nicholl, *The Lodger*, 181. BCB 1.128^v.
62. BCB 3.100^r.
63. BCB 3.96^{r-v}.
64. T. W. Craik (ed.), *The Merry Wives of Windsor* (Oxford and New York: Oxford University Press, 1990), 5–6; Giorgio Melchiori (ed.), *The Merry Wives of Windsor* (London: Thomson Learning, 2000), 24.
65. Nicholl, *The Lodger*, 177–8; J. W. Lever, 'Shakespeare's French Fruits', *Shakespeare Survey* 6 (1953), 79–89.
66. Mary Anne Everett Green (ed.), *Calendar of State Papers, Domestic Series 1598–1601* (London: Longmans, Green and Co., 1869), 299, 314.
67. Ibid., 327–8, 413, 419.
68. Ibid., 442.
69. Nicholl, *The Lodger*, 358; Lever writes, 'One suspects that for several years Shakespeare gave only desultory attention to his French studies. But around 1598—perhaps through finding himself in the Gallic environment of the Mountjoy household—there are clear signs of a revival of interest', in *Shakespeare's French Fruits*, 84.

70. John Jowett (ed.), *Sir Thomas More* (London and New York: A&C Black, 2011), 28.
71. Ibid., 18–22, 437–53.
72. Ibid., 139.

CONCLUSION

1. Smyth (BCB 4. 96^v–97^r). Skelton (BCB 5. 217^v). 'Stranger', 'Russell', and 'Jone', LMA, St Bride Fleet Street, Register of burials, 1595–1653, P69/BRI/A/004/MS06538. 'Unknown' woman, St Giles Cripplegate, Composite Register, 1561–1606/7, P69/GIS/A/002/MS06419, 5 July 1603.
2. Hudson (BCB 5. 141^v).
3. Amey Bennett (BCB 5. 10^r).
4. Katherine Floyd or Flood and Francis Bacon (BCB 4. 196^r–198^v, 220^r). Joseph Foster, *The Register of Admissions to Gray's Inn, 1521–1889* (London: Hansard, 1889), 56, 123.
5. Wilkinson (BCB 2.37^r). Thewe (BCB 4. 51^r). Harrison (BCB 4. 380^v). Carr (BCB 5. 242^v).
6. LMA, St Helen Bishopsgate, Composite Register: baptisms 1598–1654, marriages 1606–53, burials 1598–1630, P69/HEL/A/002/MS06831, baptism, 31 August 1612, burial 2 September. Vanessa Harding cites the case of Job in *The Dead and the Living in Paris and London, 1500–1670* (Cambridge and New York: Cambridge University Press, 2002), 58. I owe this latter and the Anthony Munday reference to Lena Cowen Orlin.
7. See Chambers, *Elizabethan Stage*, ii. 419–23.

| *Further Reading*

A useful historical starting point is A. L. Beier and Roger Finlay, *London 1500–1700: The making of the metropolis* (London and New York: Longman, 1986). This collection of essays offers an authoritative series of perspectives on London's early modern social history. An invaluable volume is Ben Weinreb, Christopher Hibbert, and John Keay, *The London Encyclopaedia* (London: Macmillan, 2005, 3rd edition), a compendious volume with concise entries on all major aspects of London's topography, buildings, and history, together with helpful illustrations. Lawrence Manley (ed.), *London in the Age of Shakespeare: An Anthology* (London: Croom Helm, 1986) has a short but informative introduction and contains a variety of relevant extracts from poems, official records, sermons, and accounts of London, organized into discrete sections. Manley's *Literature and Culture in Early Modern London* (Cambridge and New York: Cambridge University Press, 1995) gives an in-depth study of London from the early sixteenth century to the period of the Civil War, drawn mainly from literary sources. Lena Cowen Orlin (ed.), *Material London, ca. 1600* (Philadelphia: University of Pennsylvania Press, 2000) brings together a collection of essays on London from literary and historical scholars of the early modern era. Gail Kern Paster, *The Idea of the City in the Age of Shakespeare* (Athens: University of Georgia Press, 1985), discusses Shakespeare's constructions of those other cities of Rome, Athens, Syracuse, and Vienna through which Shakespeare filtered his awareness of urban life. Paul Seaver has an excellent short account of 'Middleton's London' in Gary Taylor and John Lavagnino, *Thomas Middleton: The Collected Works* (Oxford: Clarendon Press, 2007). An accessible and informative account of 'Thomas Dekker and London' may be found in Stanley Wells, *Shakespeare & Co.* (London: Allen Lane, 2006). For Jonson and Marston's links to the capital, see Fran C. Chalfant, *Ben Jonson's London: A Jacobean Placename Dictionary* (Athens, Georgia: University of Georgia Press, 1978); Jonathan Haynes, *The Social Relations of Ben Jonson's Theatre* (Cambridge and New York: Cambridge University Press, 1992); Janet Dillon, *Theatre, Court and City, 1595–1610* (Cambridge and New York: Cambridge University Press, 2008), 109–36; James D. Mardock, *Our Scene is London: Ben Jonson's City and the Space of the Author* (Abingdon and New York: Routledge, 2008); Philip J. Finkelpearl, *John Marston of the Middle Temple: An Elizabethan Dramatist in his Social Setting* (Cambridge, MA: Harvard University Press,

1969). Hannah Crawforth, Sarah Dustagheer, and Jennifer Young, *Shakespeare in London* (London: Bloomsbury, 2014) argues that aspects of the capital inspired Shakespeare's writing. Lisa Picard, *Elizabeth's London: Everyday Life in Elizabethan London* (London: Weidenfeld and Nicolson, 2003) is an accessible work for the general reader and has much for specialists too.

MAPS AND PANORAMAS

The changing nature of London from the mid-sixteenth century through to the end of the eighteenth century can be traced through a series of publications by the Guildhall and London Topographical Society. Howard Colvin and Susan Foister, *The Panorama of London circa 1544, by Anthonis van den Wyngaerde* (London: London Topographical Society/Ashmolean Museum, 1996) authoritatively presents Wyngaerde's drawings in all their detail and beauty. Adrian Prockter and Robert Taylor, *The A-Z of Elizabethan London* (Kent: Guildhall/Harry Margary, 1979) reproduces the 'Agas' map with an introduction and index. Ralph Hyde (int.), *The A-Z of Restoration London* presents the 1676 map by John Ogilby and William Morgan (London: London Topographical Society, 1992). Ralph Hyde, *The A-Z of Georgian London* gives the 1738–47 map of the city by John Rocque (London: London Topographical Society/Harry Margary, 1982). Paul Laxton (int.), *The A-Z of Regency London* reproduces the map compiled by Richard Horwood in 1792–9 and updated by William Faden in 1813 (London: London Topographical Society/Harry Margary, 1985). Ann Saunders and John Schofield, *Tudor London: A map and a View* (London: London Topographical Society/Museum of London, 2001) gives valuable discussion of three sections of the Copperplate map and its contexts. John Schofield, *The London Surveys of Ralph Treswell* (London: London Topographical Society, 1987) presents fascinating illustrations and discussion of the houses, chambers, gardens, privies, and streets of early-seventeenth-century London. Peter Whitfield, *London: A Life in Maps* (London: The British Library, 2006) is well-illustrated but not always reliable. Dorian Gerhold, *London Plotted: Plans of London Buildings c.1450–1720* (London: London Topographical Society, 2016) presents a superb collection of early plans of areas and localities. Ida Darlington and J. L. Howgego, *Printed Maps of London, 1553–1850* (London: Dawson, 1978) remains an authoritative reference guide.

LONDON'S ADMINISTRATION AND SOCIAL CHANGE

F. F. Foster, *The Politics of Stability: A Portrait of the Rulers in Elizabethan London* (London: Royal Historical Society, 1977) is concise and helpful. Steve

Rappaport, *Worlds Within Worlds: Structures of life in Sixteenth-Century London* (Cambridge and New York: Cambridge University Press, 1989) and Ian Archer, *The Pursuit of Stability: Social Relations in Early Modern London* (Cambridge and New York: Cambridge University Press, 1992) are essential reading for anyone interested in the social history of the period. Roger Finlay, *Population and Metropolis: The Demography of London 1580–1650* (Cambridge and New York: Cambridge University Press, 1981) is the most detailed study of London's demographic to date. A. B. Beaven, *The Aldermen of the City of London* (London: Eden Fisher, 1908) remains a useful source of ward-by-ward information on London's civic rulers. Books by Rappaport, Archer, and Finlay refine some of the essays in Beier and Finlay, *London 1500–1700*. Laura Hunt Yungblut, *Strangers Settled Here Amongst Us: Policies, Perceptions and the Presence of Aliens in Elizabethan England* (London: Routledge, 1996) gives an accessible account of the situation of aliens mainly resident in early modern London. Jacob Selwood, *Diversity and Difference in Early Modern London* (Farnham and Burlington, VT: Ashgate, 2010) gives a key account of the status and challenges facing strangers and foreigners in the capital. Valerie Pearl, *London and the Outbreak of the Puritan Revolution: City Government and National Politics 1625–1643* (Oxford: Oxford University Press, 1961) has valuable comment on London's transitions from 1550 to 1650. Paul Griffiths, *Lost Londons: Change, Crime and Control in the Capital City, 1550–1660* (Cambridge and New York: Cambridge University Press, 2008) offers a compendious study of criminality in the period, drawing mainly on the archives of Bridewell Hospital. Jonathan Andrews, Asa Briggs, Roy Porter, Penny Tucker, and Keir Waddington, *The History of Bethlem* is a *tour de force* history of an early modern institution, Bethlem Hospital or 'Bedlam'. Carol Kazmierczak Manzione, *Christ's Hospital of London, 1552–1598* (Selinsgrove and London: Susquehanna University Press, 1995) gives a useful account of this educational 'hospital' mainly for orphans. Originally published in 1908, George Unwin, *The Gilds and Companies of London* (with an introduction by William F. Kahl, 1962) is showing its age but remains a valuable resource (London: Frank Cass, 1963). Susan Brigden, *London and the Reformation* (Oxford and New York: Oxford University Press, 1989) is an important study of the City's adaptation through traumatic years of political, ideological, and religious change. Paul Slack, *The Impact of Plague in Tudor and Stuart England* (Oxford and New York: Oxford University Press, 1989), especially chapter 6, gives a detailed study of the effects of infection on the population and economy.

OTHER STUDIES

Many biographies of Shakespeare are invaluable on his time in London, especially S. Schoenbaum, *William Shakespeare: A Documentary Life* (Oxford:

Clarendon Press, 1975), René Weis, *Shakespeare Revealed: A Biography* (London: John Murray, 2007), and Lois Potter, *The Life of William Shakespeare: A Critical Biography* (Chichester: John Wiley, 2012). So, too, is Robert Bearman's *Shakespeare's Money: How Much Did He Make and What Did This Mean?* (Oxford and New York: Oxford University Press, 2016). There is much to learn about the theatrical context in William Ingram's *A London Life in the Brazen Age: Francis Langley, 1548–1602* (Cambridge, MA: Harvard University Press, 1978). Various aspects of London's social life are fascinatingly explored in Paul Griffiths and Mark S. R. Jenner (eds), *Londinopolis: Essays in the cultural and social history of early modern London* (Manchester and New York: Manchester University Press, 2000). Other valuable studies are listed below. J. F. Merritt, *The Social World of Early Modern Westminster: Abbey, Court and Community, 1525–1640* (Manchester and New York: Manchester University Press, 2005). Julian Bowsher, *Shakespeare's London Theatreland: Archaeology, History and Drama* (London: Museum of London Archaeology, 2012). Andrew Gurr, *Playgoing in Shakespeare's London* (Cambridge and New York: Cambridge University Press, 2004). William Ingram, *The Business of Playing: The Beginnings of Adult Professional Theatre in Elizabethan London* (Ithaca, NY and London: Cornell University Press, 1992). Charles Nicholl, *The Lodger: Shakespeare on Silver Street* (London: Penguin Books, 2007). Lena Cowen Orlin, *Locating Privacy in Tudor London* (Oxford and New York: Oxford University Press, 2007). Eleanor Hubbard, *City Women: Money, Sex and the Social Order in Early Modern London* (Oxford and New York: Oxford University Press, 2012). Jacob Selwood, *Diversity and Difference in Early Modern London* (Farnham and Burlington, VT: Ashgate, 2010). Nigel Goose and Lien Luu, *Immigrants in Tudor and Early Stuart England* (Brighton: Sussex Academic Press, 2005). Miranda Kaufmann has a chapter on 'John Reasonable' whom she names 'Reasonable Blackman' in *Black Tudors: The Untold Story* (London: Oneworld, 2017). The detailed notes in C. L. Kingsford's *John Stow: A Survey of London, Reprinted from the Text of 1603* (Oxford: Clarendon Press, 1908) make it still the necessary edition of Stow. John R. Elliott and Alan H. Nelson's beautifully produced three-volume *Inns of Court* (Woodbridge: Boydell & Brewer, 2011) is an example of the importance of the REED volumes in general. The second chapter of Robert Tittler, *The Face of the City: Civic Portraiture and Civic Identity in Early Modern England* (Manchester and New York: Manchester University Press, 2007) contains a useful account of paintings commissioned by the livery companies. Edward Town's 'A Biographical Dictionary of London Painters, 1547–1625', *Walpole Society* (2014), 1–235, is a monumental piece of original research and an important source for early modernists. Simon Alford's

London's Triumph: Merchant Adventurers and the Tudor City (London: Allen Lane, 2017) is written for the general reader and has a useful discussion of the Royal Exchange. Paul Menzer has some very worthwhile comment on playing in the City in *The Hamlets: Cues, Qs, and Remembered Texts* (Newark: University of Delaware Press, 2008), 140–61.